Communications in Computer and Information Science 2445

Rationale
The CCIS series is devoted to the publication of proceedings of computer science conferences. Its aim is to efficiently disseminate original research results in informatics in printed and electronic form. While the focus is on publication of peer-reviewed full papers presenting mature work, inclusion of reviewed short papers reporting on work in progress is welcome, too. Besides globally relevant meetings with internationally representative program committees guaranteeing a strict peer-reviewing and paper selection process, conferences run by societies or of high regional or national relevance are also considered for publication.

Topics
The topical scope of CCIS spans the entire spectrum of informatics ranging from foundational topics in the theory of computing to information and communications science and technology and a broad variety of interdisciplinary application fields.

Information for Volume Editors and Authors
Publication in CCIS is free of charge. No royalties are paid, however, we offer registered conference participants temporary free access to the online version of the conference proceedings on SpringerLink (http://link.springer.com) by means of an http referrer from the conference website and/or a number of complimentary printed copies, as specified in the official acceptance email of the event.

CCIS proceedings can be published in time for distribution at conferences or as post-proceedings, and delivered in the form of printed books and/or electronically as USBs and/or e-content licenses for accessing proceedings at SpringerLink. Furthermore, CCIS proceedings are included in the CCIS electronic book series hosted in the SpringerLink digital library at http://link.springer.com/bookseries/7899. Conferences publishing in CCIS are allowed to use Online Conference Service (OCS) for managing the whole proceedings lifecycle (from submission and reviewing to preparing for publication) free of charge.

Publication process
The language of publication is exclusively English. Authors publishing in CCIS have to sign the Springer CCIS copyright transfer form, however, they are free to use their material published in CCIS for substantially changed, more elaborate subsequent publications elsewhere. For the preparation of the camera-ready papers/files, authors have to strictly adhere to the Springer CCIS Authors' Instructions and are strongly encouraged to use the CCIS LaTeX style files or templates.

Abstracting/Indexing
CCIS is abstracted/indexed in DBLP, Google Scholar, EI-Compendex, Mathematical Reviews, SCImago, Scopus. CCIS volumes are also submitted for the inclusion in ISI Proceedings.

How to start
To start the evaluation of your proposal for inclusion in the CCIS series, please send an e-mail to ccis@springer.com

Andrei Chugunov · Olga Filatova ·
Yury Kabanov · Harekrishna Misra ·
Leonid Smorgunov · Wei Zhang
Editors

Digital Transformation in Governance and Society

7th International Conference, DTGS 2024
St. Petersburg, Russia, June 24–26, 2024
Revised Selected Papers

Springer

Editors
Andrei Chugunov
ITMO University
St. Petersburg, Russia

Olga Filatova
ITMO University
St. Petersburg, Russia

Yury Kabanov
HSE University
St. Petersburg, Russia

Harekrishna Misra
BML Munjal University
Kapriwas, Haryana, India

Leonid Smorgunov
St. Petersburg State University
St. Petersburg, Russia

Wei Zhang
Huazhong University of Science
and Technology
Wuhan, China

ISSN 1865-0929 ISSN 1865-0937 (electronic)
Communications in Computer and Information Science
ISBN 978-3-031-90719-7 ISBN 978-3-031-90720-3 (eBook)
https://doi.org/10.1007/978-3-031-90720-3

This Springer imprint is published by the registered company Springer Nature Switzerland AG
The registered company address is: Gewerbestrasse 11, 6330 Cham, Switzerland

Preface

The International Conference "Digital Transformation in Governance and Society" (DTGS 2024) was held during June 24–26, 2024, in St. Petersburg, Russia, within the framework of the joint international conference "Internet and Modern Society" (IMS).

This year the conference united two academic forums previously hosted by ITMO University: the conference on Digital Transformation & Global Society (DTGS) as well as the conference on Electronic Governance and Open Society: Challenges in Eurasia (EGOSE). The updated title of the event—Digital Transformation in Governance and Society—reflects the new focus of the conference on the role of digital technologies in governance and societal processes across the globe.

Overall, 35 submissions were reviewed and evaluated by the international Program Committee, and 10 papers were selected, with an acceptance rate of 29 percent. Each paper received at least three reviews; a double-blind peer review procedure was applied. Participants in the Young Scholars' Forum also received additional feedback from nine members of the Awards Committee. The best paper presented at the Forum, authored by Fady Ayad and Anna Sytnik, is also included in the volume.

The papers selected reflect the multidimensional and interdisciplinary scope of DTGS 2024. They report developments in such topics as digital governance, smart cities, and communication on social media, with special emphasis on the experience of developing countries. They also highlight the importance of building citizens' capacities and trust in the processes of digital transformation. The papers have important implications for both academia and practitioners in the field of digital governance.

We express our gratitude to the members of the Program Committee for their help in selecting the papers for the conference. We would like to thank the Awards Committee members who participated in the evaluation of the Young Scholars' Forum papers: Alena Suvorova, Ilia Dunichkin, and Yury Kabanov (HSE University), Radomir Bolgov and Dmitry Prokudin (St. Petersburg State University), Andrei Chugunov, Olga Filatova, and Igor Kuprienko (ITMO University), as well as Maxim Bakaev (Novosibirsk State Technical University).

We are also grateful to the moderators of the sessions, including Yury Kabanov (HSE University), Leonid Smorgunov (St. Petersburg State University), Lyudmila Vidiasova, and Igor Kuprienko (ITMO University).

We thank our partners, organizers, and hosts, and all those who made this event possible and successful.

June 2024

Olga Filatova
Andrei Chugunov
Yury Kabanov
Harekrishna Misra
Leonid Smorgunov
Wei Zhang

Organization

Program Chairs

Andrei Chugunov	ITMO University, Russia
Olga Filatova	ITMO University, Russia
Yury Kabanov	HSE University, ITMO University, Russia
Harekrishna Misra	BML Munjal University, India
Leonid Smorgunov	St. Petersburg State University, Russia
Wei Zhang	Huazhong University of Science and Technology, China

Program Committee

Ayman Alarabiat	Al-Balqa Applied University, Jordan
Maxim Bakaev	Novosibirsk State Technical University, Russia
Svetlana Bodrunova	St. Petersburg State University, Russia
Radomir Bolgov	St. Petersburg State University, Russia
Mikhail Bundin	Lobachevsky State University of Nizhni Novgorod, Russia
Anna Chizhik	St. Petersburg State University, Russia
Andrei Chugunov	ITMO University, Russia
Shefali S. Dash	National Informatics Centre, India
Saravanan Devadoss	Sri Manakula Vinayagar Group of Institutions, India
Ruben Elamiryan	Public Administration Academy of the Republic of Armenia, Armenia
Olga Filatova	ITMO University, Russia
Salah Kabanda	University of Cape Town, South Africa
Yury Kabanov	HSE University, ITMO University, Russia
Igor Khodachek	European University in St. Petersburg, Russia
Olessia Koltsova	HSE University, Russia
Aleksei Martynov	Lobachevsky State University of Nizhni Novgorod, Russia
Harekrishna Misra	BML Munjal University, India
Dmitry Prokudin	St. Petersburg State University, Russia
Aleksandr Riabushko	Independent researcher, Russia
Bogdan Romanov	University of Tartu, Estonia

Jenny Marcela Sanchez-Torres	Universidad Nacional de Colombia, Colombia
Anna Smoliarova	St. Petersburg State University, Russia
Leonid Smorgunov	St. Petersburg State University, Russia
Alexander Sokolov	Demidov Yaroslavl State University, Russia
Evgeny Styrin	HSE University, Russia
Irina Tolstikova	ITMO University, Russia
Dmitrii Trutnev	ITMO University, Russia
Lyudmila Vidiasova	ITMO University, Russia
Daniil Volkovskii	HSE University, Russia
Can Yang	Chongqing University, China
Wei Zhang	Huazhong University of Science and Technology, China

Contents

Israeli Digital Diplomacy Towards Arab States: Social Media Engagement Analysis

Fady Ayad(✉) and Anna Sytnik

St. Petersburg State University, 7/9 Universitetskaya Emb., St Petersburg 199034, Russia
st13571@student.spbu.ru, a.sytnik@spbu.ru

Abstract. This paper investigates the role of digital diplomacy in Israeli-Arab relations, particularly since the signing of the Abraham Accords in September 2020. Israel has leveraged social media and digital platforms to promote normalization agreements, emphasizing economic cooperation and regional stability. Despite substantial engagement on these platforms, negative sentiments towards normalization remain prevalent. The study utilizes quantitative analysis and the Digital Diplomacy Index to assess the effectiveness of Israel's digital diplomacy efforts. Findings indicate significant engagement but also highlight ongoing challenges, including geopolitical dynamics and historical tensions, in fostering positive Arab-Israeli relations.

Keywords: Digital Diplomacy · Israeli-Arab Relations · Abraham Accords · Social Media Engagement

1 Introduction

One of the central pillars of Israeli diplomacy towards Arab nations in recent years has been the promotion of normalization agreements, exemplified by the Abraham Accords. Israel has used social media platforms, official websites, and digital campaigns to communicate the advantages of these agreements, emphasizing economic cooperation, tourism opportunities, and regional stability.

While Israeli digital diplomacy towards Arab nations presents numerous opportunities, it is not without its challenges. Navigating complex geopolitical dynamics, addressing historical tensions and present conflicts are ongoing challenges. Nevertheless, digital diplomacy remains a critical tool in Israel's efforts to nurture peaceful relations, enhance regional stability, and promote economic cooperation with its Arab neighbors.

Israel has created a digital diplomacy bureau under the ministry of foreign affairs responsible for the digital diplomacy efforts of the country, which makes Israel very active on social media. It maintains social media accounts in more than 50 languages, reaching around 2 billion impressions a year. The ministry uses various social media platforms, including X, Facebook, TikTok, Instagram, and LinkedIn, to reach to the public and world leaders. In addition to social media, the ministry is also exploring the use of AI and metaverse for digital diplomacy activities [1].

A. Chugunov et al. (Eds.): DTGS 2024, CCIS 2445, pp. 1–14, 2025.
https://doi.org/10.1007/978-3-031-90720-3_1

Israeli digital diplomacy differs from that of any other country, as it is not merely used to enhance international communication or increase external openness. Instead, it serves as a tool for managing the extended Arab Israeli conflict, aiming to normalize the ties.

This research conducts an examination of the official social media presence of the Israeli Ministry of Foreign Affairs directed to the Arab countries, specifically focusing on the Ministry's officially managed Facebook and Twitter accounts. The goal of the research is to uncover and explain the role of digital diplomacy in the current international relations arena with Israeli-Arab case study as example. Therefore, the study poses a central question.

RQ: To what extent does Israel utilize the digital channels to shape the public opinion in the Arab region?

The study period begins with the signing of the Abraham Accords, a series of bilateral agreements for Arab-Israeli normalization, between Israel and the United Arab Emirates in September 2020. The Abraham Accords have been effective since September 15, 2020, and have led to new forms of cooperation in the Middle East and marked a new phase in the Israeli-Palestinian crisis [2]. The study tracks Israeli digital diplomacy towards the Arab region until 2023 focusing on the Israeli assault on the occupied Palestinian territories began in early May 2021, particularly in "Sheikh Jarrah." and 2023 crisis in Gaza.

2 Literature Review

2.1 Israeli Digital Diplomacy

Digital diplomacy refers to the use of digital technologies and online platforms to achieve diplomatic objectives. It involves various government-sponsored efforts aimed at communicating directly with foreign publics to establish a dialogue designed to inform and influence [3]. Scholars delve into digital diplomacy role in the Israeli-Palestinian Conflict and the broader Middle Eastern region. For instance, the study of the interplay between the use of force in conflicts and rhetorical efforts in shaping international discourse highlights the significance of digital diplomacy in the Israeli-Palestinian context. Israel's "Hasbara" and the Palestinian "Sumud" strategies leverage social media platforms like Twitter and Facebook to influence public opinion and the international community. This approach allows both sides to bypass traditional media, making social media a pivotal tool in digital diplomacy [6].

An analysis of the visual framing of the 2014 Gaza War by the Israeli Ministry of Foreign Affairs on social media platforms reveals how visual content emphasized Israel's security concerns and portrayed Hamas as a terrorist organization. This framing significantly influenced public opinion, particularly in the United States, highlighting the power of social media in shaping perceptions [7]. A case study on the United Arab Emirates (UAE) addresses challenges in implementing digital diplomacy, such as state security, media regulations, limited digital tool usage, and linguistic barriers. The study concludes that balancing digital empowerment with regulation is crucial for successful digital diplomacy in the UAE [8]. An article on how Gulf Cooperation Council (GCC) countries used social media during the first 100 days of the blockade finds that social media was crucial for communicating positions and engaging local and international communities, underscoring the importance and challenges of digital diplomacy in globalization [9].

Overall, the literature on Israeli digital diplomacy highlights the significance of social media performance, integration within broader foreign policy towards Arab nations, and the impact of the digital divide in the Middle East. These studies collectively underscore the transformative and challenging nature of digital diplomacy in contemporary international relations. However, there are no studies that provide an in-depth analysis of Israel's current strategy towards Arab states through the lens of the rapidly evolving field of digital diplomacy.

2.2 Israeli Digital Diplomacy Strategic Engagement Towards Arab States

Digital diplomacy is considered one of the pivotal activities of the Israeli Ministry of Foreign Affairs, as the Ministry is intensively active in the digital arena. The Israeli Ministry of Foreign Affairs launched its initial online presence in 2009, a noteworthy milestone that involved the creation of the ministry's Twitter account. In 2011, the formation and evolution of the digital diplomacy department commenced, as it became evident that digital diplomacy is a fundamental responsibility of the ministry of foreign affairs. Yiftah Curiel, the former head of the department, played a pivotal role in this process. In 2011, the Arabic team launched the "Israel in Arabic" pages on X and Facebook. This was followed by the establishment of "Israel in Gulf" in 2013, which served as a virtual embassy at the time. More recently, the team created "Israel in Iraqi," which stood out due to its administrator, Linda Menuhin. According to Menuhin, the "Israel in Iraqi" page was created in response to the positive feedback received from Iraqis on the main "Israel in Arabic" page [10]. Currently, David Saranga is the head of the digital diplomacy department and Sapir Levi, head of the Arabic New Media Desk for Israel's Foreign Ministry [11] (Fig. 1).

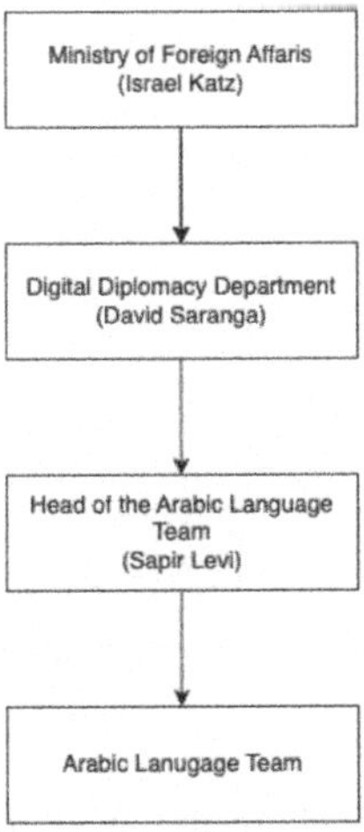

Fig. 1. Israeli Digital Diplomacy Department Hierarchy

In a recent interview [12] with the Trusted Middle East news agency, Saranga and Sapir Levi, expounded upon the prevailing challenges they encounter and the strategies they employ to attain their ultimate objective, as previously mentioned. Their discussion underscored the significance of countering misinformation and propagating Israel's message to counteract negativity in the Arab world. Their primary goals encompass managing the ongoing conflict with Hamas and addressing terrorist menaces supported by Iran. The digital warfare entails active engagement on diverse social media platforms in numerous languages, with the aim of reaching a broader spectrum of individuals and shaping the international narrative. Assessing the success of achieving this goal is of particular interest. The main goal according to David Saranga is ensure the viral dissemination of the Israeli message before that of the Palestinians, as he perceives his team to be at the forefront of this ongoing Gaza war [13].

Israeli Digital Diplomacy Engagement Layers.
Israeli Ministry of Foreign Affairs highlights four levels of influence of digital diplomacy [14]. Digital diplomacy initiatives aim to influence discussion topics by spreading messages across online platforms, shaping both traditional media and local social media agendas. Engaging audiences with digital diplomacy content are crucial; diplomatic entities craft content that resonates with the cultural and normative frameworks of their target audiences to encourage sharing and commentary. Shifting attitudes towards foreign policy is also a key goal, requiring ongoing dialogue between diplomats and online communities and leveraging the interactive nature of social networking sites. Ultimately, on the fourth layer, the aim is to change behaviors among foreign populations, gaining acceptance of a nation's foreign policies and support from national policymakers. However, achieving this goal is challenging, highlighting the complexity of digital diplomatic efforts (Fig. 2).

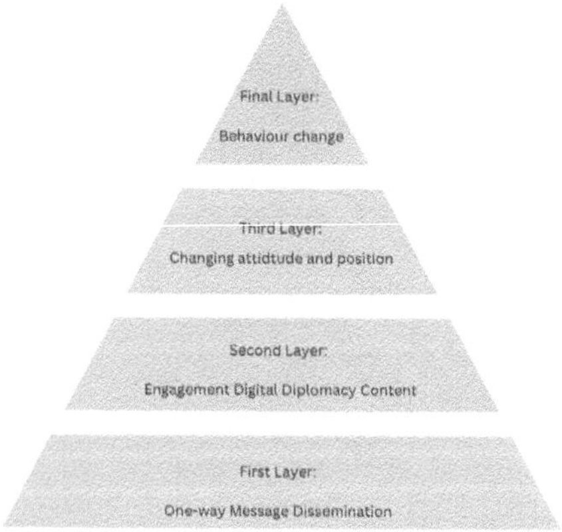

Fig. 2. Layers of online influence [14]

Digital Diplomacy and Engagement. In the academic literature on digital diplomacy and engagement, layers of online influence correspond to levels of engagement analysis.

One-way message dissemination can be assessed using message frequency analysis [15] or agenda analysis [16]. Second level of engagement analysis requires focusing on reactions, namely, the number of comments [16]. Likes are taken as the overall positive effect of the post, and shares are considered as the degree of importance of the message for the audience [17]. It is also important to assess the total number of users informed through digital diplomacy channels, for example, by using of surveys [18]. The last two levels require the most sophisticated methodologies. Scholars combine topic modeling with sentiment analysis of comments under digital diplomacy posts [19] Studying user profiles and comparing their preferences with the results of a quantitative content analysis of the diplomatic mission agenda allow to draw conclusions about the effectiveness of promoting the interests of the country [20].

3 Sample and Method

This study adopts a quantitative and qualitative approaches to the analysis of Israeli digital diplomacy, employing a systematic methodology that encompasses several critical stages.

3.1 Data Collection

We collected data from August 2020 to October 2023 using the Popsters.ru tool from accounts managed by the Israeli Ministry of Foreign Affairs or Israeli embassies in Arabic-speaking countries identified based on their descriptions in the information sections, verification signs, and references in the literature review. Popsters.ru was utilized to compile posts, tweets, and other relevant data from Facebook and X (formerly Twitter). The resulting dataset includes 7,691 posts from Facebook and 27,212 tweets from X. This comprehensive dataset offers a detailed view of the social media presence and engagement strategies employed by the Israeli Ministry of Foreign Affairs across different platforms.

3.2 Data Processing

We removed duplications and ensured data completeness and accuracy. The analysis involved several key steps. First, descriptive statistics was used to summarize engagement patterns. Second, comparative analysis helped to identify variations in message framing across platforms and languages. Third, correlation analysis was used to explore relationships between specific message frames and engagement levels. Engagement levels across platforms were assessed using metrics such as likes, shares, comments, retweets, and reactions. This facilitated a comparative analysis of engagement trends on Facebook and X, helping to identify the types of content and narratives that resonated most with audiences.

3.3 Qualitative Analysis

We applied content analysis for detailed examination of the themes, narratives, and framing of messages across different posts and tweets. We also use document analysis to analyze the first digital diplomacy conference held by the Israeli Ministry of Foreign Affairs. It was hosted at Tel Aviv University, focusing on their assessment of digital diplomacy performance, as well as their definition and objectives of digital diplomacy.

3.4 Digital Diplomacy Index

The study also utilized the Digital Diplomacy Index (DDI) [21] criteria to evaluate the performance of Israeli digital diplomacy. The Digital Diplomacy Index (DDI) is a reliable and important index that measures the digital engagement and performance of countries in the arena of digital diplomacy, assessing G20 countries influence on the online scene of international relations on Twitter.

According to the website of the Digital Diplomacy Index (DDI), the methodology relies on four key factors: the reachability, which assesses the accessibility of the diplomatic network, including language diversity (or in this case, dialects); format proficiency, which measures the percentage of posts that contain visuals or videos out of the total number of posts; vocality, which refers to the average number of monthly posts published; and message efficiency, which indicates the quantity of engagement with the posts.

4 Results

The Israeli Ministry of Foreign Affairs manages several Facebook pages aimed at engaging with Arab audiences and improving Israel's image in the Middle East (Fig. 3). The most prominent of these pages is "Israel Speaks Arabic", which attracts 45% of the followers and employs propaganda strategies to portray Israel as a rational, democratic, and peace-loving state that cooperates with its Arab neighbors. The second most popular page is managed by Avichay Adraee, the head of the Arab media division of the IDF Spokesperson's Unit, with 34% of the followers. His Facebook page focuses on presenting the Israeli military's perspective on events and conflicts in the region.

In X, the situation with leadership of accounts is identical, where they are joined by the Prime Minister of the State of Israel account (19%), the official account of the Office of the Prime Minister of Israel, sharing updates on the Prime Minister's activities, policies, and statements, with a focus on reaching an international audience (Fig. 4).

With regards to the vocal nature and active engagement of accounts in promoting and maintaining posting sustainability, Facebook pages, on average, produce approximately 190 posts per month (Fig. 5).

There is a relatively higher number of posts observed in September and October 2020, coinciding with the announcement of the Abraham Accords and the establishment of new ties with the UAE and Bahrain. Additionally, there was an increase in posts in December and January, focusing on celebrations and references to peace, as well as the historical and cultural ties with Morocco and Sudan, following their participation in the

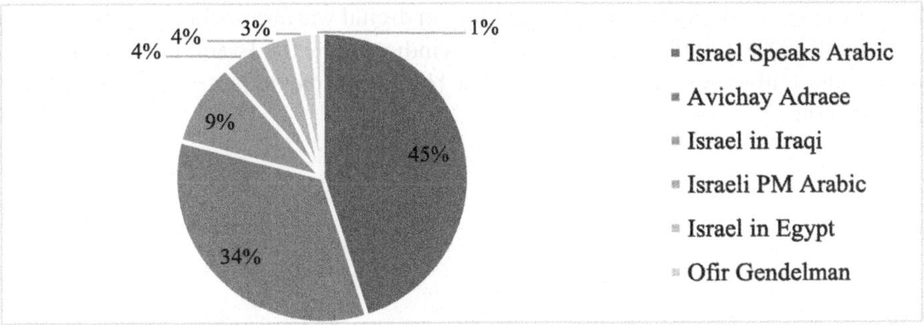

Fig. 3. Israeli Facebook Pages Reachability

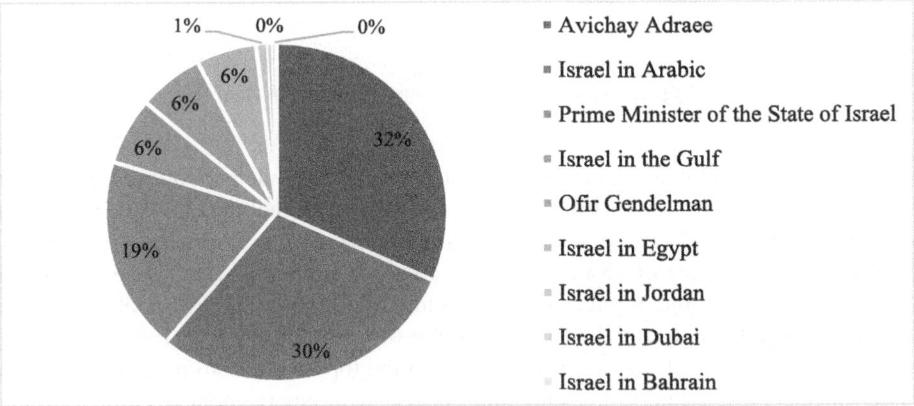

Fig. 4. Israeli X (formerly Twitter) Accounts Reachability

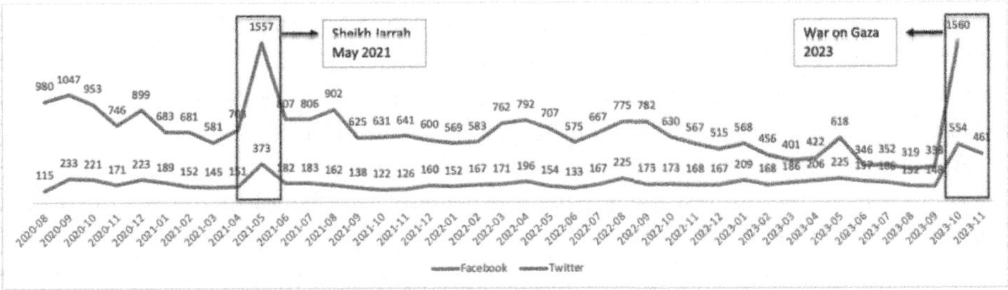

Fig. 5. The Posting Peak Timing

accords. Furthermore, there was a surge in posting activity in May 2021, primarily in response to the events occurring in the Sheikh Jarrah neighborhood in East Jerusalem. This heightened posting rate aimed to counter misinformation, as stated in the objectives, and to correct the portrayal of IDF personnel. The peak in posting activity occurred during the initial stages of the Gaza war in October 2023, with more than 500 posts.

These efforts were directed towards engaging in digital warfare within the online sphere, involving the Arab population and Hamas, as indicated by the Israeli Digital Diplomacy Bureau, and embassies, in order to combat Hamas propaganda, as emphasized in the Israeli discourse.

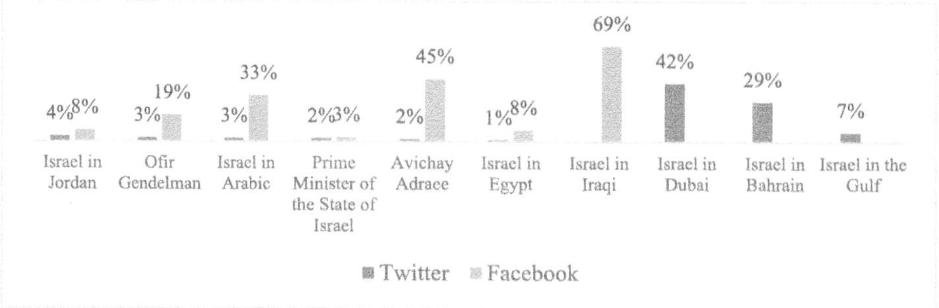

Fig. 6. Social Media Accounts Engagement Rate

It is evident that the accounts that exist on both platforms demonstrate a higher level of engagement on Facebook (Fig. 6). On Facebook, The Israel in Iraqi page stands out with an impressive 69% engagement rate. Similarly, the Avichay Adraee page maintains a solid engagement rate of 45%, suggesting effective content and audience interaction strategies. However, not all pages share the same rate. The Israeli PM Arabic page has the lowest engagement rate at just 3%. On the other hand, Israel in Egypt and Israel in Jordan pages, both at 8%. Falling in between the top and bottom performers are the Israel Speaks Arabic and Ofir Gendelman pages, with engagement rates of 33% and 19%, respectively.

The most active account appears to be "Israel in Dubai", which has the highest 42% engagement rate across all the analyzed accounts. The next most engaged account is "Israel in Bahrain" at 29%. Followed by, "Israel in the Gulf" has 7% engagement rate. Other accounts with lower engagement include "Israel in Jordan" (4%), "Ofir Gendelman" (3%), "Israel in Arabic" (3%), the "Prime Minister of the State of Israel" (2%), "Avichay Adraee" (2%), and "Israel in Egypt" (1%) (Table 1).

Based on the table showing Facebook accounts' engagement rates by message type, video posts have the highest engagement, especially for "Israel in Iraqi" (145%) and "Avichay Adraee" (72%). Text posts also show strong engagement, notably for "Israel in Iraqi" (69%) and "Avichay Adraee" (45%). Image posts are lower but still significant for some accounts. Link posts generally have the lowest engagement, with "Prime Minister of the State of Israel" at just 1% (Table 2).

The table reveals that video posts attract the highest engagement, especially for "Israel in Dubai" (56%) and "Israel in Bahrain" (27%). "Israel in Dubai" also excels in other message types, with links (55%) and images (52%) showing high engagement. Conversely, "Israel in Jordan," "Israel in Egypt," and the "Prime Minister of the State of Israel" have consistently low engagement across all message types (Table 3).

Political content is the predominant category across nearly all pages, comprising an 48.6% of the content. Military content, while less prominent overall at 10.2%, holds a

Table 1. Facebook Accounts Engagement Rate by Message Type

Page Name/Post Type	Image	Text	Video	Link
Israel in Arabic	25%	33%	55%	6%
Avichay Adraee	29%	45%	72%	14%
Israel in Iraqi	44%	69%	45%	40%
Prime Minister of the State of Israel	3%	3%	5%	1%
Israel in Egypt	9%	8%	6%	2%
Israel in Jordan	8%	8%	12%	6%
Ofir Gendelman	21%	19%	26%	5%

Table 2. Twitter Accounts Engagement Rate by Message Type

Page Name/Message Type	Image	Text	Video	Link
Israel in Jordan	5%	4%	2%	4%
Israel in Egypt	2%	1%	1%	2%
Israel in Bahrain	43%	29%	27%	39%
Israel in Dubai	52%	42%	56%	55%
Ofir Gendelman	3%	3%	11%	5%
Israel in Arabic	3%	3%	4%	3%
Avichay Adraee	2%	2%	3%	2%
Prime Minister of the State of Israel	2%	2%	4%	3%
Israel in the Gulf	7%	7%	9%	8%

notable presence on Avichay Adraee's page, implying a particular emphasis on security and defense matters as the IDF Arabic spokesman. Religious content is consistently high across all pages, averaging 10.6%. Surprisingly, scientific content is present to a significant extent on certain pages, particularly Israel in Egypt (17.4%) and Israel in Jordan (17.1%), with an average of 8% overall. Cultural (3.4%) and historical (5.9%) themes are employed to varying degrees, with the highest proportion of historical content observed on the Israel in Jordan page (Table 4).

The overall average for political content across all accounts is 56.5%, making it the most prominent category. Military Content, the "Avichay Adraee" account (46.4%) has the highest prevalence of military content. While, the religious Content, "Israel in Egypt" (10.8%) and "Israel Arabic" (10.3%) accounts have notably high percentages of religious tweets, with an overall average of 6.8% across all accounts. Social content is fairly evenly distributed, with the "Israel in Egypt" account (10.0%) having the highest percentage and an overall average of 5.6%. Economic, Historical, Cultural, Scientific, and Art Content: These categories exhibit a more diverse distribution across the accounts.

Table 3. Facebook Pages and Message Topic

Page/Message Topic	Avichay Adraee	Israel Arabic	Israel in Egypt	Israel in Iraqi	Israel in Jordan	Israeli PM Arabic	Ofir Gendelman	**Grand Total**
Social	3,8%	10,6%	10,4%	8,2%	9,8%	2,0%	6,4%	**7,0%**
Economic	0,8%	3,2%	3,9%	3,5%	5,7%	1,1%	1,8%	**2,7%**
Historical	3,5%	7,8%	6,4%	11,8%	11,1%	0,6%	2,8%	**5,9%**
Cultural	3,8%	3,4%	3,2%	10,5%	4,2%	0,2%	0,9%	**3,4%**
Religious	9,4%	11,7%	13,5%	21,9%	13,3%	2,9%	6,1%	**10,6%**
Political	41,3%	39,9%	39,1%	25,6%	30,6%	84,0%	62,2%	**48,6%**
Military	31,4%	9,3%	3,2%	2,5%	2,6%	7,1%	12,9%	**10,2%**
Scientific	3,1%	9,3%	17,4%	10,9%	17,1%	1,5%	3,5%	**8,0%**
Art	3,1%	4,9%	2,9%	5,1%	5,5%	0,6%	3,4%	**3,5%**

Table 4. X Accounts and Message Topic

Accounts/Message Topic	Avichay Adraee	Israel Arabic	Israel Dubai	Israel in Bahrain	Israel in Egypt	Israel in Jordan	Israel in the Gulf	Israeli PM	Ofir Gendelman	**Grand Total**
Social	3,2%	8,3%	5,4%	5,6%	10,0%	6,0%	7,1%	3,8%	3,3%	**5,6%**
Economic	1,4%	3,9%	1,1%	0,4%	5,9%	2,6%	3,2%	3,1%	1,5%	**2,7%**
Historical	2,1%	6,5%	4,4%	2,8%	6,3%	8,5%	10,7%	1,3%	1,8%	**4,4%**
Cultural	2,0%	3,4%	2,8%	0,4%	3,3%	0,9%	4,4%	0,9%	0,7%	**2,3%**
Religious	5,8%	10,3%	5,2%	9,1%	10,8%	8,5%	7,4%	3,1%	3,7%	**6,8%**
Political	35,0%	51,1%	75,5%	77,5%	41,8%	52,1%	56,1%	71,3%	78,2%	**56,5%**
Military	46,4%	5,1%	1,1%	0,7%	2,6%	12,0%	2,4%	10,5%	6,9%	**14,0%**
Scientific	2,2%	7,8%	2,9%	2,1%	16,3%	6,8%	4,9%	4,0%	2,2%	**5,0%**
Art	1,9%	3,5%	1,4%	1,4%	3,0%	2,6%	3,8%	2,0%	1,6%	**2,5%**

After a thorough analysis of the post clusters and categories, it becomes evident that the most prevalent and emphasized categories in the Israeli strategy are political and military categories, with the other clusters following suit.

5 Conclusion

In conclusion, Israeli digital diplomacy towards Arab states, particularly in the period following the Abraham Accords, exemplifies a strategic and multifaceted approach aimed at fostering regional stability and economic cooperation. Through the extensive use of social media, Israel has achieved notable reachability of messages, particularly during conflicts such as those in Sheikh Jarrah and Gaza, indicating a militarization of its digital efforts to manage public perception. Despite these successes, challenges persist due to historical tensions and geopolitical dynamics. Israel excels in message dissemination and engagement, yet remains on the third level of digital diplomacy influence, as there is no clear evidence of changing perspectives or behaviors among Arab populations. This is supported by ongoing boycotting campaigns against Israeli products on social media.

Appendix 1

Facebook Pages

- Israel Speaks Arabic https://www.facebook.com/IsraelArabic.

This page serves as the predominant Arabic-language portrayal of the State of Israel on Facebook. With an impressive follower count of 3.3 million, it signifies a significant interest among Arabic-speaking users in actively engaging with Israeli content. The noteworthy follower count highlights the effectiveness of this page in promoting dialogue and fostering mutual understanding with Arabic-speaking audiences.

- Avichay Adraee https://www.facebook.com/IDFarabicAvichayAdraee.

Avichay Adraee, a prominent figure in the Israeli military, possesses a considerable online following of 2.5 million individuals on his Facebook page. In his capacity as a spokesperson for the Israeli military, his page assumes a pivotal role in disseminating official information and actively engaging with a diverse global audience. The substantial number of followers serves as a testament to his significant influence in shaping public discourse and perceptions surrounding Israeli military affairs.

- Israel in Iraqi https://www.facebook.com/IsraelinIraqi.

With a follower count of 705,851, the page "Israel in Iraqi" functions as a platform for facilitating dialogue between Israel and the Iraqi population. Its government sponsorship reflects a deliberate endeavor to connect with Iraqi audiences via social media. Although the number of followers may appear modest in comparison to other pages, it nonetheless demonstrates considerable interest and engagement within the Iraqi demographic.

- Israeli PM Arabic https://facebook.com/IsraeliPM.Arabic.

The Facebook page of the Israeli Prime Minister serves as a platform for disseminating news regarding the esteemed prime minister and his public addresses. The page's description explicitly states that it is the official Arabic page for Prime Minister Benjamin Netanyahu. Presently, the page boasts an impressive following of 320,066 individuals.

- Israel in Egypt https://www.facebook.com/IsraelinEgypt.

The mentioned page represents the official webpage of the consulate and embassy in Cairo. While it may not exhibit the same level of activity as other pages, it serves as a manifestation of the strategic objective to establish a dedicated digital diplomacy office within embassies, complementing the primary bureau in the Ministry of Foreign Affairs. As of now, the page boasts a substantial following of 263,943 individuals.

- Israel in Jordan https://www.facebook.com/IsraelinJordan.

This is the embassy page in Jordan, which currently has a relatively low number of followers—only 78,064. However, it is important to highlight that the page has been displaying a significant level of activity, possibly due to the ongoing conflict in Gaza and the strained relations between Jordan and its population.

- Ofir Gendelman https://facebook.com/OfirGendelmanpmo.

This is the Facebook page of Ofir Gendelman, an official government spokesperson for the Israeli Prime Minister, catering to the Arabic media. The page showcases Arabic posts discussing a wide range of topics, including military operations, humanitarian situations, and religious events in the region. Additionally, it provides videos and updates on current affairs, with a particular emphasis on Israel's interactions with Gaza and the broader Arab world. The page currently boasts a follower count of 198,549.

X Accounts

- Israel in Arabic https://twitter.com/IsraelArabic.

This page functions as the official Arabic-language representation of the State of Israel on social media. With a follower count exceeding half a million, it reflects a notable level of interest among Arabic-speaking audiences in actively engaging with Israeli content. The considerable number of followers implies a possible means for the Israeli government to effectively communicate its narratives and messages to Arabic-speaking populations, thereby promoting dialogue and fostering mutual understanding.

- Israel in the Gulf https://twitter.com/IsraelintheGulf.

Despite having a follower count that is comparatively lower than the "Israel in Arabic" page, the presence of a dedicated page for the Gulf region signifies the Israeli government's acknowledgement of the strategic significance of fostering connections with the Gulf states. The moderate number of followers suggests a certain level of interest in Israeli affairs within the Gulf region, although it may be lower compared to other contexts.

- Avichay Adraee https://twitter.com/AvichayAdraee.

This page portrays a prominent figure within the Israeli military, functioning as a medium for communication and engagement. Boasting a substantial following of over half a million individuals, it underscores the noteworthy role of individual personalities in molding public discourse and perspectives. The significant number of followers serves as a testament to the far-reaching impact of Avichay Adraee as a representative for the Israeli military, thereby magnifying the government's endeavors in conveying its messages.

- Prime Minister of the State of Israel https://twitter.com/Israelipm_ar.

As the section dedicated to the Israeli Prime Minister, this platform functions as a medium for official communications and updates from the highest position in the nation. Although the number of followers is significant, it is worth mentioning that it is lower compared to other pages examined in this research. Notwithstanding, the page continues to be a vital element of the Israeli government's digital communication strategy, enabling direct interaction with both national and international audiences.

- Ofir Gendelman https://twitter.com/ofirgendelman.

This is a X (formerly Twitter) profile page attributed to Ofir Gendelman, who holds the position of spokesperson for the Prime Minister of Israel in the Arab world. The page exhibits a range of posts authored by Ofir Gendelman, encompassing updates on Israeli Defense Forces (IDF) operations in Gaza, and observations pertaining to Arab television channels. The profile also includes a concise biography highlighting Ofir Gendelman as a media personality situated in Jerusalem, Israel. The current count of followers is 109,752.

- Israel in Dubai https://twitter.com/ofirgendelman.

This page is the official account of the Consulate-General of Israel in Dubai. It provides updates and information related to Israel in Dubai. The account has 8,016 followers.

- Israel in Bahrain https://twitter.com/IsraelinBahrain.

This page is the official account of the Israeli Embassy in the Kingdom of Bahrain. It posts updates and reposts content related to Israel and Bahrain relations. The account has 5,870 followers.

- Israel in Egypt https://twitter.com/IsraelinEgypt.

This page is X (formerly Twitter) account for the Israeli Embassy in Egypt. It focuses on strengthening relationships and cooperation between Israel and Egypt in various fields. The account has a total of 101.4 K followers.

- Israel in Jordan https://twitter.com/IsraelinJordan.

This page is the official page of the Israeli Embassy in Jordan. It is dedicated to enhancing diplomatic relations, economic growth, and friendship between Israel and Jordan. The page has approximately 20.5 K followers.

References

1. The next frontier: Israel taps AI and metaverse for aid in digital diplomacy (2023). Timesofisrael.com. https://www.timesofisrael.com/the-next-frontier-israel-taps-ai-and-metaverse-for-aid-in-digital-diplomacy/. Accessed 10 May 2024
2. The Abraham Accords: Unlocking Sustainable and Inclusive Growth Across the Middle East | UAE Embassy in Washington, DC (2020). https://www.uae-embassy.org/abraham-accords-sustainable-inclusive-growth. Accessed 10 May 2024
3. Westcott, N.: Digital diplomacy: the impact of the internet on international relations (2008)
4. Ali, D.: Electronic diplomacy: A study of the nature, requirements, and implications. ResearchGate; University of Human Development (2019). https://www.researchgate.net/publication/332418327_Electronic_diplomacy_A_study_of_the_nature_requirements_and_implications. Accessed 10 Mar 2024

5. Nweke, E.: Diplomacy in the era of digital governance: theory and Impact. Inf. Knowl. Manage. **2**(3) (2012). https://www.iiste.org/Journals/index.php/IKM/article/download/1784/1737. Accessed 10 Mar 2024
6. Kretschmer, L.-M.: Imagine there is war and it is tweeted live – an analysis of digital diplomacy in the israeli-palestinian conflict. Global Media J. – Germ. Ed. **7**(1) (2017). https://globalmediajournal.de/index.php/gmj/article/view/37. Accessed 10 May 2024
7. Manor, I., Crilley, R.: Visually framing the Gaza War of 2014: the Israel ministry of foreign affairs on Twitter. Media, War Conflict **11**(4), 369–391 (2018)
8. Antwi-Boateng, O., Al Mazrouei, K.A.M.: The challenges of digital diplomacy in the era of globalization: the case of the United Arab Emirates. Int. J. Commun. **15**, 19 (2021)
9. Al-Mansouri, T., Al-Mohannadi, H., Feroun, M.: Digital diplomacy during the first 100 days: How GCC ministries of foreign affairs and ministers tweeted the blockade. QScience Connect **2021**(2), 1 (2021)
10. Shamir, J.: Pursuing normalization with Iraq, Israeli digital diplomacy plays the heritage card - Israel News, Haaretz.com, Haaretz (2021). https://www.haaretz.com/israel-news/2021-01-30/ty-article/.premium/israel-pursuing-normalization-iraq-digital-diplomacy/0000017f-f133-df98-a5ff-f3bf29fe0000. Accessed 10 May 2024
11. Klee, M.: Israel's social media chief swears twitter messaging is working, rolling stone (2023). https://www.rollingstone.com/culture/culture-features/israel-social-media-twitter-messaging-david-saranga-1234874381/. Accessed 10 May 2024
12. Friedson, F.: Keyboard warriors: Fighting for Israel's digital story. The Jerusalem Post, JPost.com (2023). https://www.jpost.com/business-and-innovation/article-776252. Accessed 10 May 2024
13. Ruth, M.E.: Meet Israel's new digital diplomacy chief", Jewish Insider (2022). https://jewishinsider.com/2022/12/david-saranga-israel-digital-diplomacy-social-media-twitter/ Accessed 20 Apr 2024
14. Israel Ministry of Foreign Affairs, "Summary of Israel's 1st digital diplomacy", Digital Diplomacy Blog, p. 31 (2016). https://digdipblog.com/wp-content/uploads/2014/02/summary_of_israels_1st_digital_diplomacy.pdf. Accessed 5 Apr 2024
15. Ittefaq, M.: Digital diplomacy via social networks: a cross-national analysis of governmental usage of Facebook and Twitter for digital engagement. J. Contemp. Eastern Asia **18**(1) (2019)
16. Bjola, C., Jiang, L.: Social media and public diplomacy. Digit. Diplomacy: Theory Pract., 71–88 (2015)
17. Saxton, G.D., Waters, R.D.: What do stakeholders like on Facebook? Examining public reactions to nonprofit organizations' informational, promotional, and community-building messages. J. Publ. Relat. Res. **26**(3), 280–299 (2014)
18. Bolgov, R., Bogdanovich, S., Yag'ya, V., Ermolina, M.: How to measure the digital diplomacy efficiency: problems and constraints. In: Digital Transformation and Global Society: First International Conference, DTGS 2016, St. Petersburg, Russia, June 22–24 2016, Revised Selected Papers 1, pp. 180–188. Springer International Publishing (2016)
19. Wang, Y. Weibo diplomacy: management, measurement and challenges (Doctoral dissertation, King's College London) **161** (2021)
20. Garud-Patkar, N.: Is digital diplomacy an effective foreign policy tool? Evaluating India's digital diplomacy through agenda-building in South Asia. Place Brand. Public Dipl. **18**, 128–143 (2022)
21. DDI | About – Methodology (2024). https://digital-diplomacy-index.com/about/. Accessed 10 May 2024

Human Capital (Non-)mediatized? Media and Communication Competencies as an Element of Human Capital in the Strategies of Russian Regions

Svetlana S. Bodrunova[1(✉)] and Natalia Belyakova[2]

[1] St. Petersburg State University, 7-9 Universitetskaya nab., St. Petersburg 199004, Russia
s.bodrunova@spbu.ru

[2] Higher School of Economics, National Research University, 3A Kantemirovskaya ul., St. Petersburg 194100, Russia

Abstract. Regional development in many countries has been shown to be interlinked with and dependent upon the development of human capital in regions. Today, human capital gets digitalized, and digital competencies are seen as a crucial component of human capital. However, among them, competencies on modern media use and communication receive much less attention than digital competencies needed for professions or document processing. Most strategies of the Russian regions calculated till 2030 focus much upon regional human capital. However, in them, human capital is predominantly interpreted in terms of demographics, education, or culture, not communicative capabilities. Moreover, there is a lack of understanding whether competencies linked to communication, Internet use, and media literacy remain overlooked in the regional strategic planning, gradually take their proper place in regional strategic planning, or are seen as digital threats, rather than digital opportunities. In order to address these gaps notable both in academic research and regional strategic planning, we conduct qualitative coding for eight selected full texts of the Russian regional development strategies renewed in 2023. Our results show that the strategies are inert enough in how they, in general, (do not) link human capital to digital media and communication skills. This path dependence creates an obstacle for setting media education as a strategic regional goal for next decades. The strategies non-systemically mention digital competencies as 'intermediary' capital, but next-to-never assess the current state of media/communicative competencies and do not set exact and measurable priorities in this area of human capital. We discover 'four detachments' of media/communication from regional development, which future indicators for evaluation of communicative human capital may tackle.

Keywords: regional development · human capital · strategy · policy analysis · media use · communicative competencies · media literacy · Russia · regions

A. Chugunov et al. (Eds.): DTGS 2024, CCIS 2445, pp. 15–31, 2025.
https://doi.org/10.1007/978-3-031-90720-3_2

1 Introduction

Regional development in many countries has been shown to be interlinked with and dependent upon the development of human capital in regions [1]. However, in the predominant majority of recent studies on regional development, human capital is measured via levels of education, business productivity [1], inter-regional migration [2] and migration attractivity of regions, or occupational skills [3]. However, since late 2000s, aspects of human capital development based on information technologies have started to be counted in in terms of regional development [4].

Today, human capital gets digitalized, and digital competencies are seen as a crucial component of human capital in Europe [5] and the USA, as well as in China and Russia [6, 7]. However, among them, competencies of use of modern media use and communication receive much less attention than digital competencies needed for professions or document processing. This does not correspond to the everyday practices of socialization and pastime of both urban and rural dwellers, as well as to the rising political importance of today's mediatized communication and media use [8]. This is why it is necessary to address media and communicative competencies, both in regional strategic planning and in research, as a crucial element of human capital relevant for both everyday life and regional development.

Most development strategies of the Russian regions calculated till 2030 focus notably enough upon regional human capital in its various forms. However, today's research shows that, in the Russian political decision-making, human capital is predominantly interpreted in terms of demographics, education, or culture, just as in international studies and foreign human capital policies [1, 9]. Today's research on Russian regional development vs. human capital that shapes it is diverse enough to highlight regional differences in human capital growth in digital economy [10] and digital capital itself [11]. However, particular competencies within the generalized understanding of human capital, e.g. media and communication ones, remain largely understudied.

In particular, there are three areas that need immediate research. First, it is the issue of presence (or, rather, absence) of media and communicative competencies in the strategies and the actual place that media competencies take in strategic development of the Russian regions (see **RQ1** below). Second, it is the question on how media and communication competencies relate to the notion of human capital, enhance and reinterpret it (see **RQ2**). Third, the recent global polarization and the rise of online crime have both contributed to reshaping strategic thinking on many levels of the country's administration. This has, i.a., led to re-interpreting communication- and digitalization-related issues as digital threats, rather than digital opportunities. Thus, it is necessary to see whether communication competencies are seen more as a resource (part of the extant human capital), development goal, or digital threat (see **RQ3**).

In order to analyse how human capital is addressed and conceptualized in the newest versions of the development strategies of the Russian regions and whether media and communicative competencies are part of it, we link the extant studies on human and communicative capital to the practices of strategic regional planning. First, we discover the conceptual gap in human capital studie. Here, we base our argument upon the works on digital capital [12] and techno-capital [13]. We also show that today's research on communicative capital and communicative capitalism does not contain substantial studies on human communicative capital as an asset.

Second, we introduce the term 'communicative human capital' as a particular type of human capital that comprises competencies of two types: 1) those of media use for socio-political and human development purposes, and 2) those of mediated social communication for everyday use and education. For both (1) and (2), one needs to take into account direct use of media/social media for development, as well as abilities of individual countering digital threats, following media hygiene and heathy use of gadgets, and media literacy.

Third, we conduct qualitative coding as advised by Krippendorff [14] for full texts of the development strategies in 8 pilot regions, all the strategies renewed in 2023. The basis for the selection of regions is the works by Zubarevich [15] who has monitored regional development in Russia since the late 1990s, stratifying the regions according to dominant patterns of socio-economic behavior; in our current work, we employ her data on per capita gross regional product 1999 to 2017, as it allows for clear assessment of development dynamics. The overall number of pages coded manually is 1,500 +.

As a result, we make conclusions on the degrees and forms of involvement of human communicative capital into the regional strategic vision of development. In particular, we delineate the vision by regional governments towards media and communication competencies, define gaps in their strategic as a part of human capital, and formulate recommendations for raising this type of capital in the upcoming future.

2 Media and Communication Competencies as a Part of Human Capital: In Search of Conceptualization

2.1 Social, Cultural, Informational, Digital, or Technological? The Approaches to Communicative Human Capital and Gaps in Conceptualization

Today, the field that studies media and communicative competencies as a part of human capital is in the making; or, more precise, it is next to non-extant. In its current form, it has several significant gaps that need to be delineated.

First, these competencies are, overall, very rarely studied within the academic discourses on human capital. Development of human capital is researched upon in the context of digital economy and/or creative economy, while media and communication literacy are mostly studied within research on digital citizenship [16], quality of everyday life [17], and digital threats to (mental) health and counteraction against malcontent. In Western research, there is almost no direct linkage between media/communication skills and human capital in terms of territorial/national development. Since the early 2000s, the focus in the Western studies has been more on personal life-long development – individuals 'learning to be part of knowledge economy' [18]. This vision went in line with seeing digital divides and inequalities as a threat jeopardizing individual-level competition capacities and quality of life [19], rather than economic prosperity of societies on the whole, not speaking of seeing competencies in media and communication as a part of national and/or regional human resource.

Second, in parallel, a wide enough conceptualization of digital /technological/informational capital has emerged. A line of works has rethought Bourdieu's notion of social capital [20] for technologically-enhanced social environments. It started from the studies that expanded cultural capital for it to include information technology (but not as digital competencies) [20], and specified 'informational capital' [22], mostly as information technology capabilities and know-hows [23]. In a decade, the plea for measurable parameters of volume of knowledge-and-skills capital in specific fields [24], as well as the introduction of 'technological capital' [25, 26] and 'digital capital' [27, 28], allowed for coming closer to involving individual digital capacities into the vision on human capital as a societal-level category. However, 'communicative capital' or 'media human capital' as would-be-terms delineating media competencies as a part of human capital were not introduced. Today, 'techno-capital' [13] looks like the term closest to the one that we seek, as 'digital capital' is too wide and includes all aspects of human capital linked to digitalization, while 'techno-capital' implies information technologies for everyday use.

Third, there is a so far truly thin (but growing) stream of works that deals with the concept of 'communication/communicative capital' – seemingly, the concept we are looking for to define the distinct part of media-use- and mediatized-communication-related human capital. However, the 'media/communicative capital' has received various conceptualizations, most of which miss the point for us. In particular, there is a line of post-Bourdieu research that shows how *individual* social capital of *influence* grows via communication and media consumption [12], with implications for civic engagement [29], news credibility [30], strategic communication, branding and promotion strategies [31], and political influence [32]. It is also employed to interpret the power of media corporations as actors of capitalist economies; this, we one can easily see, is quite far from what we are looking for. However, a tiny research stream that explores the organizational-level effects of communicative capital in large-scale organizations actually comes quite close to our focus, as 'communication capital' in such works is seen as an organizational asset [33] (while we see it as a societal-level asset, a part of human capital that serves for regional development).

The post-Marxist line of research accentuates that communicative capital is the heart of communicative capitalism – a form of late capitalism in which values heralded as central to democracy materialize via networked communications technologies. 'Ideals of access, inclusion, discussion, and participation are realized through expansions, intensifications, and interconnections of global telecommunications' [34: 4]. This line also includes works on the capitalist and enslaving nature of digital labor, including the one produced when one uses social media for their own benefits [35, 36]. Another left-leaning line of research is represented by the works on digital inequalities, including those in digital capital having impact upon media use in the Russian regions [37], as well as upon the structure of online communities in the country [38]. In some other works, 'communication capital' is seen as the aggregate of means that technically allow for communication in the benefit of an entity [39], which, again, takes the concept too far away from human capital.

All the abovementioned leaves a distinct research gap on how media/communication competencies turn into human capital, including the one that may be employed for regional development. For delineating media/communicative capital as a type of human capital employed for development from other meanings of communicative capital, we suggest calling it 'communicative human capital' (CHC), analogously to 'digital human capital' [40] used occasionally as a clarifying term instead of 'digital capital.'

2.2 Communicative Human Capital: Searching for a Definition

To explore the concept of communicative human capital, we will first take a closer look at how one may deconstruct a close enough term of digital human capital.

Here, we need to accentuate that digital human capital as a concept is blurred in academic reflections upon it: Its vision ranges from a precondition of further development to its goal, its resource, and/or a metric of overall regional/national development. This prevents proper linking of digital human capital to regional development, besides several important attempts.

One of the telling attempts to conceptualize the linkage between regional development, human capital, and digitalization is that by Bannykh [41]. She sees digital human capital as both a process (with which one could disagree) and a result of accumulation of knowledge, experience, and know-hows by economic entities in the digital realm. For her, the process of formation of digital human capital has three stages, including: 1) capital as potential of access to ICT and Internet; 2) capital as accumulation of knowledge and skills in the digital realm; 3) transformation of the digital capital into social, economic, and cultural one, which implies its application to professional and personal life. If so, the regional digital capital, for her, is the process and the result of accumulation of digital capital on personal and organizational levels within the territory of a region [41: 674]. We do not fully share this logic, as we cannot agree that potential and accumulated capital need to be called the same way; however, what we see useful here is that, evidently, digital capital occupies an intermediary mental position that encompasses conditions for formation of digital skills, the accumulation of them, and their realization with the result of producing the 'final' forms of social capital. This logic of seeing digital capital (including communicative one) as an 'intermediary' form of capital may also be traced in the Digital Economy federal program and other legislative initiatives; we expect it to also show up in the regional strategies.

This is why, in the aforementioned absence of clear and shared understanding of communicative human capital, we will orient ourselves to two definitions of digital capital and techno-capital – by Ragnedda [13] and Choi et al. [12], respectively. They both see technologies-based capital in a twofold way, as accumulation of digital competencies (information, telecoms, digital safety, content production, and problem solution) and digital technologies *per se* as conditions for the growth of competencies. However, while agreeing that technologies need to find their proper place in conceptualization of digital human capital, we disagree with the vision that sees technologies *per se* as a part of human capital; rather, we see it as a factor, pre-condition, or pre-asset for human capital development.

Thus, we introduce the term 'communicative human capital' as a particular type of human capital that is built on the notion of communicative competencies, rather than on communicative technologies.

Our vision of communicative competencies comprises seven types of them:

1) Consumer competencies:
   a. Direct use competencies
   b. Media hygiene and development of healthy mediatized lifestyles
   c. Media literacy
   d. Countering digital communicative threats
2) Participatory competencies – media/communication deployment…:
   a. …for socio-political self-development and social change
   b. …for personal/group professional development
   c. …in creative industries and the public sphere

Here, competencies are seen as a foundation and core of CHC. However, in a wider view, analogously to digital human capital, one may view CHC as a constellation of infrastructural and competence-related accumulated assets, especially when competencies are undetachable from the competencies stated above (e.g., discussion clubs, media literacy courses etc.). However, we needn't forget that digital capital and communicative human capital differ in an important aspect, namely their political implications. Thus, digital capital is mostly viewed as a 'safe' democratization tool of e-governance – that is, ICT-based facilitation of relations between citizens and authorities. Unlike that, CHC may include both infrastructure and competencies for public discussion and deliberation, which may lead to both higher involvement of citizens into political decision-making *and* political turbulence. This is why CHC may be seen by political decision-makers (including the elaborators of regional strategies) as a digital threat not only in terms of malcontent and misuse of communicative infrastructure, but also as a threat to powerful via (il)legitimate enabling of citizens' voice. Due to current macroregional tensions and the growing world polarization, 'consolidational' trends may appear in strategic thinking of regional authorities; we will include both pro- and anti-deliberation positions into our analysis, if discover any.

CHC may also be seen on two levels – the strategic one and the competence (pragmatic) one. The strategic level implies that CHC is discussed in the strategies of the state/regional development where the current demands to CHC, as well as shortcomings in its development, are stated. The pragmatic level would study the ongoing states of competencies and the overall CHC development. Thus, our thought results into creating a two-dimensional research design that, first, explores the strategic level of CHC and then studies the consumer and participatory competencies of regional populaces.

In this paper, we focus on the strategic level of CHC in the Russian regions. Below, we explore how various types of human capital, either directly communicative or in some way connected to communication and/or media use, are discussed in the Russian research and the Russian regional strategies of development.

2.3 Communicative Human Capital in a Multi-speed Society: The Case of Russian Regions

The Russian regional development has been a special focus of both academic research and industrial/governmental analytics. Many of such studies demonstrate that, since at least the late Soviet times, Russia has been experiencing multi-speed development, and not in its better sense. Thus, multi-speed transition to the fifth and sixth technological waves [42–44] was accompanied by multi-dimensional socio-economic clustering of regions based on social values, patterns of labor distribution and consumption, and personal economic behavior [15] mirrored in the fragmentation of the Russian media system [45, 46] and political preferences of the population. In these conditions, digital transformation and digitalization have become a metric of regional development and competitiveness [47]. However, it is also seen as a precondition for regional development, in particular for its competitiveness [47] and for the development of human capital [48]. In many Russian-language essays on regional development, digital skills are also viewed as a development goal or a source for developing of other parameters of human capital and, more generally, regional progress.

In the late 2010s, Russia still lagged behind the developed countries in terms of use of of ICT technologies for regional development, especially in rural areas [10]. However, today, one may state that basic conditions for equal and low-barrier use of ICTs in everyday life have been established in all the federal districts of Russia. Thus, use of personal computers reaches 87% +, Internet use does not drop lower than 91% (in Siberia), and even use of ICTs for communication with authorities varies from 64% to nearly 88% in 2022 [40: 94–96]. Based on Rosstat data, Borodkin [40] postulates the absence of significant digital inequalities between Russian regions; moreover, in 2018 to 2022, he sees a 'progressive increase in digitalization in all regions of the Russian Federation' [40: 88]. However, other studies show that, today, federal districts vary by the salience of digital divide and possibilities for accumulation of individual digital capital [37]. In the 2010s, they used to vary notably in terms of access to smartphones and organizational access to hi-speed Internet [11], though platformized communication was available throughout the country, even if used in varying ways (e.g., there are cases of use of popular messengers for newsgroup formation in the Far Eastern region, while other regions use social media platforms like VK.com for the same practice). Today, the differences in digital inclusion only start to gradually diminish [37].

2.4 Regional Strategic Planning: Human Capital *and/or* Digital Economy vs. Regional Socio-economic Development

Today, all the three aspects of our focus, namely socio-economic development of Russian regions, human capital, and digitalization are expected to be interlinked in the strategic planning developed by the regions; for socio-economic development vs. digital economy, this is openly demanded by Ministry of Economic Development [49].

Despite that, the rare cases of exploratory analysis of strategic interlinkage between the two, e.g. those of translocation of the goals of the 'Digital Economy' federal program to regional strategies of Urals regions [49], shows that, on the strategic level, the regional goals only partly mirror the federal program, and do so in half of the district only. Thus, we do not expect that media/communicative aspects of the digital transformation would occupy any significant space in the regional strategies; but, the smaller the attention, the bigger lacuna we could discover, and the bigger shift would be needed in strategic regional planning. There are also impressive attempts of elaboration of indexing criteria for digitalization of the Russian regions [50]; however, media/communication capital is completely omitted in them, which only confirms that a large-scale gap exists in practical thinking over digitalization in regional development, mirroring the gap in theorizing communicative human capital and its regional dimension. We will partly employ the exploratory approach by Elokhov and colleagues [49] in our study (see below), but we will also amplify it by additional parameters suitable for future indexing, as suggested in [50].

We also cannot help noting that, while strategies demand interlinking socio-economic and digital development, the impact of digital transformation upon regional growth is a contested terrain in Russian regional studies. Thus, modeling [51] demonstrates the positive impact of digital economy upon regional growth, but there are studies with other qualitative and quantitative methods that undermine their real-life interrelatedness, especially the positive impact of digitalization upon the regional GDP [52, 53]. Assessment of efficiency of the regional communicative capital is much beyond the goals of this paper; but we need to note that communicative skills and media use have not yet at all been seen as a factor of regional development, and we still need to (dis)prove their (ir)relevance in this respect.

Human capital is, as stated above, another parameter of regional development on which cluster analysis of regions is made [54] and regional scenarios are forecasted [55]. However, no research shows how the two parameters – human capital and digital economy – could interrelate in regional development. This is why we will focus on exploring media/communication capital as a part of digital human capital in regional strategies, to see how exactly the two development parameters intertwine and what relations are implied between them by the regional authorities.

3 Method

3.1 The Research Questions

Having in mind all the aforementioned, we can now concretize our research questions in the following way:

RQ1. How are media and/or communicative infrastructure and competencies conceptualized in the development strategies of the Russian regions? What conceptual space, if any, do they occupy in the strategies?

RQ2:

a) Is media/communicative capital seen as a part of human capital? What are the relations between media use and/or communicative competencies, on one hand, and human capital, on the other?
b) If media/communicative capital is not discussed at all, what are the relations between digital capital and human capital?

RQ3. How is media/communicative capital (or digital capital, if the former is absent) interpreted in the strategies? Is it seen as an 'intermediary' capital (a pre-requisite, condition, resource, or factor of development), as 'goal capital', or a digital/political threat?

3.2 The Exploratory Methodology and the Research Focus

Our methodology partly echoes that of [56, 57] but focuses more on interrelation between communicative human capital and regional development. We have developed a codebook with 11 interpretive variables, among them:

- section, subsection, and exact page of the discovered quote;
- specific context of the quote;
- priority vision (communicative or digital capital as a challenge, resource, perspective, goal, threat, other, mixed, undefined);
- topicality (media literacy, media use and Internet communication, digital literacy, other, mixed, undefined);
- problem statement in the quote and/or in the context of the quote;
- statistical evidence (yes/no and the actual data);
- general interpretation by a coder.

We have employed 4 pre-trained coders to code the texts of eight regional strategies. The approach to coding is as advised by Krippendorff [14].

Based on Ragnedda's definition [13] and our reflections stated above, we have defined the scope of our analysis to instruct the coders. What we, in particular, aimed to find in the strategy texts and to code was the following [13]:

- general assessment of the media/communicative competencies in relation to human capital and/or regional development;
- measurement and mapping of communicative skills and/or media consumption;
- measurement/mapping of content production by population in relation to human capital, productivity growth, problem solving, or regional competitiveness;
- measurement or any other type of discussion on media/communicative threats and the capacities of population to struggle with them;
- discussion on communication as a threat to political regime and the necessity of counter-action;
- reviewing of and strategic planning for the development of landscapes for formation of media/communicative competencies, such as media/digital educational initiatives, media schooling and higher education, media camps etc.

We amplify the coding with a case study on Lipetsk region, where we show how strategic thinking on media and communication demonstrates inertia in perception by the authorities and multi-dimensional detachment between the key development goals.

3.3 Sampling of the Strategies

As this is a pilot study needed for method testing and refinement, we have selected eight regions for our analysis. In our selection, we have followed the logic that emerged in the report by economic geographer Natalia Zubarevich [15]; additionally, we wanted to avoid the impact of the major crises of the 2020s and, thus, have used the data on regional stability and capital published by Zubarevich before the crises, in 2019. Zubarevich's report contains the data on per capita gross regional product for 1999 to 2017 that depicts the stable inequality of the Russian regions, providing for three groups of regions (and Tyumen as a positive outlier), namely developed ones, mid-developed ones, and outsiders. Each region is given a position within three waves of research (1999, 2008, 2017), which allows for tracing individual development of a region juxtaposed to the other regions' trajectories pf economic growth. This classification differs significantly from the 'four Russias' classification provided by Zubarevich in her earlier works [58] and used in our earlier studies on fragmentation of public communication in Russia [45, 46, 59], but we prefer the per capita GRP data, as they allow for tracing both the stable inequalities and the growth dynamics of individual regions.

We have selected two regions from each group, making sure that their position remained the same from 1999 to 2017. Of the developed ones, these were Perm Krai and Orenburg region; of mid-developed, Vologda and Lipetsk regions; of outsiders, Zabaikalsky Krai and Pskov region. Then, we have added two regions whose position has drastically improved between 1999 and 2017, to see whether, for these regions, communicative (or digital) capital stands out in importance. The two regions were Amursky Krai and Kamchatsky Krai. The volume of analysed text was 1,500 + standard pages.

4 Results

4.1 RQ1: The Place of Media/Communication Capital in the Regional Strategies

The regions mostly do not place communication capital development within strategic goals or priorities; public and citizen communication is discussed at the end of strategies, if ever at all. Digital competencies are discussed to a larger extent, but mostly in professional aspects, in terms of e-governance (access to state digital services), education for IT, facilitation of medical services, infrastructural development, and formation of accessible environments. Thus, on one hand, the 'intermediary' role of digital competencies is confirmed, while the regions do not see communicative skills as important *per se*. On the other hand, though, the 'infrastructural' vision clearly dominates over the competence-oriented one, and digitalization is not interlinked with the regional priorities well enough. The only exception is the leader region of Perm Krai where a sustainable program called 'Development of information society' clearly connects digital development as an all-encompassing contour to the goals of diversification in major production sectors, green economy, creative economy, tourism and hospitality, human capital, and territorial development. Most regions, though, put attention into digitalizing local TV services and, more generally, access to regional and national news. Orenburg, another developed region, also links environmental protection to digital growth.

Mid-developed regions demonstrate attention to both digital development and traditional media, though not in terms of competencies development but infrastructurally. The Lipetsk region (see below) notably cares for communication development but does not contextualize it via social capital, public sphere, or other developmental goals.

The regions lagging behind in overall economic development seem to set a bit more ambitious goals in the digital realm but overlook communication. Thus, Zabaikalsky Krai sets several infrastructural goals related to raising digital capital, including hi-speed connection to state digital services and digital switchover of the local state TV channel, as well as several competence-oriented goals (e.g., opening a 'digital university'). Kamchatsky Krai aims at finding chances for breakthrough in growth of creative industries. Border regions, such as Zabaikalsky and Amursky Krai, emphasize linkages between digital communication and preservation of cultural identity.

4.2 RQ2: The Linkages Between Digital/Communication Development and Human Capital

In most regions, the link between human capital as a goal and communication or digital development is very weak and fragmented. No region mentions communicative capital as a strategic goal; moreover, in all the regions, the strategic goals of digital development and human capital development are detached from each other. Media education as a key instrument of raising communicative competencies is virtually absent; so are soft communicative skills for development, from information hygiene and false information detection to participation in public discussion on key regional projects and collaborative projecting to deliberative participation via open communication milieus to mediatized social relations to cybercrime alertness.

The linkages between digital development and human capital mostly lies, for the regions, in three aspects: 1) in raising populational skills of using state digital services; 2) in how they prioritize education on digital technologies, with no clear goals of this education explained, and 3) in provision of infrastructure (from Internet access, to virtual libraries and concert halls, as in Zabaikalsky Krai, to digital tourist attractions) that, evidently, implies the rise of communicative skills and digital embeddedness of citizens. However, all the regions also state shortage of IT staff for the digital shift, less developed regions being especially concerned over it.

4.3 RQ3: The Interpretation of Media/Communicative Environment and Skills

Both infrastructural and competence-oriented communicative and digital capital (even if not called this way) are seen in the strategies in a wide variety of ways – as a goal, perspective, asset, resource, challenge, problem, risk, and threat (in cybercrime and its prevention), thus reconfirming the 'intermediary' vision of digital and communicative capital in terms of its developmental roles.

As a goal, communicative competencies are present within strategizing on digital transformation of education, enhancement of educational capacities/environments, and access to digitalized services, from state documentation to virtual cultural facilities. As a resource, three regions see media use competencies (web portal use capacities) as resources for inclusion of the disabled and, again, provision of equal access to services, from smart cities to telemedicine, for creation of digitalized/mediatized access to compensates for geographical and logistic asymmetry of regions. Media competencies are not seen as a public threat, except for the cybercrime-related use of media; but neither they are seen as a public asset needed for public sphere development.

4.4 A Case Study: Lipetsk Region

To explore deeper the typical logic of detachment between communicative human capital, on one hand, and premises and goals of the regional development, on the other, we have taken Lipetsk region as a case study. In this region, media and communication are salient enough in the regional strategy, but inertia and distortions in perception of the media landscape and public roles of media lead to conceptual gaps in strategic planning. These gaps come from four types of detachment of communicative human capital from:

- *digital economy.* Strategic goal setting mentions development of social networks (G4) and communicative spaces in the city, with no explanation of how social networks would work in terms of social capital or economic growth. In the development scenario, digital development ('Speed of communication and information processing: online [as a noun], clouds, networks, facilities, big data, AI, VR') is not linked to communication and media consumption. This demonstrates an 'infrastructural' vision where provision of facilities is seen as a 'magic wand', a per se growth factor and a goal at the same time, as if infrastructural changes were the capital itself. This echoes the vision in Russian academic writing and national projects that sees infrastructure accumulation as a part of digital/communicative capital, without the necessity to develop skills for using it. Thus, the development of digital economy does not include the development of new media/communicative skills for the wide population. Interestingly, the region sees well enough 'the growing demand on information services and creative industry services, [as well as] changes in the structure of media consumption towards new publicly available platforms' (p. 264), but continues to see 'media' as TV and newspapers, despite describing the competition of traditional media with multiple 'new gatekeepers in town' [55], including what the region calls 'free agents' (assumingly, independent digital media based in the blogosphere, social networks, and/or messengers) and brand media. Traditional media, especially the politically relevant TV and newspapers, are also viewed 'infrastructurally', and the major goal is seen as provision of TV service and publishing more copies of newspapers – again, despite the noted shift in media use patterns. The detachment is, though, not full, as the region reports on the regional state-owned TV channel as non-included in the national TV multiplex and its readiness to start digital broadcasting. Just as well, the region sees the goals in 'developing new media, including Internet outlets, rearrangement of editorial offices, expansion [of media] on social networks, opening [of media] on new platforms', along with the growth of attractivity of the regional media for audiences and advertisers. But this vision is not supported by that on why expansion of new media formats would be beneficial for the regional publics;
- *human capital:* Both the development of traditional media and digital economy are detached from human capital development. Thus, priority G3 (human capital) does not contain any digital or communicative competencies, and priority G4 (technologies) does not mention human capital. The efficiency metrics suggested till 2024 contained neither digital nor communicative competencies in public or professional human capital development. In the strategic goals, both human capital and urban communicative spaces are mentioned but not interlinked; development of ICT infrastructures is not linked to human capital; and the goal of development of digital competencies is contextualized via knowledge of state digital services, not everyday communicative practices or political roles of media. In 2.4 'Policy on human capital accumulation', no goals related digital, media-use, or communicative competencies are set. The 'infrastructural' vision on traditional media is also detached from human capital

development, though not completely. In particular, human capital is linked to media via the statement on staff shortage in the media sphere and competition on qualified professionals between traditional media, 'free agents', and brands, and... the region sets a goal of raising salaries for media professionals in order to prevent(!) their flow to new media and brand media, rather than of stimulating a diverse digital media landscape. At the same time, one of the sub-goals within media development is seen as 'growth of adaptability of the staff in media and publishing to the new and changing conditions and formats (social networks, Internet media, and Smart TV)' (p. 269); that is, only professional media-related human capital is taken into account by the region. This logic also shows up in the fact that the only signs of media education as strategy elements are mentions of trainings for governmental staff on public communication and the focus of the local branch of RANEPA academy on studying communicative competencies, and media education for populace is not mentioned in the strategy;

- *political participation:* Once in the text, 'involvement of citizens into public life' is mentioned (p. 279), but the instruments for that are described in a soundly paternalistic way ('interaction of authorities with opinion leaders', 'speaking to the people in the language comprehensible to them', 'lowering communicative barriers, both vertical and horizontal' – assumingly, between the power chimneys and between the authorities and the people). No clear deliberative goals are set in development of human capital, digital economy, or media and communication infrastructure in the region. On the other hand, public communication is neither seen as a threat for political stability and is, in general, perceived as a strategic sub-field for development. We would also stress the controversial view on the current level of development of the Lipetsk media landscape, as it is described as well-developed and under-developed at the same time.
- *regional development potential:* As stated above, neither digital nor communicative /media-use skills are set as evaluation parameters of regional growth; nor even the communicative infrastructure is set as a clear metric, with the exception of Internet use reaching over 90% in the nearest future.

5 Discussion and Conclusion

Our analysis of the Russia regional development strategies has revealed a large-scale lacuna in their orientation to communicative human capital, from capital accumulation to control to political participation and many more. Media use and mediatized communication are not seen as human capital-creating assets, as they can be (and are) in reality. Being largely overlooked, they do not invoke statistical measurement, strategic goal-setting, or problem statement; however, neither they are described as a major threat.

We have also spotted four types of detachment of media/communication as a regional development asset from other resources/assets/goals, including the detachment from digital economy, human capital, and political participation; this reduced vision on communication leads to the fourth type of detachment, which is overlooking the communicative human capital as a strategic parameter of regional development.

The vision of media and communication development in the regions reviewed, both developed and outsiders, is still subjected to a certain inertia of: 1) seeing traditional communication formats as leading, and 2) the 'infrastructural' view upon the media landscape that needs developing in terms of tech facilities and staff professionalism, with the necessity of media education disregarded. Communicative competencies are seen as self-forming (or not discussed at all), and this leads to overlooking both the public participation potential they bring on and digital threats caused by them. Despite the well-developed world study area on media education, Russian regions do not see educating people about complicated communication environments as their goal, limiting themselves to spreading knowledge on state digital services and provision of communication infrastructure. The crucial link between the two parts of communicative human capital, the facilities one and the competencies one [13], thus does not form.

In our small sample, we did not detect striking regional differences; rather, there is a striking similarity of approaches in regions of varying GRP per capita. This may be conditioned by how communicative capital is disregarded in the federal-level goal-setting documents, which needs further study. Yet, we have seen systemic difference in how Perm Krai has made digitalization (including media) a contour for reaching the goals of advancing to the sixth technological wave. A trend that we can trace is.

However small the sample, it still allows for suggesting criteria for deeper assessment of communicative human capital in the regional strategies. These may be linked to the 'four detachments' of communication from human capital, digital economy, public sphere, and overall prosperity of the Russian regions.

Acknowledgements. Svetlana S. Bodrunova's work is supported by Center for International Media Research at St. Petersburg State University, Russia. Natalia Belyakova's work is supported by Projecting and Educational Laboratory of Communications in Creative Industries at National Research University – Higher School of Economics, Russia.

References

1. Gennaioli, N., La Porta, R., Lopez-de-Silanes, F., Shleifer, A.: Human capital and regional development. Q. J. Econ. **128**(1), 105–164 (2013)
2. Faggian, A., Modrego, F., McCann, P.: Human capital and regional development. In: Capello, R., Nijkamp, P. (eds.) Handbook of regional growth and development theories: Revised and extended second edition, pp. 149–171. Edward Elgar Publishing (2019)
3. Mellander, C., Florida, R.: The rise of skills: Human capital, the creative class, and regional development. In: Fischer, M. M., Nijkamp, P. (eds.) Handbook of regional science: Second and extended edition, pp., 707–719. Springer, Heidelberg (2021)
4. Schaffer, A., Siegele, J.: Efficient use of regional transport infrastructure, communication networks, and human capital. J. Infrastruct. Syst. **15**(4), 263–272 (2009)
5. The European Reference Framework for Key Competences for Lifelong Learning. Brussels: European Commission (2018). https://op.europa.eu/en/publication-detail/-/publication/297a33c8-a1f3%E2%80%9311e9%E2%80%939d01%E2%80%9301aa75ed71a1/language-en. Accessed 12 May 2024
6. Decree of the President of the Russian Federation as of May 7, 2018, #204, On national goals and strategic targets of development of the Russian Federation for the period till the year of 2024 https://base.garant.ru/71937200/. Accessed 12 May 2024
7. Decree of the President of the Russian Federation as of July 21, 2020, #474, On national development goals of the Russian Federation for the period till the year of 2030. http://www.kremlin.ru/acts/bank/45726. Accessed 12 May 2024

8. Salleh, S.M., Shamshudeen, R.I., Abas, W.A.W., Tamam, E.: Determining media use competencies in media literacy curriculum design for the digital society: a modified 2-wave Delphi method. SEARCH (Malaysia) **11**(1), 17–36 (2019)
9. Human development report 2023/2024: Breaking the gridlock: Reimagining cooperation in a polarized world. United Nations Development Programme. https://hdr.undp.org/system/files/documents/global-report-document/hdr2023%E2%80%9324reporten.pdf. Accessed 12 June 2024
10. Minaev, N.N., Zharova, E.A.: Analysis of accumulation of human capital in the Russian regions as conditioned by technological shifts and digital economy transition [Analiz nakopleniya chelovecheskogo kapitala v regionakh Rossii v usloviyakh tekhnologicheskikh sdvigov i perekhoda k tsifrovoy ekonomike]. Ekonomika truda **8**(6), 565–584 (2021)
11. Gladkova, A., Vartanova, E., Ragnedda, M.: Digital divide and digital capital in multiethnic Russian society. J. Multicultural Discourses **15**(2), 126–147 (2020)
12. Choi, J.R., Straubhaar, J., Skouras, M., Park, S., Santillana, M., Strover, S.: Techno-capital: theorizing media and information literacy through information technology capabilities. New Media Soc. **23**(7), 1989–2011 (2021)
13. Ragnedda, M.: Conceptualizing digital capital. Telematics Inform. **35**(8), 2366–2375 (2018)
14. Krippendorff, K.: Content Analysis: An Introduction to Its Methodology. Sage (2018)
15. Zubarevich, N.V.: Trends in development of the Russian regions [Tendentsii razvitiya rossiyskih regionov]: A report to the Federation Council of the Federal Assembly of the Russian Federation (2019). https://www.youtube.com/watch?v=_zwWcxU43Tk. Assessed 12 June 2024
16. Hunt, E.A.: Media literacy and digital citizenship. In: Halpern-Felsher, B. (ed.) Encyclopedia of Child and Adolescent Health, vol. 3, pp. 372–384. Elsevier (2023)
17. Zdravkova, E.: Media literacy as a key competency for the safe and effective use of media. In: ICERI2019 Proceedings, pp. 7467–7473. IATED (2019)
18. Grant, L. Learning to be part of the knowledge economy: digital divides and media literacy. Futurelab, Bristol (2007)
19. Trappel, J.: Digital media inequalities: policies against divides, distrust and discrimination. Nordicom (2019)
20. Bourdieu, P.: Forms of capital. In: Biggart, N. W. (ed.) Readings in Economic Sociology, pp. 280–291. Blackwell Publishers, Oxford (2008)
21. Emmison, M., Frow, J.: Information technology as cultural capital. Aust. Univ. Rev. **41**(1), 41–45 (1998)
22. Van Dijk, J.: The Deepening Divide: Inequality in the Information Society. Sage (2005)
23. Rojas, V., Straubhaar, J.D., Roychowdhury, D., Okur, O.: Communities, cultural capital, and the digital divide. In: Bucy, E.P., Newhagen, J.E. (eds.) Media Access, pp. 127–150. Routledge, New York (2003)
24. Van Deursen, A., Helsper, E.J.: The third-level digital divide: who benefits most from being online? Commun. Inf. Technol. Ann. **10**, 29–53 (2015)
25. Straubhaar, J.D., Spence, J., Tufekci, Z., Lentz, R.G.: Inequity in the Technopolis: Race, Class, Gender, and the Digital Divide in Austin. University of Texas Press, Austin (2012)
26. McConnell, C.: Digital Inclusion and Techno-capital in Austin. Texas. The University of Texas at Austin, Austin (2014)
27. Ignatow, G., Robinson, L.: Pierre Bourdieu: theorizing the digital. Inf. Commun. Soc. **20**(7), 950–966 (2017)
28. Rojas, H., Shah, D.V., Friedland, L.A.: A communicative approach to social capital. J. Commun. **61**(4), 689–712 (2011)
29. Jeffres, L.W., Jian, G., Yoon, S.: Conceptualizing communication capital for a changing environment. Commun. Q. **61**(5), 539–563 (2013)

30. Lee, S., Nah, S., Chung, D. S., Kim, J.: Predicting AI news credibility: Communicative or social capital or both? In: Nah, S., McNealy, J. E., Kim, J. H., Joo, J. (eds.) Communicating Artificial Intelligence (AI): Theory, Research, and Practice, pp. 60–79. Routledge (2020)
31. Dekalov, V.V.: Communicative capital: conceptualization of the concept. Vestnik Sankt-Peterburgskogo universiteta: Sociology **10**(4), 397–409 (2017)
32. Rykov, I.: Virtual Community as a Social Field: Inequality and Communicative Capital [Virtual'noe soobshchestvo kak sotsial'noe pole: neravenstvo i kommunikativnyi kapital]. Zhurnal sotsiologii i sotsial'noi antropologii **4**, 44–60 (2013)
33. Malmelin, N.: Communication capital: modelling corporate communications as an organizational asset. Corp. Commun.: Int. J. **12**(3), 298–310 (2007)
34. Dean, J.: Communicative capitalism and class struggle. Spheres: J. Digit. Cultures **1**, 1–16 (2014)
35. Fuchs, C.: Labor in Informational Capitalism and on the Internet. Inf. Soc. **26**, 179–196 (2010)
36. Brophy, E., de Peuter, G.: Labours of mobility: communicative capitalism and the smartphone cybertariat. In: Herman, A., Hadlaw, J., Swiss, T. (eds.) Theories of the Mobile Internet: Materialities and Imaginaries, pp. 60–84. Routledge, London (2014)
37. Gladkova, A., Ragnedda, M.: Exploring digital inequalities in Russia: an interregional comparative analysis. Online Inf. Rev. **44**(4), 767–786 (2020)
38. Rykov, I.: Network Inequality and the Structure of Inline Communities [Setevoe neravenstvo i struktura onlain-soobshchestv]. Zhurnal sotsiologii i sotsial'noi antropologii **4**(81), 144–156 (2015)
39. Corrado, C.A.: Communication capital, Metcalfe's Law, and US productivity growth. Economics Program Working Papers, EPWP #11–01 (2011). https://citese-erx.ist.psu.edu/document?repid=rep1&type=pdf&doi=762de314cf72f01383fd031340921cfb7adcb3b6. Accessed 12 May 2024
40. Borodkin, M: Digital social capital of Russian regions: theoretical approaches and practical aspects [Tsifrovoy sotsial'niy kapital rossiyskih regionov: teoreticheskie podhody i prakticheskie aspekty]. Soc. Secur. Insights **7**(1), 87–102 (2024)
41. Bannykh, G.A.: Digital capital of a region as its competitiveness condition in today's economy [Tsifrovoy kapital regiona kak usloviye ego konkurentosposobnosti v sovremennoy ekonomike]. In: Russian regions in the focus of change (conference proceedings), pp. 674–676 (2020)
42. Bodrunov, S.D.: Transition to a prospective technological wave: analysis versus the concepts of new industrial society and noonomy [Perehod k perspektivnomu tehnologicheskomu ukladu: analiz s pozitsii kontseptsiy NIO.2 i noonomiki]. Ekonomicheskoe vozrozhdenie Rossii **3**(57), 5–12 (2018)
43. Mil'ner, B. Z.: The concept of knowledge management in modern organizations [Kontseptsiya upravleniya znaniyami v sovremennyh organizatsiyah]. Rossiyskiy zhurnal menedzhmenta **1**, 57–76 (2003)
44. Naumov, S.V.: Management of international competitiveness within the primary practical goals of modernization of the Russian economy [Upravleniye mezhdunarodnoy konkurentosposobnostyu v sisteme pervoocherednykh prakticheskikh zadach modernizatsii ekonomiki Rossii]. Ves' mir, Moscow (2015)
45. Bodrunova, S.S., Litvinenko, A.A.: Four Russias in communication: fragmentation of the Russian public sphere in the 2010s. In: Dobek-Ostrowska, B., Glowacki, M. (eds.) Democracy and Media in Central and Eastern Europe 25 Years On, pp. 63–79. Peter Lang (2015)
46. Bodrunova, S., Litvinenko, A.: Fragmentation of society and media hybridisation in today's Russia: how Facebook voices collective demands. J. Soc. Policy Res. **14**(1), 113–124 (2016)
47. Svistunova, I.G., Shutova, O.A., Sakhnyuk, T.I., Sakhnyuk, P.A., Korshikova, M.V.: Formation and development of human capital of rural territories with the help of new information and

communication technologies: Barriers and perspectives. In: Popkova, E. G., Ostrovskaya, V. N. (eds.) Perspectives on the use of New Information and Communication Technology (ICT) in the Modern Economy, pp. 716–722. Springer, Cham (2019)
48. Vartanova, E.L.: Post-Soviet transformations of media and journalism [Postsovetskie transformatsii SMI i zhurnalistiki]. MediaMir, Moscow (2013)
49. Guidelines on elaboration and correction of a strategy of socio-economic development of a region of the Russian Federation and its realization plan, approved by the order of the Ministry of Economic Development of the Russian Federation, #132 as of March 23, 2017. http://docs.cntd.ru/document/456054578. Accessed 12 May 2024
50. Elokhov, A.M., Alexandrova, T.V., Bulgakova, I.N.: Requirements of the National Program 'Digital Economy of the Russian Federation' as mirrored in the development strategies of the regions of the Ural Federal District [Otrazheniye trebovaniy Natsionalnoy Programmy «Tsifrovaya Ekonomika Rossiyskoy Federatsii» v strategiyakh razvitiya regionov Uralskogo federalnogo okruga]. Vestnik Yuzhno-Uralskogo gosudarstvennogo universiteta: Ekonomika i menedzhment **17**(1), 36–48 (2023)
51. Kaurova, O.V., Maloletko, A.N., Matrayeva, L.V., Korolkova, N.A.: Composing indicators for assessing the level of development of the digital economy in the region (regional digital environment) [Opredeleniye sostava pokazateley otsenki urovnya razvitiya tsifrovoy ekonomiki v regione (regionalnoy tsifrovoy sredy)]. Fundamentalnyye i prikladnyye issledovaniya kooperativnogo sektora ekonomiki **1**, 138–149 (2020)
52. Mirolyubova, T.V., Radionova, M.V.: Evaluation of impact factors of digital transformation upon regional economic growth [Otsenka vliyaniya faktorov tsifrovoy transformatsii na regionalnyy ekonomicheskiy rost]. Regionologiya **29**(3(116)), 486–510 (2021)
53. Abdurakhmanova, G.I., Vishnevskiy, K.O., Volkova, G.L., Gokhberg, L. M.: Indicators of digital economy: 2018: statistical yearbook [Indikatory tsifrovoy ekonomiki: 2018: statisticheskiy sbornik]. NRU-HSE, Moscow (2018)
54. Nikolayev, M. A., Makhotayeva, M. Yu., Gusarova, V. N.: Analysis of impact of digitalization processes upon economic development of regions [Analiz vliyaniya protsessov tsifrovizatsii na ekonomicheskoye razvitiye regionov]. π-Economy **13**(4), 46–56 (2020)
55. Trifonov, Y.V., Sochkov, A.L., Mironov, E.A.: Typology of Russian regions by human capital development based on neural network cluster analysis [Tipologiya rossiyskikh regionov s tochki zreniya razvitiya chelovecheskogo kapitala na baze neyrosetevogo klasternogo analiza]. Vestnik Nizhegorodskogo universiteta im. Lobachevskogo: Sotsialnyye nauki **4**(64), 23–34 (2021)
56. Akindinova, N.V., Yasin, E.G., Avdeyeva, D.A.: Growth scenarios for the Russian economy with human capital calculated in [Stsenarii rosta rossiyskoy ekonomiki s uchetom vklada chelovecheskogo kapitala]: A conference report. NRU – HSE, Moscow (2019) [in Russian]. scinapse.io/papers/3018517577. Accessed 12 May 2024
57. Dovbysh, O.: New gatekeepers in town: How groups in social networking sites influence information flows in Russia's provinces. Soc. Media + Soc. **7**(2), 20563051211013253 (2021)
58. Zubarevich, N.V.: Four Russias [Chetyre Rossii]. Vedomosti, December 30, 2011, vedomosti.ru/opinion/articles/2011/12/30/chetyre_rossii. Accessed 12 June 2024
59. Nigmatullina, K., Bodrunova, S. S., Rodossky, N., Nepiyushchikh, D.: Discourse of complaining on social networks in Russia: Cumulative opinions vs. decentering of institutions. In: Fifth Networks in the Global World Conference, pp. 3–20. Springer, Cham (2022)

Managing Information Flows of Financial Literacy in Social Media: The Russian Case

Elena Brodovskaya(✉), Roman Parma, and Vladimir Lukushin

Financial University Under the Government of the Russian Federation, Moscow, Russia
evbrodovskaya@fa.ru

Abstract. The article is devoted to the study of financial literacy information flows of the adult population of the Russian Federation in the social media. In the context of dynamic digitalisation of the financial sector, the issues of promotion of educational and training materials on competent and effective financial behaviour of citizens in social networks and messengers are becoming more and more relevant. The purpose of the study is to determine the scope, dynamics, structure and main topics of information flows of adult financial education in the Russian segment of social media, to identify the main trends in the development of the digital communication system and problem areas that require additional efforts on the part of government agencies and public structures. The design of the empirical study is based on the general principles of social media predictive analytics and includes the use of the following methods: cognitive mapping of thematic digital content, automated social media analysis of information flows. The results of the study show dysfunctionality in the management of financial education information flows and web content in terms of continuity, targeting and genre diversity of materials, which negatively affects the visibility, reach and distribution of such content. Based on the results of the research, it is possible to identify significant shifts in the direction and content of the flow of information, linked to the current social and political environment. During the study period, the gender and age composition of users involved in the process of creating and disseminating financial education materials also changed. The authors identify broad prospects for the use of social media analysis for in-depth study of the current state and trends in the development of financial behaviour, financial culture and financial literacy in Russia.

Keywords: financial literacy · financial education · electronic interaction · digital communications · social media · social networks · information flows · digital environment

1 Introduction

The current stage of development of the Russian Federation is associated with a number of complex conditions and challenges, such as increased international tensions, changes in world economy, restructuring of the national economy in the context of instability of commodity markets, increased sanctions. Multiplied by the increased dynamics of

A. Chugunov et al. (Eds.): DTGS 2024, CCIS 2445, pp. 32–46, 2025.
https://doi.org/10.1007/978-3-031-90720-3_3

socio-economic and political processes, these conditions require adequate responses and efforts, first of all, of state institutions aimed at forming a culture of financial literacy among the population, including the skills of formation and management of the household budget, creation and provision of safe environments for digital communication, installation of a responsible attitude to their civic duties.

In addition, the intensity and complexity of the observed changes in the sphere of financial literacy of the population require modernisation of approaches, new combinations of methods, development of modern tools and technologies. In Russian studies of the financial literacy of the population we still observe the predominance of empirical strategies based on surveys. The lack of empirical studies using methods of mathematical modelling, statistical processing and analysis of big data, including open digital footprints, is due to the limited number of ready-made and open databases, as well as the need for researchers of financial literacy to have modern professional skills.

The development of a new direction of social media predictive analytics within the social and human sciences focuses on the analysis, staging and forecasting of social processes based on the analysis of digital footprints, digital platforms, information flows and digital infrastructures [1]. The advantage of this approach in carrying out the tasks of studying the financial literacy of the adult population is that this methodology simplifies and optimises the study of public opinion, replacing lengthy and expensive sociological surveys.

This study represents the first experience of applying the methodology and techniques of social media predictive analytics to analyse the volume, topics, structure and technological support of financial education information flows in the Russian segment of social media. According to the results of 2022, there are 106 million social media users in Russia, which is 7 million or 7% more than in the previous year. At the same time, there is an upward trend in the national internet audience. Significant growth was observed among the older population, in particular, the share of Internet users among citizens aged 55–64 was 81% (67% in 2019); among those aged 65–74 – 53% (40% in 2019).

Thus, the digital environment become the most important source reflecting, on the one hand, the state agenda in the sphere of financial literacy of Russians, and, on the other hand, demonstrating feedback from the target groups, including through the analysis of such parameters as involvement in the information flow, the nature of response to events and triggers, the prevalence of behavioral patterns. The implementation of the methodology and techniques of social-media predictive analytics as applied to the analysis of information flows of adult financial literacy in the Russian social media also has significant opportunities for tracking the dynamics of changes, comparativist potential, and broad prospects for modeling and forecasting such processes.

2 Theoretical Review

At the government level, there has been a recognition of the need to increase the financial capability of the Russian people. The main negative factors are identified as the global manifestations of the economic crisis, the increasing complexity of services in the financial market, and the incompatibility of the population's financial knowledge with the ongoing technological changes. Improving financial literacy requires continuous, systematic and coordinated work of state and public institutions [8]. The strategy for improving financial literacy in the Russian Federation provides for differentiation of the population according to various criteria, including geographical, gender, age, social and professional [2]. Such an approach implies building targeted interaction with different social groups based on the requests and expectations of their representatives.

Globally, the digitisation of financial products and services increases the need for competent use of digital technologies. For example, current OECD guidelines aim to identify and promote effective initiatives to improve digital and financial literacy, considering the specific characteristics, benefits and risks of digital financial services and channels. Key measures aim to promote the evaluation of financial education programmes in digital or traditional formats, as well as the use of big data (collected from various sources such as government reports, mobile apps or online platforms) to evaluate digitally delivered financial education programmes [6].

Research shows that digitalisation has an ambivalent impact on the financial sector. Along with new opportunities, the digital transformation of the financial sector increases the risks associated with fraud and other economic crimes, cyber-attacks on financial systems at various levels, and the growth of the creditworthiness of the population that has access to the execution of such services in a remote format [4]. In this case, it is necessary to consider digitalisation in the complex of conditions and characteristics of the environment it creates for the user. Most of authors are convinced that excessive cyberoptimism in relation to personal financial behaviour can lead to the realisation of many threats that reduce the personal trust of citizens in digital financial instruments.

Sociological measures of financial literacy usually include indicators of financial knowledge, financial behaviour and financial attitudes [3, 10]. In the sociological dimension, financial literacy is determined by a system of factors that influence financial behaviour, as well as correct it in a negative direction, constituting risks for the welfare and security of citizens. On the other hand, the sociological measurement of financial literacy is aimed precisely at the positive correction of financial behaviour by determining the extent and type of spread of the most correct strategies and models of financial behaviour of citizens, which not only prevent such risks, but also create positive effects.

Several studies look at digital financial literacy in a substantive way. An important aspect of the studies is to determine the relationship between financial literacy, use of the internet and social media, use of digital financial products and financial access. For example, a study in China showed that internet use does not have a direct impact on financial inclusion. What does have a direct impact is the level of financial literacy and the use of digital financial products, which are facilitated by the popularity of the internet. The use of the global network and digital financial products play multiple mediating roles between financial literacy and financial access. Chinese researchers believe that to achieve the goal of promoting financial inclusion, it is necessary to improve consumers' financial literacy and promote the use of digital financial products [12].

The results of Russian researchers indicate that the level of financial literacy of Russian citizens does not correspond to the objective reality and the requirements of the digital age. In the medium and long term, this circumstance cannot provide the necessary basis for the country's advanced development. To solve this problem, some researchers suggest creating a mass financial culture. In the modern world, the category of "financial literacy" comes closer to the concept of "financial behaviour". In the latter case, attention is paid not to the theoretical knowledge of a person, but to the ability of its practical implementation, including considering changing external circumstances [7, 13]. Nowadays the priority task is to create financial literacy in the mass society, to spread the most successful practices of competent and rational financial behaviour, to expand the set of tools and technologies of financial education [11].

Local researchers pay special attention to the efforts of state and municipal authorities and other actors involved in activities to increase the level of financial literacy of the population and rationalise financial behaviour strategies. The implementation of these programmes and activities is the responsibility of a wide range of political and economic actors interested in limiting the negative effects of irresponsible and uneducated financial behaviour of citizens. Much attention is now being paid to the role of information resources created or supported by the state, local governments, the non-profit sector, business and educational institutions to disseminate relevant information on protecting and saving funds, combating financial fraud, competent use of various financial services widely available on the market, including insurance, credit and investment. The role of modern information resources in promoting such knowledge cannot be underestimated [5, 9, 14].

The theoretical review conducted reveals a significant deficit in the use of social media analysis capabilities, including the monitoring of digital footprints of internet users and thematic information flows. Domestic and foreign studies on financial literacy are dominated by subjective assessments or conclusions based on external statistics and purely interpretative models. Less common are data-driven works based on the results of sociological research, using the methods and tools of traditional sociology. At the same time, under current conditions, such research practices demonstrate their limitations, lack of self-sufficiency and poor applicability to the analysis of large and dynamic social processes. The present empirical analysis is aimed at identifying and analysing information flows of financial literacy as a reflection of objective markers and predictors of the level and specifics of financial literacy of the adult population of the Russian Federation.

3 Methods and Tools

The presented study of information flows of adult financial literacy in social media was carried out in two stages.

A qualitative and quantitative analysis of the submissions was carried out between 2021 and 2022, using a common set of evaluation indicators. The total number of reports was 1200. IBM SPSS Statistics was used for statistical processing of the collected database. The main methods of data processing were axial and cross-tabulation types of analysis. These analytical options allowed to identify the main problem area of content management of digital financial literacy communities, to study the specificity of content features of messages in online financial literacy network groups of different regional clusters, as well as to conduct cross-temporal analysis of structural and content features of information flows generated by financial literacy communities in 2021 and 2022. An additional result of the application of cognitive mapping was the creation of a dictionary of search queries (markers), i.e. words and phrases whose presence in a digital document ensures its relevance to the information flow under study.

In the second phase of the study, an automated social media analysis of adult financial education information flows was conducted using the online social media monitoring service IQBuzz based on selected search queries. As part of the preliminary work, the initial list of queries was adjusted based on the following criteria: consistency with the topic of this study, high contextualisation of the construct, frequency of use in the total volume of the information flow. As a result of the preparatory work, a lexicon of search queries was created, containing 200 sentences. The total volume of accumulated information flow for 2021–2022 exceeded 1.5 million publications published in more than 30 popular sites. The use of automated social media analysis in this study ensured the discovery of the weight, dynamics and topics characteristics of information flows, as well as demographic indicators of the digital audience involved in these information flows.

4 Results

Based on the results of the study, it can be said that there are significant problems with the management of information flows and financial education web content in Russian social media. According to the survey data, the dominant genre of financial education materials is advertising and news (about 60% of the total volume of published content). This is quite understandable given the significant representation of commercial organisations among the founders of digital financial education groups. At the same time, it is clear that the objectives of financial education are much broader than just advertising and information about new financial and banking products. Important genres may include analytical materials that objectively reflect the situation on the financial market and possible strategies of financial behaviour, as well as advice on individual issues, maintenance of targeted thematic sections of financial literacy, including tips, instructions, checklists and other useful content genres for mass users.

Comparing the results of the 2021 and 2022 analyses, we can see some positive shifts (Fig. 1). In particular, the share of advertising and news content has fallen by more than 20%, while information and analysis documents and financial education have increased their representation by around 10% and 5% respectively. In general, however, the fifth and fourth shares of materials of this content are clearly insufficient to fulfil the tasks of effectively advising the population on strategies of financial behaviour and solving financial problems. It is particularly noteworthy that such an important genre of financial literacy materials as "advice, instructions on saving, deposits, doing business" is presented in less than a quarter of all thematic publications. Considering the problems common to most Russian regions, including low indicators of small and medium business development, high level of adult population's indebtedness, low-income level and some others, the wide introduction and dissemination of this genre of financial education materials requires special attention.

Another challenge in managing the content of online financial literacy communities is that most content is not clearly targeted to a specific audience. Too general a flow of

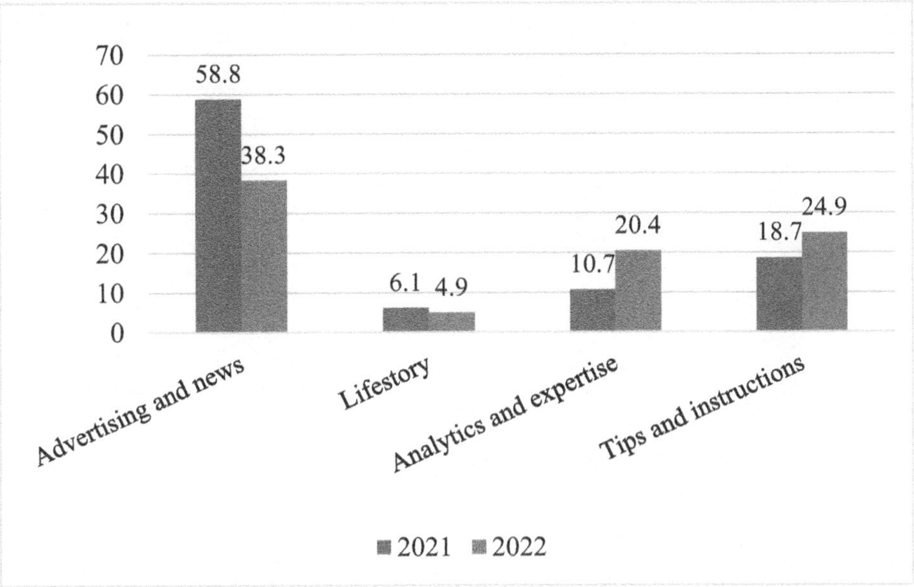

Fig. 1. The ratio of the genre structure of messages in the information flow of financial literacy in 2021 and 2022, in %.

information means a lack of targeting in the work of digital financial education groups. Targeting means tailoring content to the interests, needs and problems of a specific part of the audience, united by one or more common characteristics. According to the research data, targeting as a technology of work of digital communities with the target audience is to some extent realised in relation to the community of entrepreneurs and future businessmen. To the greatest extent, it is characteristic of groups at the regional level, with the most favourable economic conditions for the development of entrepreneurship, high indicators of socio-economic development. To a much lesser extent, it is characteristic of such social groups as people in difficult life situations, families with many children, pensioners, citizens with high levels of credit, students, people with disabilities. These social groups are the most vulnerable in terms of risky financial behaviour and are the target area of state structures in the field of financial education.

Compared to 2021, this contradiction remains quite acute (Fig. 2). Content not aimed at specific problem groups and target groups has increased to two thirds of the total volume. In addition, the targeting of professional communities and entrepreneurs, including potential entrepreneurs, has even halved. The targeting of people in difficult life situations increased slightly, but 2.5% of the messages is within the statistical margin of error. Moreover, such a low percentage of materials targeted at this social group is obviously insufficient to address the issues of overcoming difficult financial problems of a certain part of the population.

The background triggers in the context of which financial education materials are disseminated are also of research interest. These are events, processes and phenomena of social and political life that have a direct impact on the formation and adjustment

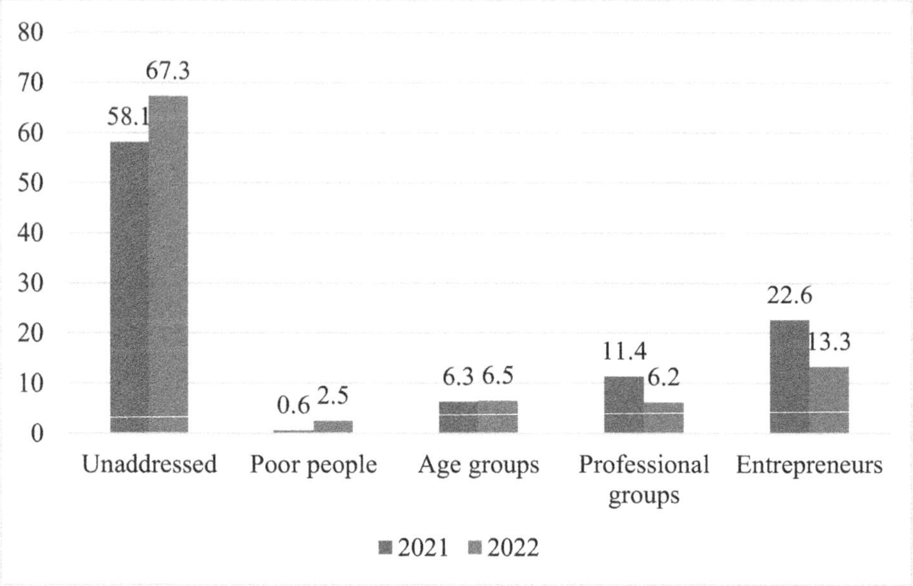

Fig. 2. Addressing of messages in the information flow of financial literacy in 2021 and 2022, in %.

of strategies of financial behaviour of citizens (Fig. 3). In 2022, the dominant triggers for the creation of materials on financial literacy are sanctions, financial and economic restrictions and other related processes that lead to changes in financial activity in the new political and economic environment (78.9% of the total volume of publications). At a level close to statistical significance are also triggers related to external pressure on Russians in the context of a special military operation (5.6%), high inflation (5.5%), termination or suspension of work of a few large foreign companies and brands in Russia (4.2%), volatility of the ruble exchange rate and stock market (3.1%).

Note that the use of background triggers to create financial literacy materials is not really regionally specific: sanctions are equally represented as the dominant contextual background of most relevant documents in all regional communities. At the same time, however, this disparity poses a significant content management challenge for financial literacy communities. Materials that respond to contradictions related to external pressure on Russian financial activity, the impact of mobilisation on this activity, and a number of other contexts are extremely important for ensuring the necessary thematic balance in financial education information flows.

The next problem among the difficulties in managing online financial literacy content is the low representation of materials focused on the development of specific financial literacy competencies in the target audience (Fig. 4). According to the research data, more than a quarter of the thematic materials do not focus on the development of any financial literacy competencies in the audience. In a further quarter of the materials, such competences are weakly expressed. This situation is particularly typical for regional financial education communities. At the same time, the share of such materials has halved

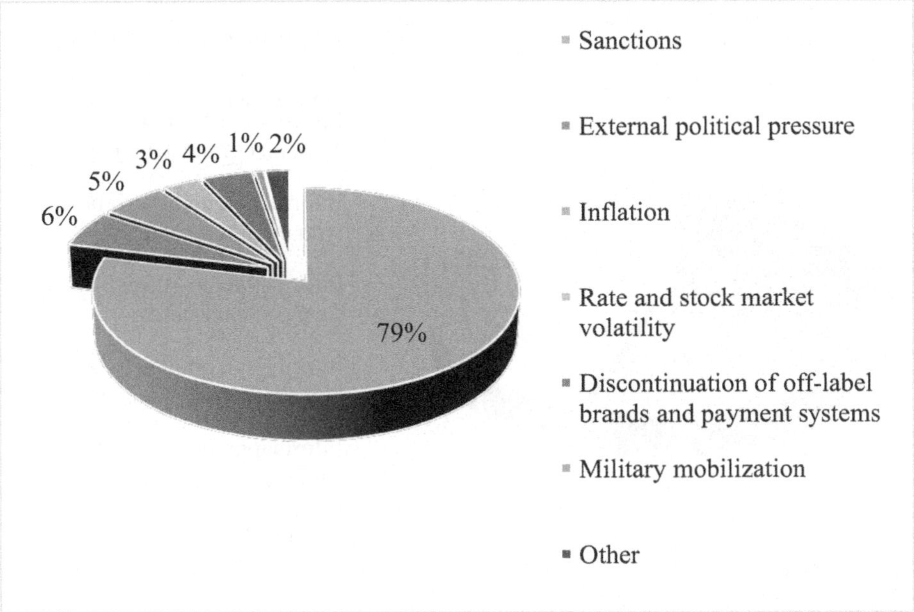

Fig. 3. Ratio of background triggers in the context of which the materials of financial literacy communities are broadcast, in %.

compared to 2021, which represents a positive trend towards strengthening not only the informative but also the educational significance of financial literacy information flows for the population (from 49.4% in 2021 to 26.7% in 2022).

Among the definable competences that the studied materials aim to form, the ability to invest in new conditions, including investment in one's own business, is noticeably represented (19.5%). A significant concern is the relatively high number of documents in social media on how to file for bankruptcy (8.2%). The materials emphasise the so-called "ease" of solving all financial problems through this procedure. However, these materials do not reflect either the possibility of avoiding the solution of financial problems through bankruptcy or significant negative consequences of this procedure. Quite a significant part of the materials reflects the answers to the questions about the possibilities of saving personal funds in the conditions of economic crisis and reduction of incomes (7.3%). A significant positive change compared to 2021 is the growth of social media documents on investment opportunities. At the same time, a negative trend can be observed in the growth of materials on passive economic strategy (saving personal funds versus active strategy-opportunities to increase income, for example, from professional activities).

According to the results of the automated social media analysis of financial education information flows, an increase in the total volume of messages can be observed throughout 2022. At the same time, the information flow is characterised by high daily activity. In January-March the daily amplitude of the flow was 2–3 thousand publications, in April-August 4–5 thousand publications, in September-October 6–7 thousand publications. The general peaks of information activity are connected mainly with the current

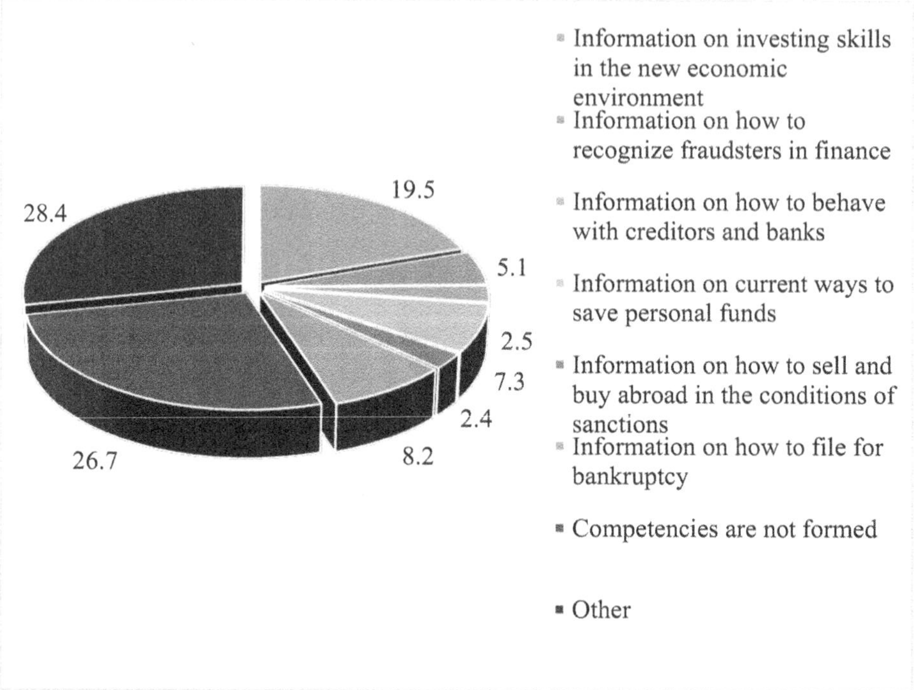

Fig. 4. The ratio of materials aimed at developing financial literacy competencies in the information flow in 2022, in %.

events of social and political life, which have a significant impact on the information support of financial literacy of the population in the current year.

In particular, the peaks of activity in the first half of the year will be determined by events on the national securities market (suspension and partial resumption of trading on the Moscow Exchange), the tightening of sanctions policy of Western countries (disconnection of major Russian banks from the SWIFT, blocking of mobile banking applications), the departure from Russia of major commercial brands or the suspension of operations of major international companies. In the second half of 2022, financial flows will also continue to be influenced by external events, including the announcement of partial mobilisation in Russia and further aggravation of the geopolitical situation.

Thus, the general dynamics of the flow of information on financial literacy is mainly provided by the influence of external factors and is largely formed by various events-triggers for the mass Internet audience, which determines its jump-intensive character with the transition from one major event in the social and economic sphere to another. This trend is developing against the background of a decrease in the volume of content directly related to the financial education of the population, regardless of the degree of commercialisation of the content source. Since March 2022, the background activity associated with the increasing pace of the information agenda, the development of a set of problems in the social and economic sphere actually overshadows the state-controlled flows aimed at the systemic development of financial literacy among the population.

Information activity reached the highest levels in November under the influence of the new season of discounts and sales ('Black Friday') traditionally organised by large retail chains. The great attention of the mass Internet audience to seasonal sales, discounts, competitions and lotteries is also explained by the need to save, save money and achieve financial stability.

Based on the results of the comparison of digital data, differences in the representation and promotion of financial literacy of the population in social media are recorded (Fig. 5). The total weight of the information flow increased by almost 2.5 times over the same period, from 480 thousand to 1.1 million publications. At the same time, the average daily amplitude of the flow increased from 1–2 thousand to 4–5 thousand publications. The inclusion of the current information agenda makes the flow of financial education more even. Nevertheless, it is an artificial expansion of the information presence due to the current information agenda and the influence of external factors and events on the promotion of financial literacy on the Internet that was recorded this year. Differences in the volume of information flow in January-February remain insignificant, while the largest gap in the distribution of daily publications has been sharply manifested since March of this year, corresponding to the beginning of a new round of the economic crisis and increased global political tensions. A comparison of the data from the cognitive mapping of digital content and the monitoring of social media shows that the representation of thematic, managed streams aimed at the acquisition of new competences and skills of citizens in the financial sphere remains at the same level.

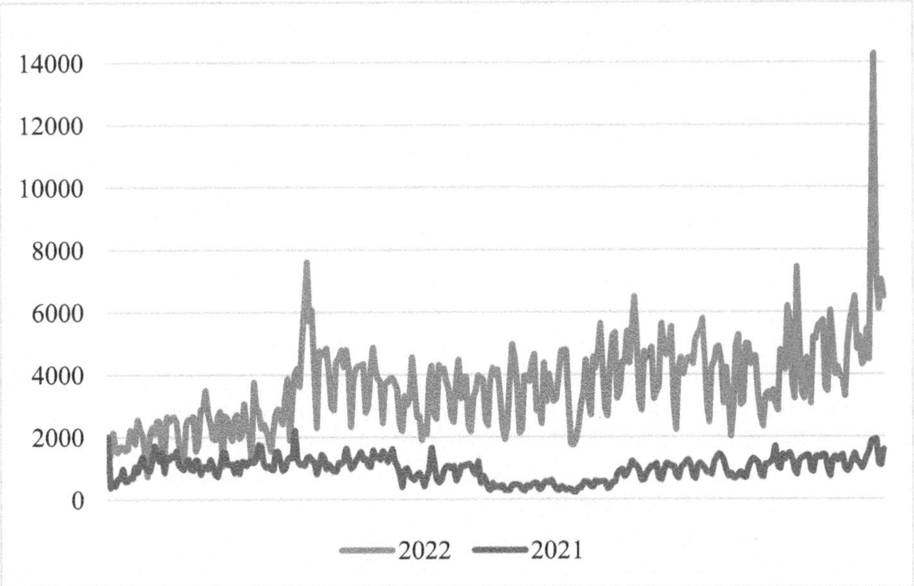

Fig. 5. Daily dynamics of the information flow of financial literacy in the Russian segment of social media in 2021–2022 (by publications)

The general content of the information flow was analysed by determining the semantic core-the most frequently used lexical constructions in the total volume of the collected publications. Within the semantic core, the following categories can be distinguished 1) constructions aimed at saving money or the budget ("savings", "save", "keep", "valuable"); 2) constructions aimed at easing the financial and tax burden ("support", "help", "preferential", "free", "want", "discount", "get"); 3) constructions aimed at activating labour functions ("work", "earn", "engage", "monetary", "can", "make", "income", "salary"); 4) constructions reflecting the influence of current social and political events on the processes of financial education ("rate", "military", "ruble", "currency", "dollar", "inflation", "sanction", "sanctions", "country"); 5) constructions reflecting the actual financial difficulties of the most problematic social groups ("allowances", "family", "parents", "child"). The data obtained allow us to assert the dominance of discourses of saving and preservation of personal resources against the background of the deterioration of the general economic situation. In the third quarter of 2022, the use of savings markers increases significantly and is supplemented by markers of assistance and support for the most problematic and socially unprotected segments of the population. In addition, the high frequency of use of markers of socially important processes confirms the fact of their impact on the processes of promoting financial literacy of the population in the current year.

Under the conditions of a difficult macroeconomic situation and a general deterioration of socio-economic indicators at both federal and regional levels, the content of the financial education information flow is changing. Whereas a year earlier the core of the flow was made up of messages aimed at incremental growth through personal activity and additional income (investments, cryptocurrencies, small businesses, etc.), from the beginning of 2022 to the current moment, discourses on saving clearly dominate. The prevalence of messages aimed at saving personal and family funds, using them competently, planning personal and family budgets and looking for benefits is recorded throughout the year, with a roughly twofold increase towards the end of the study period. In addition, the thematic seasonality recorded a year earlier has been lost, when bursts of information activity were provided by internal events and contexts that changed over the seasons of the year. The general content of the flow of information is thus unified and subordinated to the actual events and phenomena of political life.

As a result, the structure of the flow of information is also changing. The development of large amounts of information and increased news activity has led to the dominance of content publication formats rather than commentary. Despite the fact that overall user activity has remained at the same level, there is much more content on relevant topics, also due to the activity of large media and other information resources. At the same time, the problem of weak representation of the regional agenda, which has become even more overshadowed by the federal agenda, remains relevant.

Internet users living in the largest cities (primarily Moscow) continue to accumulate up to 80% of the total information flow in 2022 (73% a year earlier). Moscow users account for the bulk of thematic publications on the topic of financial literacy. On the one hand, this is due to the high standard of living, the spread of modern financial services and the existence of a steady demand of the population of megacities for financial education. On the other hand, the lowest representation in the information flow is demonstrated by users living in regions with a low level of financial education. In these subjects the demand for such information has not been formed yet due to objective factors. These regions are the points of application of the greatest efforts on the part of the state and civil society (Republic of Ingushetia, Republic of Tyva, Republic of Dagestan, Republic of Altai, etc.).

In the final stage of the monitoring, the socio-demographic characteristics of the users involved in the financial literacy information flows in social media were analysed. In particular, the total number of Intermet users-authors of financial literacy content (more than 100 thousand authors) is distributed by gender and age. At the end of 2022, the dominance of the female audience is recorded, accounting on average for up to 64% of the total structure of users involved in the flow of information. Throughout the year, the representation of the female audience shows a steady increase. Seasonal events and phenomena of social life are the circumstances that ensure the increased involvement of the middle-aged female audience in the information flow. For example, seasons of discounts, sales, special offers from retail chains and popular brands, and other opportunities to save family funds during this period of the year. In addition, the discourse on saving and saving on the part of the female audience increased significantly after the announcement of the start of the military mobilisation of citizens.

The adult population (36–45 years old) is the most represented in the information flow. As a rule, the members of this social group have a family and children, secondary or higher education and a permanent job. The representation of this audience is about one third of the total audience of the information flow in social media (Fig. 6). This age group is more likely than others to use rational models of online information consumption, actively using social networks and messengers as a tool to find useful information for everyday use. There is a significant imbalance in the representation of age groups,

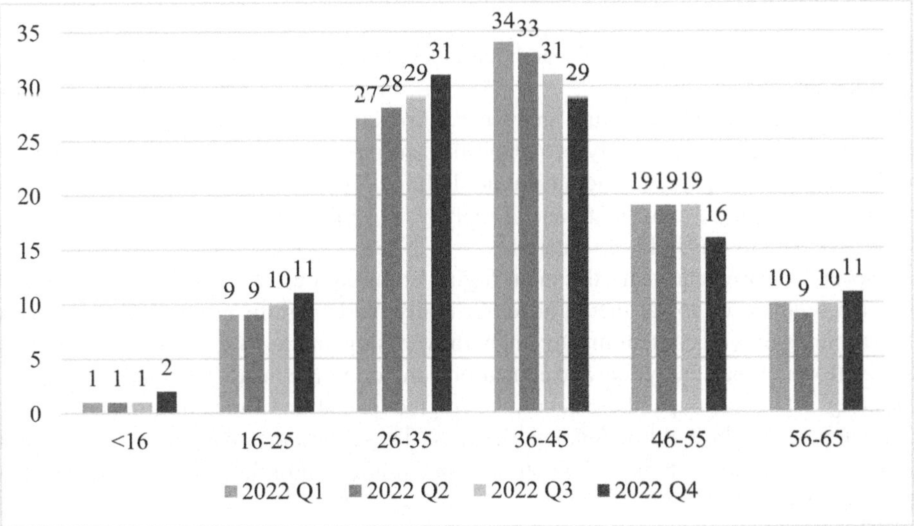

Fig. 6. Distribution of age groups of Internet users in the structure of authors of the financial literacy information flow by quarters of 2022, in %.

including the "disconnection" of young people (8% on average for users aged 16–25) and representatives of the retired and pre-retired (11% in general). This perceived imbalance is a direct consequence of problems with the flow of information and management of web content, limited localisation of key financial education publications and messages, poor integration and management of the population's financial education streams.

5 Discussion

In recent years, the basic characteristics of the flow of financial education information in Russia have changed as a result of changes in the information agenda and the socio-political environment, which is crucial for determining the strategies of the population's financial behaviour. The facts considered in this empirical study are a direct consequence of the changes in the key demands and attitudes of the target groups of financial education under the influence of negative factors of the external environment. Among other things, the results of the empirical study create a space for the application of efforts on the part of authorized public authorities and civil society institutions in the sphere of digitalization of the main programs of financial education of the population, increasing the scale, quality and technology of financial literacy projects for the adult population of the Russian Federation. Given the external context and the preservation of significant risk factors in the development of the financial and economic system of the country, comprehensive work with various public groups to improve the level of financial literacy is a strategic state task, a mechanism to prevent and limit in advance the effects of sanctions pressure, negative social consequences of the crisis situation, as well as a means of ensuring the processes of import substitution and sovereignty of the national economy.

6 Conclusion

Based on the results of the research conducted, the following conclusions can be formulated:

First, the conducted literature analysis confirms the existence of a significant deficit in the use of social media analysis capabilities, automated analysis of digital footprints, statistical processing and mathematical modelling of data on the financial activity of the population and the level of its financial literacy, as well as the fact of the prevalence of subjective data in this field of research.

Secondly, in recent years the main digital communities of financial literacy in the Russian segment of social media have not really made significant progress in solving the problems of web content management: advertising and news content still dominate, while informational, analytical and educational materials are in great shortage; there is no targeting of target groups, there is no focus on the formation of meaningful and specific competencies in the field of financial literacy. These circumstances predetermine low user interest in the content of the communities studied and relatively low user activity around thematic content.

Third, according to the results of the study, some changes in the trajectory of development of financial literacy information flows of the adult population were recorded. For example, a significant increase in the volume of information flows of financial literacy in

2022 due to external contexts and current socio-political events against the background of growing demand for financial education among Internet users. This trend is developing against the background of a narrowing of the volume of materials directly related to the financial education of the population, regardless of the degree of commercialisation of the content source.

Fourthly, the transformation of the dominant strategy of financial behaviour of Russians in the digital space is recorded, due to the transition from investing and increasing funds to the “survival strategy”, which consists in preserving and saving existing resources and money. Starting from the third quarter of 2022, the frequency of use of savings markers will enter the growth phase and will be supplemented by markers of assistance and support for the most problematic and socially unprotected segments of the population. At the same time, targeted work with the most vulnerable social groups will be weak and non-systematic, determining the priority area of application of digital communication technologies by state and public structures.

Fifthly, the change in the gender and age structure of the audience of financial education information flows was noted, which is expressed in the dominance of the female audience living in the largest Russian cities. Seasonal events and phenomena of social life are the circumstances that ensure increased involvement of middle-aged female audience in the information flow. For example, seasons of discounts, sales, special offers of retail chains and popular brands and other opportunities to save money for the family in this period of the year. The increase in the representation of the older 36–45 age group, which is most interested in developing financial literacy, is also related to external challenges and prevailing trends in the development of the financial behaviour of a significant part of the population. This social group tends to use the most rational strategies of social media use, including the search and practical application of useful information in everyday life.

The presented empirical study is the first attempt to use the methods and tools of social media predictive analytics to analyse the current state and trends in the development of financial literacy of the adult population of the Russian Federation. The results obtained demonstrate the functionality and applicability of these methods, broad prospects for further use to identify problem areas, the best regional and federal practices in promoting financial literacy in the social media space, improving the effectiveness of interaction with the population on financial education using modern technologies of digital communication.

References

1. Brodovskaya, E.V., Dombrovskaya, A.Y., Karzubov, D.N., Sinyakov, A.V.: Developing methodology for «smart» search for political process markers in social media. Monit. Public Opin. Econ. Soc. Changes **5**, 79–104 (2017). https://doi.org/10.14515/monitoring.2017.5.06
2. Decree of the Government of the Russian Federation of September 25, 2017 N 2039-r «On Approval of the Strategy for Improving Financial Literacy in the Russian Federation for 2017–2023». http://government.ru/docs/29441/. Acceded 01 Jan 2024
3. Dulina, N.V., Moiseeva, D.V., Tokarev, V.V.: Financial literacy: from the concept definition to the methods of measuring tech (the case of «Volgograd omnibus»). Logos et Praxis **1**, 88–94 (2013)

4. Financial literacy in the context of digitalization: main risks and their management. Moscow: Institute of National Projects (2020). https://vashifinancy.ru/upload/materials/Digitalization.pdf. Acceded 01 Jan 2024
5. Golubeva, K.A.: Subjective and objective factors which influence financial culture formation. Soc. Sociol. Psychol. Pedagogics **1**, 53–57 (2022). https://doi.org/10.24158/spp.2022.1.7
6. Guidance on Digitalization and Financial Literacy: G20/OECD INFE Policy Guidance. Paris: OECD Publishing (2018). https://www.oecd.org/finance/financial-education/g20-oecd-infe-policy-guidance-digitalisation-financial-literacy-2018.htm. Acceded 01 Jan 2024
7. Kunizheva, D.A.: Financial subjectivity as a criterion for assessing financial culture. Sociopolitical Sci. **12**(5), 71–77 (2022). https://doi.org/10.33693/2223-0092-2022-12-5-71-77
8. Kuznetsov, O.V., Ivanov, A.V., Vorovskii, N.V., Shevalkin, I.S.: Institutionalization of financial literacy of the adult population of Russia. Financ. Theor. Pract. **24**(1), 34–45 (2020). https://doi.org/10.26794/2587-5671-2020-24-1-34-45
9. Litvinova, S.A.: Improving the financial literacy of the population as a factor in the growth of human capital. Probl. Mod. Econ. **3**(59), 221–223 (2016)
10. Makar, S.V., Yarasheva, A.V., Markov, D.I.: Financial behavior as a result of the interaction of people in the socio-economic space. Financ. Theor. Pract. **26**(3), 157–168 (2022). https://doi.org/10.26794/2587-5671-2022-26-3-157-168
11. Safronova, T., Chernousova, N., Safronova, M. Financial literacy and financial capability: interdependence of concepts and possibilities to form them in a school course of mathematics. Propósitos y Representaciones. **8**(3) (2020). https://doi.org/10.20511/pyr2020.v8n3.504
12. Shen, Y., Hueng, J.C., Hu, W.: Using digital technology to improve financial inclusion in China. Appl. Econ. Lett. **27**(1), 30–34 (2020). https://doi.org/10.1080/13504851.2019.1606401
13. Silina, S.N., Stupin, V.Y.: From financial literacy to financial culture, Bulletin of the Baltic Federal University. Ser. Philol. Pedagogy Psychol **4**, 71–79 (2017)
14. Vdovin, S.M., Averina, O.I., Gorbunova, N.A., Moskaleva, E.G.: Financial literacy in the context of the lifelong education. Integr. Educ. **22**(3), 441–459 (2018). https://doi.org/10.15507/1991-9468.092.022.201803.441-459

Interface Elements and Trust in Online Media: A Conjoint Analysis Approach

Elena Artemenko and Liliia Faizova(✉)

HSE University, St. Petersburg, Russia
faizowa.lil@yandex.ru

Abstract. In the age of the Internet, where misinformation is spread with great ease, trustworthiness of news sources has become an important issue. The aim of this study is to assess how users perceive credibility of different online news interfaces by employing experimental methodology. An online experiment was conducted using the conjoint analysis approach. Participants were recruited to complete a series of surveys, which displayed different news interfaces, each with varying elements (e.g. menu type, presence of the author). Participants scored their perception of the credibility of each interface. Through conjoint analysis, the results were used to identify which element combinations have the strongest effects on credibility perception for different user groups. Findings from the logistic regression on the whole sample revealed that the presence of all elements is important, but has a detrimental impact on trust. Conversely, the k-means cluster analysis identified five distinct user segments based on demographic and conjoint data. Based on these clusters, the study offers recommendations for developing a trustworthy news interface. This study provides valuable insights into how users evaluate credibility of online news interfaces, and contribute to the development of strategies for improving trust in online news.

Keywords: Credibility · Online news · Social media · UX-analytics · Conjoint analysis

1 Introduction

Modern communication is becoming more computer-mediated, with social media taking the lead in the dissemination of news content both true and fake. As Shu & Liu [28] point out, social media possesses good opportunities for dissemination of fake news and misleading information, as it is easily accessed, low cost, and provides opportunities for rapid information circulation.

Thus, the issue of trust in online information and the factors that can modulate trust is currently one of the most relevant in the study of computer-mediated communication. It is important to address here, that there are many ways to reach online news, and according to Bentley et al., online news websites play a crucial role as an information channel, and users reach news not only in social

A. Chugunov et al. (Eds.): DTGS 2024, CCIS 2445, pp. 47–61, 2025.
https://doi.org/10.1007/978-3-031-90720-3_4

media, but also in news sites [6]. Despite the preferred channel of news consumption, most consumers encounter news sites on a daily basis. In this context, the interface of news sites plays an important role as an intermediary between a user and information, having an impact on perceived credibility. The purpose of this research is to understand the impact of different element combinations on credibility perception for different user groups. Various visual properties of websites have been widely studied and shown to be important predictors of user trust [13,24], and specifically trust to news [29,30,36]. However, to the best of our knowledge, their joint effect on user trust has so far received little or no attention. This work contributes to covering this gap by carrying out a conjoint analysis of five visual features via an online survey experiment. In many ways, this is an exploratory study that relies on a conjoint analysis methodology that is new to this research field, yet has demonstrated high validity in other areas of research (e.g. [5,11,23]).

2 Theoretical Background

2.1 Credibility and Trust

Trust is "a psychological state comprising the intention to accept vulnerabilities based upon positive expectations of the intentions or behavior of another" [25]. In the context of measuring trust, it is important to understand that trust since long has been studied in sociology, psychology, economics and marketing, and conceptualized in a number of ways - as a rational choice, in terms of emotional attachment (psychological approach), in terms of trust in institutions (institutional approach) or in terms of subject reflexivity [31]. Trust can be also considered in its impact on behavior when different interventions are spread through online media. A study by Pagliaro et al. shows that psychological differences like moral principles in terms of trust are significant predictors of individuals' behavioral intentions in different countries [22]. Thus, trust can influence behavior. At the same time, trust itself is influenced by various factors. Among such factors, the web interface (e.g., the interface of a news site) in which the news is presented is also presented.

2.2 Surface Elements of the Interface

In the context of this work, trust is an important feature in human-computer interaction, as users receive information shaped into interfaces, and interface design, in its turn, can influence content perception [37]. In a study by Simko et al., for example, participants browsed through artificial Facebook feeds and determined the truthfulness of stories. Stimuli consisted of four groups: true-alarmist, true-denier, fake-alarmist, and fake-denier. As a result, fake articles caused more report calls, and unsuccessful participants (those who failed to detect fake news) relied more on information given in the feed as opposed to actual full article [29]. Thus, research on how interface design may impact trust into content is important and can bring new highlights in user experience shaping practices. Previous research has identified several groups of factors that can affect user's level of trust in online information sources: message or content elements, social and reputational elements, user-based elements, and surface elements. The latter are represented by graphical user interface elements which may be grouped into three main categories: (a) aesthetics, including colors and fonts, (b) usability, including navigation and device adaptability, and (c) website structure, including structural characteristics, presence of advertisements and other interface elements. The last group is of high interest in this article, as proper arrangement and organization of structural elements within an interface greatly impact the user's perception of trust and reliability in the system [36]. However, the effect of the structural features on trust to news content specifically was mostly studied in terms of the content provided in these boxes [8,19,35], while this study focuses on the presence of these elements as such. A detailed table with all surface elements found to have an impact on online trust are presented in Appendix 1.

However, as far as we know from the literature review, the impact of interface elements is usually evaluated separately, while its impact on the user is usually cumulative. According to Schenkamn, and Jönsson [27], users form their first impressions of web sites based on the overall visual appearance, rather than on a particular element. That said, interfaces should be studied as a whole product. This study focuses on the presence of interface elements as such and their combination. Thus, the first research question is:

RQ1: Is there a combination of interface elements in an online news interface which will make users trust the respective news item more?

2.3 User-Based Characteristics

User-based characteristics may play a significant role in online media trust formation. For example, according to [2], gender, age, and experience with internet usage have a significant impact on trust in online information. This study suggests that women exhibit higher trust and hold a more favorable view of online services than men; older users have higher levels of trust in e-government compared to younger individuals; and finally, a greater level of internet experience has a positive impact on users' trust. However, it is also important to know whether there are some user groups who have different preferences in the organization of a news interface. The second research question is stated as follows:

RQ2: Whether the combination of identified interface elements affecting trust will be the same for the Russian sample or different for different sample groups of people?

2.4 Interface Complexity and Trust

Although the joint influence of different interface elements has not been studied previously, the effect of interface complexity characteristic on user trust has been slightly investigated. Research on interface elements organization implies different levels of stimuli complexity. According to Chassy [9], high levels of perceived complexity resulted in low aesthetic ratings of university webpages, but fixation count correlated negatively with complexity and positively with aesthetics. That is, the more "difficult" interface is, the less appealing it is for users. Based on this idea, one can suppose that a low aesthetics site can cause rejection by users and receive less credibility ratings. However, according to Berlyne theory [7], there is an "optimal" level of complexity which results in the highest levels of aesthetics, reminding a U-curve relationship between these concepts.

In the context of the current study, stimuli materials were different not only in terms of which elements were present, but also in terms of the number of elements present. Taking this into account, the variable "complexity" was calculated for each profile; complexity was formulated as the number of present elements. Thus, in our study we also test whether this hypothesis is confirmed under the conditions of the chosen methodology for perceived trust:

H1: There will be a parabolic relationship between interface complexity and interface trust. The average levels of interface complexity will be characterized by the highest level of interface credibility compared to the extreme ones.

2.5 Conjoint Analysis

The choice of conjoint methodology (conjoint = consider jointly) lies in the possibilities of this approach: instead of asking respondents to evaluate different elements of the interface separately, they will evaluate a whole product. Choice-based conjoint methodology aims to explore the preferences and interactions of different attributes and their levels by presenting respondents with a choice of different alternatives. Respondents need to choose a variant among sets of 2–3 alternatives with different combinations of attributes and levels. Although conjoint analysis has been mostly used in marketing [26,33], it is also increasingly being used for academic purposes, including testing website feature effects on trust in news [14]. Unlike most other methods testing the independent contribution of each predictor, it allows finding the most trustful combination of features and does so experimentally.

3 Method

To test our hypotheses and research questions, we conducted a large online experiment using a conjoint analysis methodology.

3.1 Pilot Study

To understand whether there are preferred platforms of online media consumption, as well as to understand the most popular online news topics, a pretest was conducted before the main experiment. An online survey with 24 questions designed to explore online news consumption experiences was collected with 153 students of the affiliated university (mean age = 23.6, 26% male). As a result, Telegram was mentioned as the main platform of online news consumption (55% of the sample use it), followed by VK (29.4%). Although participants mentioned mobile versions of the platforms, the majority (62%) stated that they transition from mobile version to web version to verify information always or very often. The most interesting topics of online news were politics, society, health, and economics. Thus, the results of the pilot study allowed us to choose exactly the web interface as the stimulus material for the main experiment. As for the theme, health was chosen as the most neutral one.

3.2 Participants

Participants were native Russian speakers (N = 1236, Mean age = 39.4 (SD = 10.8)) recruited via *Toloka.com*, a Russian replica of Amazon Mechanical Turk, so as to represent the age and gender composition of the Russian population. Compared to the latter, the sample is expected to be a little more educated and a little lower-income, but otherwise fairly well representative of the Russian population. The average age equals 39.4 years, with the minimum equal to 18, and maximum equal to 77. There are 52% of female respondents in the sample. As for the education level, nearly half of the sample had completed a bachelor's degree (48.9%). Specialized education followed as the second most common level of education (28.8%), while unfinished education accounted for 10.8% of the sample. Finally, respondents indicated their frequency of online news consumption, with the majority (69.1%) reporting that they consume online news every day or almost every day. A smaller proportion reported consuming online news less frequently, and a few respondents declared that they never read or watched online news (1.5%). Despite this, it was determined that these respondents still provided valuable information for the construction of the news interface and were retained in the sample.

Minimal sample size, as calculated based on [21] power analysis methodology, equals 1143 which led us to aim at 1200 valid participants. All answers were anonymized before analysis, as respondents received unique codes. Given the specific motivation of crowdsourcing workers, the experiment employs a number of quality control techniques, such as exclusion of excessively fast participants, participants giving the same responses to all items and failing to answer control questions correctly.

3.3 Stimuli

As the existing literature does not provide consistent results on the structural features most important for trust production, especially in cross-cultural perspective, their choice was made based on the analysis of typical web structure among the most popular news agencies in Russia as the country of this study. After identifying 9 most visited agencies according to similarweb.com (the list included: Lenta.ru, RIA News, Dzen News, RBK News, KP.ru, Fontanka, TASS, Vesti.ru, Gazeta.ru), a traffic rank analytical company, the author developed a list of five most frequent, yet testable structural elements which are presented in Table 1. The stimulus material for the conjoint study was created to imitate the style of short news articles. It contains information on a neutral topic related to health - the impact of chocolate consumption on the cardiovascular system. Important to note that the text has questionable information and, as far as it is known from the literature, there is no scientific consensus on this topic. The stimuli text contains some links and third-party references. Overall, the news interface mimics a typical news interface with common structural elements such as news agency logo, search option, login button, date of publication, text and a photo. These common elements do not vary among the whole experiment.

Table 1. Interface elements and their levels of presentation.

Elements	Presentation Levels
Information box (weather, currency rate)	Present or absent
Live stream	Present or absent
Menu	Extended or hidden
Author of the post	Present or absent
Recommended news	Present or absent

3.4 Procedure

The online experiment was conducted using the *conjointly.com* platform - a tool designed specifically to conduct such experiments, which provides the needed possibilities to create a survey, to collect the data, and receive primary analytics. Participants were presented with 14 pairs of news web interfaces each containing the same news item and a different combination of the five listed above features (see Fig. 1). The main question of the conjoint phase sounded like follows: "Which of the following interfaces do you trust more?". To answer this question, the respondent needed to choose one of two interfaces, or choose the "I trust them equally" option. Each element was represented with two conditions: present or absent, with the same content when present. Each feature combination was randomly selected among 32 possible combinations ($2^5 = 32$). The experiment was limited to 14 tasks per participant to achieve statistical power.

Additionally, participants were asked to respond to a number of demographic questions before the experiment (including age, gender, education level, and frequency of online news consumption) and to explicitly rate the importance of the five structural features after it. To prevent participants from speeding up their completion of the survey and getting unreliable data, special control questions were added after the conjoint phase.

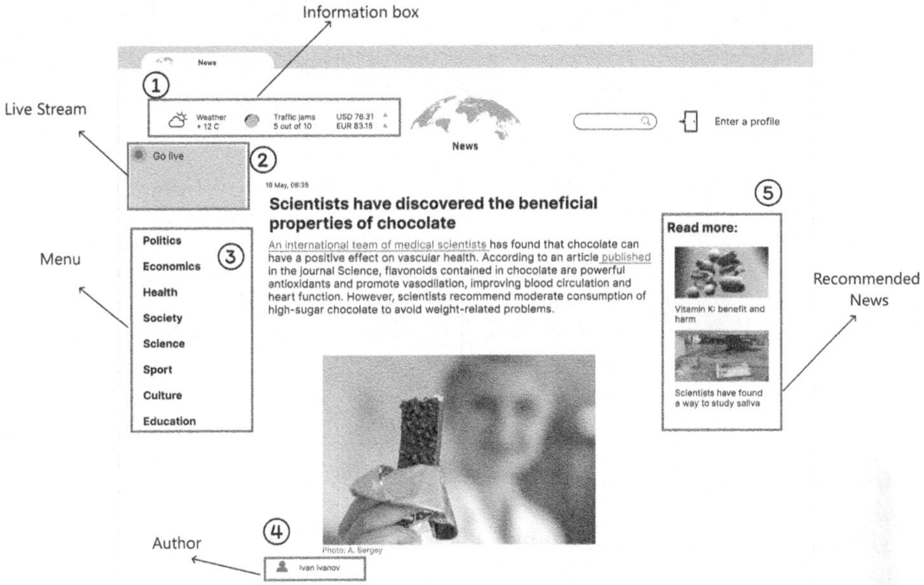

Fig. 1. Example of a stimulus material (translated from Russian). This is an example of experiment stimuli. In this profile all elements are present. Other variations include different combinations of presence or absence of the elements. 1 - Information box; 2 - Live stream; 3 - Menu; 4 - Author; 5 - Recommended news.

4 Analysis and Result

4.1 Ranking Test

The conjointly.com platform on which the experiment was implemented offers a ranking of interfaces based on participants' responses. This is a list of the most preferred interfaces and the least preferred ones. This number is calculated as the average partworths across individual respondent's total partworth utility scores for the combination. Table 2 shows the best and the worst interfaces according to the partworth ranking. However, conjoint experiments are traditionally analyzed with the use of logistic regression, and the results are described according to regression analysis [11], which will be described in the next section.

4.2 Logistic Regression

As it was already mentioned, traditionally, the results of conjoint experiments are analyzed using logistic regression [4]. Thus, the logistic regression was built based on the *sm_logit.logit* function from the Statsmodels package in Python. Overall, 34552 observations were obtained (1236 respondents, 14 questions with 2 variants each). In addition to building a logistic regression model, we also created a graph of the odds ratios to visualize the relationship between the independent

Table 2. The best and the worst interfaces according to conjointly.com ranking test.

The best interface	The worst interface
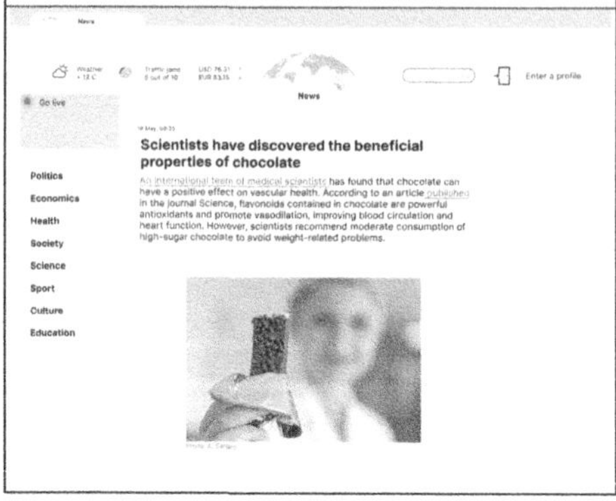	

variables and the dependent variable. The results of a logistic regression analysis can be seen in Table 3 & Fig. 2.

Table 3. Logistic regression results.

	coef	std err	z	$P > \|z\|$	[0.025	0.975]
Intercept	0.5893	0.027	21.526	0.000	0.536	0.643
Recommended	−0.0351	0.022	−1.572	0.116	−0.079	0.009
Author	−0.0253	0.022	−1.132	0.258	−0.069	0.018
Infobox	−0.0245	0.022	−1.100	0.271	−0.068	0.019
Live	−0.0185	0.022	−0.831	0.406	−0.062	0.025
Menu	0.0146	0.022	0.655	0.513	−0.029	0.058

The results of a logistic regression on elements preference on the whole sample yielded no statistical influence of interface elements on trust. Thus, RQ1 may not be answered on the whole sample.

As for the interface complexity, the variable "complexity" was calculated for each profile; complexity was formulated simply as the number of present elements. Based on this variable, a new regression model was built. However, regression models again yielded no significant results according to complexity.

4.3 Cluster Analysis

On this stage, results were analyzed with the use of clusterization methods to understand the distribution of respondents and their preferences more thoroughly. K-means clusterization method was used for this purpose. This clustering method is advantageous due to its scalability, simplicity, flexibility in specifying

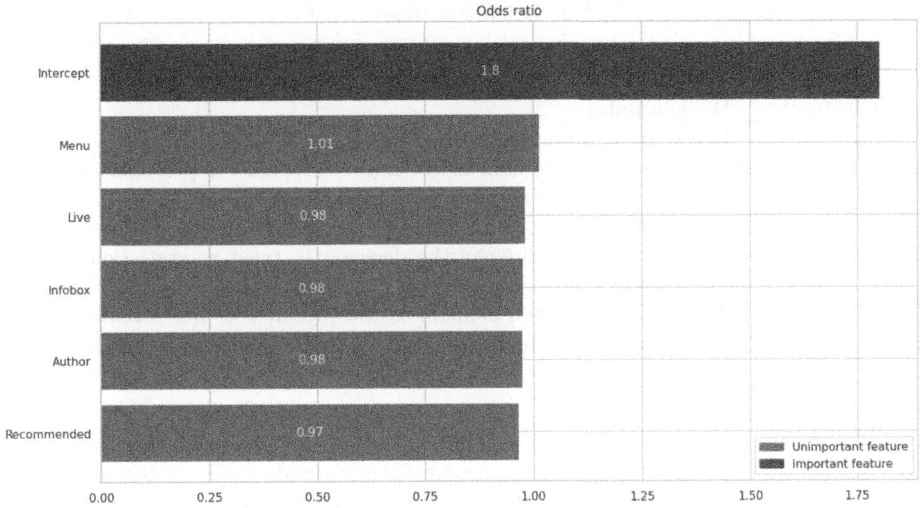

Fig. 2. Logistic regression results visualization.

the number of clusters, speed in convergence, linear complexity with respect to data points, and effectiveness for datasets with spherical clusters. While other methods like DBSCAN and hierarchical clustering have their strengths, k-means is a popular choice for its efficiency and ease of implementation. Database for clusterization included following data: age of the respondent, gender, education level, self-reported frequency of reading/watching news, and 5 columns indicating percentages of choices without specific elements (N of choices without element/N of all interfaces seen). The optimal amount of clusters was determined with the use of silhouette metric. Based on this method, there are 5 clusters in the final sample. Table 4 describes the clusters that were obtained during this stage of the analysis with the maximum number of iterations for a single run equal to 1000.

To measure the quality of the clusterization, Adjusted Rand Index (ARI) metric was used. Using ARI after K-Means clustering with different random states can show which of the obtained results is the most accurate and optimal. If the ARI value is high (close to 1), it indicates that the clustering was successful and all objects were correctly classified. If the ARI value is low (close to 0), it may indicate that the clustering results were not accurate enough and further optimization or change of algorithm parameters is required. The ARI metric was counted on 100 runs of k-means clustering, and the average number of this measure was 0.81. This result indicates the consistency and robustness of the clustering to changes in initial conditions such as random state. Overall, this value is high enough to state that the clusterization was successful and consistent.

Table 4. Cluster description.

Cluster	Description
Cluster 1	– Women only; – Read online news every day or almost every day; – Only the menu element is not significant, i.e. the presence of the extended or hidden menu does not affect the decision to trust the interface; – Other elements influence the decision to trust at statistical significance of 0.05; – The most influential element is the presence of live streaming - the chances that the interface is trusted increase 1.16 times with the presence of the live streaming element; – N = 340.
Cluster 2	– All elements are significant and positively influence the decision to trust the interface at a statistical significance of 0.05; – The most influential element is the presence of an extended menu - the chances that the interface is trusted increase 2.19 times with the presence of this element; – On average, respondents in this cluster have the highest scores for all elements in the self-reported evaluation of elements; – N = 238.
Cluster 3	– Smallest average age; – Only the menu and the extra information are significant factors, i.e. the presence of these elements increases the chances of trusting the interface by 1.21 and 1.16, respectively; – The presence of other elements, i.e. recommended news, author and live streaming are not significant features at a statistical significance of 0.05, but also positively influence the decision to trust the interface; – N = 158.
Cluster 4	– College or incomplete higher education; – Important elements affecting trust in the news interface are the presence of recommended news, a menu, and an author; – N = 136, the smallest cluster.
Cluster 5	– Men only; – Read online news every day or almost every day; – Important attributes positively influencing trust in the interface are the extended menu and the presence of live streaming; – N = 362, the largest cluster.

5 Discussion

Current research was planned with the assumption that interface construction has an important role in building trust of users. However, there are other factors which should be taken into account when researching user trust. As it was outlined in a study by [29], in most of the cases strength of trust reflects the level of users' interest. Also, different heuristics are often applied in deciding whether to trust the interface [20]. Important to mention different levels of skepticism of users, which may lead to different initial levels of their trust. For gullible users who tend to trust news more, different interface variations might not lead to drastic changes in the trust level. On the other hand, there are users who question every information piece they receive, thus even a credible interface might not be enough for them to make conclusions. This assumption should be addressed in the future studies. Also, it is important to mention that stimuli material only differentiated in the combination of elements which were included. Although users were instructed to only evaluate visual characteristics, for some users it might be important to understand the content of the news item. All stimuli material was similar in the context of text and picture, and this absence of the topic diversity has either advantages or disadvantages. Among advantages, it brings similar results for all participants throughout the whole survey process; as for the disadvantages, users could get bored and provide thoughtless answers. This is a difficult question, because just increasing the topic diversity to two different topics, it will double the stimuli material amount. This question should be also addressed in the further studies. Finally, only five interface elements were analyzed in the research. Although this is a common limitation of the conjoint-type research, that might lead to some problems regarding representation of real online news interfaces. In the future studies, it makes sense to increase the number of elements for the analysis and shorten the number of final profiles by excluding similar interfaces or obvious ones. Moreover, other sources for analyzing the relevance of different interface elements in online news should be studied, as this study only implemented nine Russian most popular sources, according to the traffic rank website.

6 Conclusion

The findings of this article point to the importance of the interface in building trust in news sources. Answering the research questions stated in the beginning, the clear answer on what features of news website layout make users trust the respective news item more could not be provided on a general sample. This research has shown that there is no one-solution-fits-all decision, and different user groups should be taken into account. Thus, clusterization analysis has provided several user groups for which different interface organizations are preferable. Among those groups, it is important to mention that almost every cluster preferred an extended menu, except the first cluster, where menu was an insignificant element. Further, presence of the author in the news interface was significant for 3 out of 5 groups, however in some clusters it highly increased trust. The same situation happened with the live translation element in the news interface - it was a significant factor influencing trust in only 3 out of 5 clusters. Interestingly, recommended news also increased trust for some clusters. And finally, the information box was significant for 3 out of 5 groups, however it does not drastically increase trust. An interesting conclusion to point is the inconsistency of self-reported data (Likert scale answers) and behavioral data (conjoint choices). When users were directly asked about their preferences regarding the presence of several interface elements and their influence on trust, users chose presence of author, extended menu and live translation to be elements with the highest rate; whereas recommended news was the lowest element by this scale. If we look at the conjoint block data, it can be clearly seen that only for some groups of users recommended news is not preferable, when other groups perceive it as an important factor in building trust. Recommendations for improving the interface of news websites can help increase user trust and improve the quality of the information provided. However, these recommendations should consider the target audience and make decisions based on their preferences.

Acknowledgments. This research was supported by the Basic Research Program at the National Research University Higher School of Economics (HSE University).

A Appendix 1

(See Table 5).

Table 5. Surface elements influencing trust.

Group	Element	Influence on trust/effect	Reference
Attractiveness	Aesthetics	In a study by Robins and Holmes, "higher aesthetic treatment" led to higher perceived credibility ratings, given the same content; a linear connection between aesthetics and credibility. In a study by Asluadi, aesthetics was operationalized as a combination of contrast, dominance, balance, and harmony. Contrast, dominance by contrast and dominance by size were 100% conclusively appreciated for all the evaluated objects/ attributes	[1,24]
	Color	A study by Hawlitschek provides inconclusive results on how color (red or blue) impacts trust, however, participants in the red color condition perceived the experimental interface as warmer than subjects in the blue color condition	[16]
	Profesionalism	According to Chaiken, an impressive presentation, perceived expertise in the content, affiliation with a respected institution, desirable features and functions, and engaging interactive elements all significantly influenced the level of trust. Professional appearance of the website was one of important conditions for perceiving the site as credible in one of the heuristics suggested by Metzger and Flanagin	[8,20]

(*continued*)

Table 5. (*continued*)

Group	Element	Influence on trust/effect	Reference
Usability	Type of the interface	The conversational interface proved to be notably more successful in fostering user trust and contentment in the decision-making tool compared to the graphical user interface. This held true regardless of the housing recommendation system's accuracy levels in different scenarios	[13]
	UX	Ease of use, navigation, interactivity are proven to increase user satisfaction, intention to use, and most importantly trust in the interface	[3,8,10,12,15,30]
Structural elements	Structure of the site	According to Tseng, the amount of text is positively correlated with trust (more text - more trust), while the amount of images suggest the opposite relationship. Findings from Wobbrock study suggest that credibility is affected by article length, image count and density, and font face and size. And the "most credible" article with 2000 total words, 15/36 px (17/41 pt) body/title serif font, one video, and four images. Hong found that only message features influence credibility perceptions (in comparison to content features)	[17,32,34,36]
	Advertisements	According to Hong, the presence of advertisements does not statistically influence trust in the interface. In a study by Kakol, however, the presence of advertisements was negatively associated with trust	[17,18]

References

1. Alsudani, F., Casey, M.: The effect of aesthetics on web credibility. In: People and Computers XXIII Celebrating People and Technology. BCS Learning & Development (2009)
2. Alzahrani, L., Al-Karaghouli, W., Weerakkody, V.: Investigating the impact of citizens' trust toward the successful adoption of e-government: a multigroup analysis of gender, age, and internet experience. Inf. Syst. Manag. **35**(2), 124–146 (2018)
3. Aubert, B.A.: The impact of interface quality on trust in web retailers. Cahier du GReSI (1), 05 (2001)
4. Backhaus, K., Erichson, B., Gensler, S., Weiber, R., Weiber, T.: Conjoint analysis. In: Multivariate Analysis: An Application-Oriented Introduction, pp. 533–599. Springer, Heidelberg (2023)
5. Bansak, K., Hainmueller, J., Hopkins, D.J., Yamamoto, T., Druckman, J.N., Green, D.P.: Conjoint survey experiments. Adv. Exp. Polit. Sci. **19**, 19–41 (2021)
6. Bentley, F., Quehl, K., Wirfs-Brock, J., Bica, M.: Understanding online news behaviors. In: Proceedings of the 2019 CHI Conference on Human Factors in Computing Systems, pp. 1–11 (2019)
7. Berlyne, D.E.: Studies in the new experimental aesthetics: steps toward an objective psychology of aesthetic appreciation. Hemisphere (1974)
8. Chaiken, S.R., Han, L., Darney, B.G., Han, L.: Factors associated with perceived trust of false abortion websites: cross-sectional online survey. J. Med. Internet Res. (2021)

9. Chassy, P., Fitzpatrick, J., Jones, et al.: Complexity and aesthetic pleasure in websites: an eye tracking study. J. Interact. Sci. (2017)
10. Cheng, T.H., Chen, S.C., Hariguna, T.: The empirical study of usability and credibility on intention usage of government-to-citizen services. J. Appl. Data Sci. **2**(2) (2021)
11. Eggers, F., Sattler, H., Teichert, T., Völckner, F.: Choice-based conjoint analysis. In: Homburg, C., Klarmann, M., Vomberg, A. (eds.) Handbook of Market Research, pp. 781–819. Springer, Cham (2022). https://doi.org/10.1007/978-3-319-57413-4_23
12. Faisal, C.N., et al.: Web design attributes in building user trust, satisfaction, and loyalty for a high uncertainty avoidance culture. IEEE Trans. Human-Mach. Syst. **47**(6), 847–859 (2016)
13. Gupta, A., Basu, D., Ghantasala, R., Qiu, S., Gadiraju, U.: To trust or not to trust: how a conversational interface affects trust in a decision support system. In: Proceedings of the ACM Web Conference 2022, pp. 3531–3540 (2022)
14. Halbach, P., Burbach, L., Ziefle, M., Calero Valdez, A.: News articles on social media: showing balanced content adds more credibility than trust badges or user ratings. In: International Conference on Human-Computer Interaction, pp. 439–460. Springer, Heidelberg (2023). https://doi.org/10.1007/978-3-031-35748-0_31
15. Hallem, Y., Abbes, I., Hikkerova, L., Taga, M.: A trust model for collaborative redistribution platforms: a platform design issue. Technol. Forecast. Soc. Chang. **170**, 120943 (2021)
16. Hawlitschek, F., Jansen, L.E., Lux, E., Teubner, T., Weinhardt, C.: Colors and trust: the influence of user interface design on trust and reciprocity. In: 2016 49th Hawaii International Conference on System Sciences (HICSS), pp. 590–599. IEEE (2016)
17. Hong, T.: The influence of structural and message features on web site credibility. J. Am. Soc. Inf. Sci. Technol. **57**(1), 114–127 (2006)
18. Kakol, M., Nielek, R., Wierzbicki, A.: Understanding and predicting web content credibility using the content credibility corpus. Inf. Process. Manag., 1043–1061 (2017)
19. Kang, B., Höllerer, T., O'Donovan, J.: Believe it or not? analyzing information credibility in microblogs. In: Proceedings of the 2015 IEEE/ACM International Conference on Advances in Social Networks Analysis 2015, pp. 611–616 (2015)
20. Metzger, M.J., Flanagin, A.J., Medders, R.B.: Social and heuristic approaches to credibility evaluation online. J. Commun. **60**(3), 413–439 (2010)
21. Orme, B.K.: Getting started with conjoint analysis: strategies for product design and pricing research (2006)
22. Pagliaro, S., Sacchi, S., Pacilli, M.G., et al.: Trust predicts covid-19 prescribed and discretionary behavioral intentions in 23 countries. PloS One **16** (2021)
23. Pelzer, E.: The potential of conjoint analysis for communication research. Commun. Res. Rep. **36**(2), 136–147 (2019)
24. Robins, D., Holmes, J.: Aesthetics and credibility in web site design. Inf. Process. Manag. **44**(1), 386–399 (2008)
25. Rousseau, D.M., Sitkin, S.B., et al.: Not so different after all: a cross-discipline view of trust. Acad. Manag. Rev. **23**(3), 393–404 (1998)
26. Sampalean, N.I., De-Magistris, T., Rama, D.: Investigating Italian consumer preferences for different characteristics of provolone valpadana using the conjoint analysis approach. Foods **9**(12), 1730 (2020)
27. Schenkman, B.N., Jönsson, F.U.: Aesthetics and preferences of web pages. Behav. Inf. Technol. **19**(5), 367–377 (2000)

28. Shu, K., Liu, H.: Detecting Fake News on Social Media. Springer, Cham (2022)
29. Simko, J., Hanakova, M., Racsko, et al.: Fake news reading on social media: an eye-tracking study. In: Proceedings of the 30th ACM Conference on Hypertext and Social Media, pp. 221–230 (2019)
30. Sousa, S., Bates, N.: Factors influencing content credibility in facebook's news feed: inside view on the united kingdom (UK) post-brexit. Human-Intell. Syst. Integrat. **3**, 69–78 (2021)
31. Tamilina, L.: A brief overview of approaches to defining social trust (2018)
32. Tseng, K.-T., Tseng, Y.-C.: The correlation between visual complexity and user trust in on-line shopping: implications for design. In: Kurosu, M. (ed.) HCI 2014. LNCS, vol. 8512, pp. 90–99. Springer, Cham (2014). https://doi.org/10.1007/978-3-319-07227-2_10
33. Wang, F., Wang, H., Cho, J.H.: Consumer preference for yogurt packaging design using conjoint analysis. Sustainability, 3463 (2022)
34. Wang, Y.D., Emurian, H.H.: An overview of online trust: concepts, elements, and implications. Comput. Human Behav. (2005)
35. Wasike, B.: When the influencer says jump! how influencer signaling affects engagement with covid-19 misinformation. Social Sci. Med. (2022)
36. Wobbrock, J.O., Hattatoglu, L., Hsu, A.K., Burger, M.A., Magee, M.J.: The goldilocks zone: young adults' credibility perceptions of online news articles based on visual appearance. New Rev. Hypermedia Multimedia **27**(1–2), 51–96 (2021)
37. Zieglmeier, V., Lehene, A.M.: Designing trustworthy user interfaces. In: Proceedings of the 33rd Australian Conference on Human-Computer Interaction, pp. 182–189 (2021)

Digital Behavior of Urban Residents: The Case-Study of St. Petersburg

Boris Nizomutdinov(✉) and Lyudmila Vidiasova

ITMO University, Kronverkskiy pr. 49, 197101 Saint-Petersburg, Russia
{boris,lavidiasova}@itmo.ru

Abstract. This paper examines the digital behavior of city residents, using the example of St. Petersburg. Digital behavior refers to the activities and interactions of people in the digital space, such as posting messages, commenting, likes and other manifestations of activity on the Internet. The relevance of studying this area is explained by the increasingly significant role of social networks, messengers and other means of communication in people's daily lives, as well as their impact on various aspects of society, including communication, electronic participation, social relations and public opinion formation. An interdisciplinary approach has been applied to the study of digital behavior, combining traditional methods of sociology and automated methods of collecting and processing information from social networks. Traditional methods of sociology allow the analysis of social processes, interactions and motivations of people, while automated methods provide extensive data analysis, pattern detection. The purpose of our study was to identify the main markers of users' digital behavior through conducting sociological surveys and analyzing the demand for digital services. We sought to assess the current situation and potential growth points, as well as apply a multidimensional approach to studying the digital strategies of city residents. The use of open data was supposed to show the prospects of the work and lay the foundation for future detailed research.

Keywords: digital behavior · strategy · social media · electronic participation

1 Introduction

As digital technologies increasingly penetrate into people's lives, they become entrenched in behavioral practices in the online environment. Thus, it becomes possible to talk about new types of activities of people in the digital environment, called digital behavior. Digital user behavior is a comprehensive concept that describes the goals, strategies, expectations, and experiences of users when interacting with digital technologies. This includes analyzing how users choose and use digital tools and platforms to achieve their personal or professional goals.

Researchers turn their attention to the phenomenon of digital behavior, considering it as an analog of an individual's behavior in the traditional sense only in the context of Internet interaction [1], including consideration of personality-driven aspects of

A. Chugunov et al. (Eds.): DTGS 2024, CCIS 2445, pp. 62–76, 2025.
https://doi.org/10.1007/978-3-031-90720-3_5

human digital life [2]. The transition to digital life is associated with the emergence of a new phenomenon of human digital, which is described in detail in the work of M.Prensky [3].

One of the most common approaches to studying digital behavior is the analysis of traffic statistics for a resource. However, this method faces significant limitations. Firstly, such data is most often inaccessible to external researchers, since attendance statistics are confidential information and are known only to platform developers. Thus, the lack of access to these data makes it impossible to use them in independent research.

An alternative approach may be to use traditional data collection methods such as focus groups. However, this method also has its drawbacks. Conducting focus groups requires significant financial and time costs. Organizing and holding meetings, attracting participants, and subsequent data processing—all this makes focus groups an expensive research method. In addition, there is a risk of group polarization of opinions, when participants may be inclined to certain points of view under the influence of other members of the group. This distortion can lead to inaccurate and biased results.

Thus, traditional methods such as analyzing attendance statistics and focus groups are not always suitable for analyzing digital behavior due to their high cost, duration, and inaccessibility of data to third-party researchers. It is necessary to search for new, more effective and accessible approaches to obtain an accurate and objective picture of digital behavior.

Therefore, the authors propose an interdisciplinary approach based on parsing open data and conducting online sociological surveys. The first approach eliminates the problem of data unavailability, since it uses open data, the second approach solves the problem of high cost, representative sampling and polarization of opinions.

To assess the parameters of digital behavior using traditional sociology methods, E.V. Brodovskaya's team uses an assessment of the importance of traditional and new communication channels, the frequency of various online communication practices, the frequency of various online entertainment practices, the relationship between Internet behavior and strategies for professional and civic adaptation [4].

Automated methods have proven themselves well in analyzing users' digital footprints. The main source of such data is social networks, which allow collecting data on user behavior online, since all published data remains open and available for collection. That is why social networks are of interest to researchers, and scientists are developing methods for collecting and analyzing such data. Correlations between the information image of users on the social network and their real psychological personality traits and personal data have been revealed [5]. The results of the research allow us to conclude that there are significant patterns that allow us to determine the age, gender or level of education based on the user's avatar and other publicly available data in his profiles.

Voluminous and complex arrays of information from social networks are currently of increasing interest to researchers studying human behavior in cities. Experimental data indicate that the huge scale and near-real-time observation are unique advantages of such data and are suitable for use in urban systems [6]. Approaches to mathematical modeling of subjective opinions and value orientations of individual citizens and society as a whole are described in order to assess and take them into account when making managerial decisions in the city, based on information from the Internet [7]. The above-mentioned subjective categories are proposed to be expressed in the form of structures of judgments, mental states, mental orientations and value systems.

To analyze content and study digital activity, it is necessary to study textual information [8]. Text mining reads the unstructured form of data to provide meaningful information patterns in the shortest period of time. Social media is an excellent source of textual data, as most people in the modern world use these sites in their daily lives to keep in touch with each other. Text analytics and machine learning methods are used to analyze digital footprints in social networks. The work of the Tikhonova O. team [9] presents an approach to studying texts from Internet social networks, using methods based on natural language analysis to extract hidden topics and thematic objects of the urban environment. The proposed approach can be used to create new information resources based on the analysis of publications and messages from citizens. In addition to text analytics, methods based on neural networks are used. Developments are underway to conduct an automated study of Internet discourse using recurrent neural networks, with messages and comments on social networks on specified topics as source data. An experiment conducted by a team of researchers at ITMO University [10] revealed the possibilities of artificial neural networks for a deeper understanding of the results of public discussions.

In addition to texts on social networks, images posted by users are actively studied, the relationship between the characteristics of Instagram users and the features of their photos is considered [11]. The personal qualities of the "Big Five" and gender are used as variables for user characteristics, the results of such studies can also be attributed to the study of digital behavior.

Summarizing the studies reviewed, we can say that the methods of text analytics, machine learning and automated data collection are promising tools for studying digital behavior. They allow not only to deeply explore the behavior and interactions on social networks, but also significantly contribute to the development of more accurate and informed conclusions about the created digital user profiles. Text analytics can reveal hidden patterns in large amounts of text data, while machine learning can improve classification and predictive behaviors based on historical data. Together, these approaches make it easier to understand the complex and dynamically changing interactions in the digital sphere. Automated data collection reduces the time and resources spent on research, and at the same time increases the accuracy and objectivity of the information collected, minimizing human errors. Thus, the use of these methods is very promising for studying the digital profile and can be recommended to researchers for a deeper understanding of the behavioral characteristics of users of social networks.

Additionally, for a deeper understanding of the term digital behavior, as well as methodologies for its study, a bibliometric analysis of scientific literature was conducted on the request "digital behavior" in the Science Direct digital library. Using appropriate clustering algorithms, groups of publications were identified based on their similarity and semantic relationships. A bibliometric analysis conducted on the basis of collected publications on the topic of digital behavior revealed the main cluster associated with social networks. This confirms that social networks are an important source of information for studying digital behavior of citizens. The identified clusters are shown in Fig. 1.

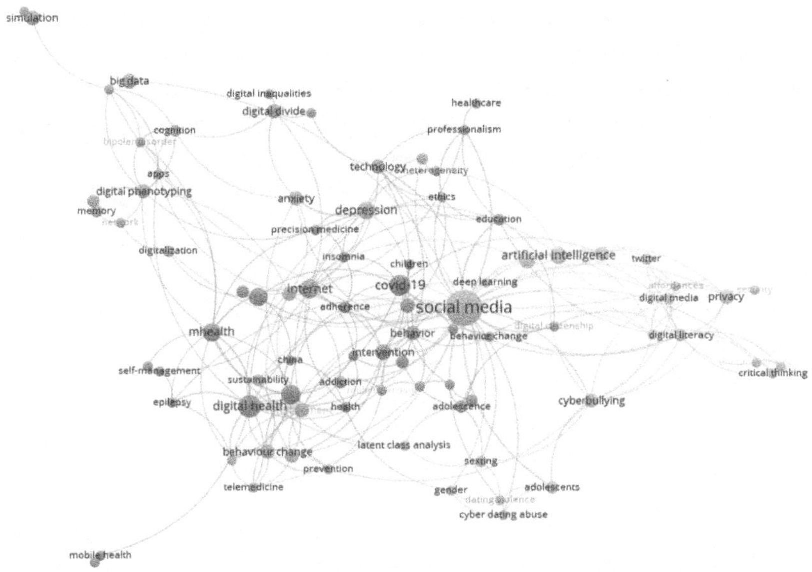

Fig. 1. The results of the bibliometric analysis of publications on the topic of digital behavior.

The result of the bibliometric analysis was the confirmation that social networks are an important tool for studying the digital behavior of citizens. However, with the existence of a number of methods for studying digital footprints, there is no comprehensive research approach that allows comparing data from the online environment with the results of surveys of respondents. This article presents a comprehensive research approach to the study of digital behavior of citizens, including a combination of traditional and automated data collection methods.

2 Research Methodology

In the course of the study, the task was set to develop an integrated approach to the study of digital behavior of citizens, combining sociological methods and automated methods of collecting and processing information from social networks. At the first step, a sociological survey was conducted, at the second stage, a method for analyzing digital behavior through data analysis in social networks was proposed.

The paper presents the results of testing the approach on the case of the St. Petersburg metropolis. Data collection, both in the case of a sociological survey and in social networks, concerned the behavior of city residents. Thus, by studying the local plot, we offer opportunities for further use of this approach in other territories.

2.1 A Sociological Survey

A sociological survey was conducted in 2023. The survey examined the use of city services (including electronic ones) and satisfaction with them. To conduct the study, a methodology for questioning respondents was developed, taking into account the need to compare the data obtained from surveys with data from social networks.

The survey was conducted using an online questionnaire. The choice of method was dictated by the need to access respondents who are users of digital services. The survey involved 500 respondents aged 18 years and older. The survey was conducted using a quota representative sample.

Based on the size of the sample population, a quota sample was compiled by gender, age and administrative regions of St. Petersburg [12]. Population data, such as gender and age composition and population of districts, were taken from the website of the Federal Statistics Service for St. Petersburg and the Leningrad Region (data for 2022 and 2023) and in the HSE ISSEK study for 2021 (data on the share of Internet users by age group) [13].

The population of St. Petersburg was divided into six age groups: 18–25 years, 26–35 years, 36–45 years, 46–55 years, 56–65 years and over 65 years (Table 1).

To conduct the survey, an online service Anketolog with a verified database of respondents was used. The database of respondents includes more than 14 thousand users from St. Petersburg.

Table 1. Research sample for the population of St. Petersburg by age and Internet use *.

Age	Amount	Internet user share	Internet users (number)	Distribution of Internet users by age
18–25	498090	100%	498090	14,8%
26–35	767811	100%	767811	22,8%
36–45	967795	100%	967795	28,7%
46–55	776581	80%	621265	18,4%
56–65	743773	50%	371887	11,0%
65 +	706358	20%	141272	4,2%
Total	4460408		3368119	100%

* according to Petrostat data for 2023 and HSE ISSEK for 2021.

2.2 Social Media Analysis

To analyze digital behavior, it is necessary to select a popular social media community for research. The "Ecosystem of Urban Services" platform, which provides statistics on the directions, was used to select the topic. This ecosystem has a role model and aggregates data on the main urban services, in particular, service usage statistics are maintained for each role. During the analysis, it was revealed that the most popular role is "Me and my health", and the maximum number of participants is involved in this role. This is in line with the results of the survey, which also showed that the most popular services are related to healthcare. The distribution of services by roles is shown in Fig. 2.

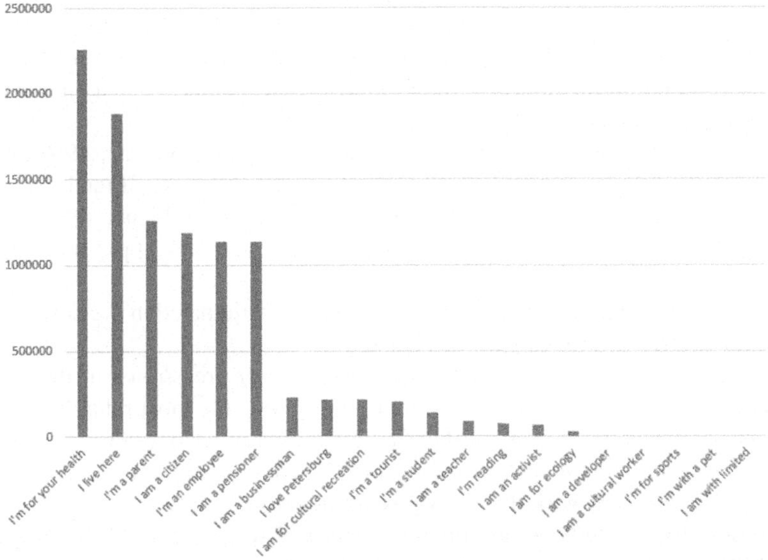

Fig. 2. The popularity of social roles according to the city services ecosystem.

Since medical services are in the greatest demand, the field of medicine was chosen at the first stage of studying digital behavior. As an example, the St. Petersburg Health Committee community was selected on the Vkontakte social network, a link to the resource - https://vk.com/komzdravspb.

3 Research Results

To assess the demand and relevance of digital city services, the questionnaire included the question "Currently, city digital services for citizens are being created in St. Petersburg. To what extent would the appearance of the following electronic services be relevant and useful for you personally?" According to the survey results, the rating of the most relevant services for citizens is as follows: health and medical services (80% consider them relevant), services for public transport passengers (76%), "Safe City" services: information, "my district police officer", mutual assistance in emergency situations (74%), services in the field of tourism and culture (67%), services for pet owners (61%), services for motorists (59%), services for schoolchildren and their parents (56%), services for doing business (56%), civil initiatives (47%).

The study assessed the frequency of use of government interaction portals. According to the survey, the penetration of the federal portal Gosuslugi portal is 95%, the Feedback Platform on the Gosuslugi is 57%, the Unified Portal of Appeals from Citizens of St.

Petersburg is 48%, the Our Petersburg portal is 49%, the Ecosystem of City Digital Services is 30%, the Ministry of Internal Affairs portal (appeals online) - 30%, the portal "Beautiful Petersburg" - 28%, the portal "Russian Public Initiative" - 24%, the portal "Your Budget - St. Petersburg" - 22%, the mini-app "I live here" - 18%.

According to the survey, 88% of city residents at least sometimes visit multi-functional centers (MFC) for state services provision, 84% contact the authorities by e-mail, 59% use chatbots of organizations and departments, 63% use feedback forms and Internet receptions on the websites of the state government, 52% - come to personal receptions at government agencies.

In addition, 54% use online portals for solving urban problems, 49% use online petition portals, 23% proactive budgeting portals, and 39% use official social media accounts. Also, 54% use online portals for solving urban problems, 49% use online petition portals, 23% use initiative budgeting portals, and 39% apply through official social media accounts.

According to the survey, every fourth respondent participated in the development of government decisions through various channels.

The study analyzed the relevance of individual user areas/roles in the context of the demand for digital services. According to the survey, the most relevant category of services is: "My Health" (88%). Further, in descending order of relevance of the roles, the following are highlighted: My vacation (82%), My family (81%), My home - St. Petersburg (77.4%), My work (64%), My retirement (45%), My studies (39%).

According to the study, approximately a third of respondents (27%) have experience in filing online complaints, which resulted in real actions by the administration or responsible organizations. At the same time, 46% of them were satisfied with the result of processing requests and solving the problem, 49.8% were not, since most often they received "unsubscribes" to their request, and another 4% found it difficult to characterize their experience as positive or negative.

Table 2 shows the contingency of emotions among respondents depending on their age when using new digital services. It can be noted that among respondents of different ages, the greatest number of negative emotions was recorded in the group of 36–45 year old.

The study examined the demand for various types of digital services. For representatives of all age groups, digital health and security services are of particular relevance. Differences were found in the demand for services for pet owners and businesses: in the oldest age group, the need for them was sharply reduced. In addition, middle-aged respondents (36–45 years old) are less likely to consider the introduction of civil initiative services as relevant (Table 3).

The survey explored strategies for using various portals. Table 4 presents the results of the distribution of respondents' answers by age group. There should be noted a decrease in use as the age of respondents increases in almost all areas. In addition, attention should be paid to the group of 46–55-year-old respondents, who demonstrate less intensive use of most portals and services, compared even to older groups.

Digital behavior was also analyzed by the frequency of use of various means of communication and access to cyberspace. Table 5 shows the distribution of users by age among those who reported frequent use of certain tools and services. According

Table 2. Distribution of respondents' emotions when using new digital services, age groups.

When I use a new digital service, I feel...	Age					
	18–25	26–35	36–45	46–55	56–65	65+
Fear, apprehension, worry	11,8%	23,5%	35,3%	11,8%	17,6%	0,0%
Anger, dissatisfaction, irritation	0,0%	31,6%	47,4%	10,5%	10,5%	0,0%
Sadness, frustration, sadness	12,0%	20,0%	44,0%	20,0%	4,0%	0,0%
Joy, pleasure, fun	15,8%	17,8%	26,7%	24,0%	12,3%	3,4%
Neutral emotions	13,6%	25,0%	27,7%	17,4%	10,6%	5,7%

to the survey, older groups demonstrate less intensity of use, among them even about 10% use a push-button telephone. The use of smartphones, instant messengers, and telegram channels is intensively included in the everyday digital behavior of respondents. However, reading news as a popular practice has already adopted a new, digital format, especially among the older generation.

It is worth noting that among respondents of all ages, people with positive experience in solving problems through digital services predominate (Table 6). At the same time, in almost all age groups, except for young people, a third prefer personal visits to authorities rather than using digital services. Representatives of older age groups act with more wariness online: they trust less online interaction with authorities, and are also afraid of putting their personal data at risk. At the same time, the majority of respondents aged 46 years and older admit that electronic services are becoming more convenient and useful over time.

As mentioned earlier, the second block of work is devoted to the development of a method for analyzing data from social networks to study digital behavior. The field of medicine was selected for the pilot study and the community of the "Health Protection Committee" was analyzed.

Using the API of the VKontakte social network, comments from users of the selected community were collected. During the analysis, the last 1000 posts were uploaded for thematic modeling and analysis of user activity. To analyze user activity, the number of comments, likes and views per post is taken into account, these parameters can be used in the study of digital activity. 6889 comments were left for these posts, which were analyzed. The results of the analysis of user activity are shown in Table 7.

Using the LDA (latent Dirichlet placement) method, thematic modeling was carried out, which made it possible to identify the key topics most actively discussed by users in this community (Table 8). The work analyzed user comments on official messages in the group.

These topics represent the most significant issues and ideas raised by the participants, and are the basis for understanding the subject of discussions within the team. During the

Table 3. Recognition of the relevance of city digital services by respondents of different age groups.

	18–25	26–35	36–45	46–55	56–65	65+
Health and medical services: email. medical record, doctor's appointment, test data	80,8	79,9	80,5	77,5	81,8	85,8
Electronic services for public transport passengers: navigation, payment	85	68,4	78,5	75,3	78,2	76,2
Electronic services to support motorists: parking payments, insurance, fines	56,1	61,4	60,4	63,5	58,2	42,9
Services for schoolchildren and their parents: email. diary, sections, circles, psychological. help, etc	47,9	51,7	63,9	62,3	45,4	47,6
Services for pet owners: veterinary medicine, vaccinations, lost searches, etc	63	66,7	59,1	59,2	60	**38,1**
Electronic services in the field of tourism and culture: navigation, excursions, virtual guides	67,1	68,5	67,3	66,6	69,1	57,1
Civic initiatives: "active citizen", voting, volunteering and sponsorship	48	47,4	**22,3**	50,6	45,4	61,9
Electronic services for business (opening and registration of enterprises, etc.)	53,4	51,8	48,6	49,6	43,7	**33,4**
Safe city: information, "my local police officer", mutual assistance in emergency situations	72,6	69,3	75,7	73,2	76,3	76,2

Table 4. Use of channels and services by respondents of different age groups (use with any frequency and frequency).

	18–25	26–35	36–45	46–55	56–65	65+
Portal "Our Petersburg"	48	54,4	50	44,1	52,7	38,1
Portal "Your Budget", St. Petersburg	27,3	33,3	20,9	14	20	4,8
Portal "Russian Public Initiative"	32,9	28,1	19,5	24,7	21,8	19
Feedback Platform (FP) - Public services, services: We decide together, Public voting	67,1	54,4	52,8	58	63,6	57,6
Public services portal Gosuslugi	97,3	95,6	94,4	95,7	92,7	95,2
Ecosystem of urban digital services	42,8	38,6	25	27,9	25,5	0

Table 5. Use of services and technologies by respondents of different age groups (frequent or very frequent use).

	18–25	26–35	36–45	46–55	56–65	65+
I use a feature phone	2,7	6,2	4,9	3,3	9,1	9,6
I use smartphone	94,5	93	93,8	92,5	90,9	81
I use messengers	93,2	86,1	80,8	81,7	70,9	66,6
I use social networks vi smartphone	83,5	84,5	84,8	69,6	61,8	52,4
I read Telegram channels	78,1	76,3	66,7	65,6	65,4	57,1
I use social networks VK	68,5	61,9	60,4	61,3	56,4	38,1
I use social networks for reading news	53,4	64	55,6	54,8	47,3	**76,2**
I use apps of social network VK	61,7	57,9	50,7	46,3	40	42,8
I use social networks and instant messengers to communicate with my neighbors	34,2	28	32,7	31,2	21,8	14,3

thematic modeling on LDA, three of the most important topics were identified, which are being discussed:

- Topic "Drugs, benefits and gratitude" is related to information about medicines, benefits when receiving medicines and expressing gratitude for the help provided.
- Topic "Medical care in the polyclinic" is related to questions about medical care provided in the polyclinic, including doctors, departments and contact numbers.
- Topic "Personal data and clarification of information" is related to the discussion and clarification of personal data, such as full name and date of birth, as well as requests for accurate information through private messages or certain groups.

These three topics are the most important and are widely discussed in the context of medical care and interaction with medical institutions.

Table 6. Agreement of respondents of different age groups with statements (agree, rather agree with the statement), % by age group.

	18–25	26–35	36–45	46–55	56–65	65 +
I plan to upgrade my mobile device in the next year	30,1	36,8	32,6	**45,1**	18,2	28,5
I believe I have optimal Internet access through my device	82,2	86	77,1	75,3	78,2	71,4
I find using chatbots useful	56,1	39,4	34	32,3	25,5	4,8
A chatbot does not allow you to get all the information; you have to look for contact with a real interlocutor	37	56,1	36,7	**65,6**	**69,1**	**61,9**
I have positive experience solving problems through digital services	46,6	45,7	40,3	44,1	43,6	23,8
I have negative experience solving problems through digital services	**20,5**	**14,9**	**11,8**	**9,7**	**9,1**	**23,8**
I consider myself an experienced user of the Internet and ICT, I easily master new programs and applications	82,2	73,7	71,9	61,3	**45,5**	**47,6**
When interacting with authorities, I prefer a personal reception than interaction via Internet services	23,3	32,5	**36,8**	31,2	34,5	33
I have no problems accessing Internet services that allow me to interact with authorities	53,5	55,2	61,8	58,8	54,5	66,6
In general, I trust interaction with authorities through Internet technologies	58,9	52,6	50	45,1	**40**	**42,9**
Thanks to the Internet, I began to solve my problems and tasks when interacting with authorities more effectively	**52,1**	**47,3**	**50,7**	36,5	40	23,8
When interacting with authorities via the Internet, compared to personal contacts, I put my personal data at risk	20,6	34,2	38,2	30,1	36,4	**52,3**
I believe that electronic services become more convenient and useful over time	68,5	69,3	70,8	**76,3**	70,9	**76,1**

As you can see, thematic modeling can also be one of the tools for analyzing digital user behavior to identify the main topics of communication.

Table 7. User activity indicators.

№	Activity Parameter	Value
1	Posts processed	1000
2	Participants	23382
3	Views per post	3804
4	Likes on the post	33
5	Comments on the post	7
6	Reposts per post	7
7	% of views to participants	16,27
8	% of likes to the participants	0,14
9	Posts per day	2,66
10	The amount of views for processed posts	3800431
11	The amount of likes for processed posts	33192
12	The amount of comments on processed posts	6943
13	The amount of reposts to processed posts	6777

Table 8. Description of the topics highlighted by the LDA method.

№	Topic	Description
1	Drugs, benefits and gratitude	The topic is related to information about drugs, benefits
2	Medical care in the polyclinic	The main topic is related to the provision of medical care in a polyclinic, including doctors, departments and a contact phone number
3	Personal data and clarification of information	This topic is related to clarifying or providing personal data through messages or a specific group
4	Getting prescriptions and medicines"	The topic is related to the process of obtaining prescriptions and medicines within healthcare, including queues and availability of medicines
5	Vaccinations and blood type of children	The topic is related to questions about vaccinations of children, blood type and communication with a doctor

(*continued*)

Table 8. (*continued*)

№	Topic	Description
6	Doctor's appointment and specialist appointment	The topic is related to the process of making an appointment with a doctor, receiving coupons and doctor's awards
7	Hospital and referral for tests	This topic is related to the hospital and the referral process for personal tests
8	Health and dental care	This topic is related to questions about health, dental care and tests
9	Neurologist, stroke and comments	This topic is related to questions about neurology, strokes, and comments from certain individuals
10	Communication and feedback	This topic is related to feedback, gratitude and getting the necessary information
11	Flu, vaccines and admission to the clinic	The topic is related to the flu, vaccines, admission to the polyclinic and the specified area
12	The city and periodic treatment	This topic is related to the specified city, periodic treatment and vaccinations
13	Toxic medicines	The topic is related to information about certain medicines that have toxic and counterfeit properties
14	Health Committee and medical examination	This topic is related to the health committee, medical examination and doctors associated with this field
15	Cardiologist and medicines	The topic is related to questions about cardiology, taking medications and disability

4 Conclusion

In conclusion of our study, it can be noted that the conducted survey among users contributed to the identification of the main markers of digital behavior. The analysis of demand for digital services made it possible to assess the current situation and potential growth points. Thanks to the pilot study of user behavior on social networks, we were able to apply a multifaceted approach to the study of digital strategies of city residents. Open data demonstrates the promise of this work and lays the foundation for future detailed research.

While a sociological survey makes it possible to collect data on the opinions and preferences of citizens, automated analysis methods have made it possible to take a snapshot of online actions that users do not always consciously perform. In the context of the study, it is situations in which the user, without thinking, searches for information and leaves data about himself on the Internet, are of particular interest.

Identifying markers of digital behavior can shed light on user needs and create useful and in-demand city services based on this information.

The analysis of the results showed that the combination of traditional sociological surveys and automated data analysis methods demonstrates the importance of an interdisciplinary approach in the study of digital behavior. Opinion polls provide detailed qualitative data reflecting the opinions, preferences and motivations of users. This allows researchers to gain a deeper understanding of the social processes and interactions taking place in the digital environment.

On the other hand, automated methods of analyzing big data collected from social networks and other digital platforms allow us to obtain quantitative indicators reflecting real user behavior. Such methods are able to identify patterns and trends in behavior that are not always obvious when conducting traditional surveys. In addition, they make it possible to analyze data in real time and cover large amounts of information, which significantly increases the scale of the study.

Together, these two approaches complement each other and provide a more comprehensive and multifaceted understanding of the digital behavior of urban residents. Traditional sociological methods bring depth and contextual awareness to research, whereas automated methods provide breadth and accuracy of data.

As a result, an interdisciplinary approach combining sociological surveys and automated data analysis allows not only to better understand the current state and potential of digital behavior, but also to use the data obtained to develop in-demand and effective urban digital services. Thus, the research not only creates a theoretical basis, but also has direct practical application, contributing to the improvement of urban digital infrastructure and communications.

The limitations of the study are related to the fact that the main focus in the analysis of social networks was on one thematic area. It is in demand among users, but does not allow extrapolation of data on users' digital behavior to other areas.

In the next stages, it is planned to implement a comprehensive project that will include the analysis of large amounts of information from social networks for a detailed description of the types and strategies of digital behavior. It is expected that this research will provide a deeper understanding of the digital environment and the behavior of its users, which, in turn, contributes to the development of more effective and targeted strategies in the field of digital development and Internet communications.

Acknowledgement. The research was conducted with the support of the grant № FSER-2024-0049 "Study of digital behavior strategies of citizens of different age groups".

References

1. Flerov, O.V., Kutaitseva, O.N.: Digital behavior as a psychological and pedagogical phenomenon (structural and content analysis). Educ. Res. Technol. **1**(42), 51–61 (2023)
2. Raven, E.V.: Discursive digital personality as a virtual copy of linguistic personality. Mod. Pedag. Educ. **5**, 193–196 (2021)
3. Prensky, M.: Sapiens digital: from digital immigrants and digital natives to digital wisdom. Innov.: J. Online Educ. **5**(3) (2009)

4. Brodovskaya, E.V., Dombrovskaya, A., Pyrma, R.V., Azarov, A.A.: Strategies of digital behavior of Russian youth in the context of the formation of civil and professional competencies. Free thought **4**, 109–118 (2019)
5. Tropnikov, A.S., Nizomutdinov, B.A., Uglova, A.B.: Application of social networks users digital fingerprints to predict their information image. In: ACM International Conference Proceeding Series: 13, Digital Governance in the Era of Disruptive Technologies and Globalisation, pp. 839–842 (2020). https://doi.org/10.1145/3428502.3428635
6. Ilieva, R.T., McPhearson, T.: Social-media data for urban sustainability. Nat. Sustain. **1**, 553–565 (2018). https://doi.org/10.1038/s41893-018-0153-6
7. Mityagin, S., Tikhonova, O.: Approaches to modeling subjective opinions and value orientations of citizens for managerial decision making in the urban environment. In: Proceedings of the International Conference on Electronic Governance and Open Society: Challenges in Eurasia EGOSE 2016, pp. 149–156 (2016) https://doi.org/10.1145/3014087.3014094
8. Salloum, S., Al-Emran, M., Monem, A., Shaalan, K.: A survey of text mining in social media: Facebook and twitter perspectives. Adv. Sci. Technol. Eng. Syst. J. **2**, 127–133 (2017). https://doi.org/10.25046/aj020115
9. Tikhonova, O., Khrulkov, A., Antonov, A., Sobolevsky, S.L., Mityagin, S.A.: Extraction of hidden topics in urban context based on the Internet publications analysis. Procedia Comput. Sci. **212**, 23–33 (2022)
10. Begen, P., Misnikov Y., Filatova O.: Application of automated tools in researching internet discourses: experience of using the recurrent neural networks for studying discussions on pension reform. In: 21st Conference on Scientific Services and Internet, CEUR Workshop Proceedings, pp. 119–130 (2019)
11. Kim, Y., Kim, J.H.: Using computer vision techniques on Instagram to link users' personalities and genders to the features of their photos: an exploratory study. Inf. Process. Manage. **54**(6), 1101–1114 (2018)
12. The population of St. Petersburg as of 01.01.2022. https://78.rosstat.gov.ru/storage/mediabank/%D0%A7%D0%B8%D1%81%D0%BB.%D0%A1%D0%9F%D0%B1%20%D0%BD%D0%B0%2001.01.2022%20.pdf. Accessed 21 Nov 2023
13. How the pandemic affected the level of digital skills of Russians (2022). https://issek.hse.ru/news/704025190.html. Accessed 21 Nov 2023

Design Approaches for Development and Implementation of AI-Driven Government Services

Andrey Nosikov(✉)

Saint Petersburg State University, 7/9 Universitetskaya nab., St. Petersburg 199034, Russia
a.nosikov@spbu.ru

Abstract. The relevance of developing government services on artificial intelligence (AI) platforms is becoming increasingly evident within the context of contemporary digital advancement. This article examines the perspectives and opportunities provided by AI platforms for enhancing government services. The research explores global practices of AI application and implementation in government services, enabling the identification of key trends, interdisciplinary scientific research results, and case studies. By employing an integrative review of interdisciplinary scientific sources, implementation cases of AI-driven government services, technical documentation, and regulatory frameworks, the comprehensive conceptualization of designs for implementing AI-driven government services is ensured. The article identifies the main components of various designs for implementing AI-driven government services, facilitating the systematization of different approaches to constructing government AI services. Thus, the article describes a taxonomy of classes of AI-driven government services and addresses the component of Sovereign AI and public-private partnerships. Additionally, an analysis of AI application in the public sector is conducted to identify key areas of application and potential advantages. The obtained results can serve as a basis for developing effective strategies for implementing AI in government agencies, taking into account various specificities.

Keywords: AI-driven government services · AI government services · taxonomy AI government services · Artificial intelligence · government services

1 Introduction

AI-driven government services encompass a wide range of applications aimed to improve the efficiency and effectiveness of public services, enabling governments to plan more effectively, target resources where they are most needed, and adapt services to user needs [1]. Additionally, AI-driven government services involve the use of AI technologies to make automated algorithmic decisions that generate efficiencies in complex and complicated local government services and operations [2].

The use of artificial intelligence (AI) in government services has become increasingly prevalent, with various applications and challenges being identified in the literature.

A. Chugunov et al. (Eds.): DTGS 2024, CCIS 2445, pp. 77–92, 2025.
https://doi.org/10.1007/978-3-031-90720-3_6

AI is being utilized in e-government services to provide personalized customer experiences, such as linking individualized data and processing individual assistance requests [3]. Additionally, AI tools have been deployed in public administration to facilitate better-informed and more rapid decision-making in multiple service domains, including policing, home office, criminal justice, and healthcare [4]. Furthermore, AI has been instrumental in enhancing governance during the management of the COVID-19 pandemic, aiding in data analysis and insights, which helped governments collect, analyze, and interpret data on the spread of the virus [5]. Moreover, the use of AI in public service design and delivery has the potential to improve the efficiency and quality of public services, leading to increased effectiveness, new forms of service delivery, evidence-based policy making, and the transformation of the public sector [6]. AI has also been employed in structural health monitoring, energy infrastructure fault detection and diagnosis, accessible customer service with chatbots, and automated transportation with autonomous shuttle buses in the context of local government [2]. However, the increasing use of AI in governance and society has raised concerns regarding accountability, transparency, reliability, safety, and trustworthiness of AI systems in government [7]. Governments are faced with the challenge of developing adequate governance frameworks to mitigate risks and maximize the potential of AI development and use [8]. In a sufficiently extensive systematic literature review of 2021 authored by Zuiderwijk, A., Chen, Y. C., & Salem, F., the following key benefits of implementing AI in public administration are highlighted: efficiency and performance benefits, risk identification and monitoring benefits, economic benefits, data and information processing benefits, service benefits, benefits for society at large, decision-making benefits, engagement and interaction benefits, sustainability benefits [9].

We can identify numerous real-life cases, technical platforms, and professional-expert discourses in various areas of public services, containing diverse elements of AI-driven government services implementation designs. However, the problem of systematizing this information is acute, as these designs entail numerous components and variables. The task of deconstructing and highlighting the most relevant components of AI-driven government services implementation designs for subsequent standardization of approach and structuring of these components for design, their components, and features, is the main focal point of this research. Thus, this study represents an attempt to provide a more integrated overview of the field of AI-driven government services implementation by combining real cases, Interdisciplinary scientific literature sources, regulatory frameworks, and information on current AI technical capabilities to ensure a comprehensive synthesis of the topic.

2 Materials and Methods

The study employed several methods based on the integrative review [10, 11]. Primarily, an Integrative Literature Review was used to provide a more structured and critical overview of the interdisciplinary field of designing and implementing AI-driven government services. The criteria for selecting scientific sources were as follows: indexed scientific publications on the research topic from the last five full years (2019 to 2023), as well as publications from the incomplete current year of 2024 (a total of six partial years).

This time frame was chosen because AI technologies demonstrated an exponential leap in capabilities during this period, which also intensified scientific, technical, consumer, and other discourses. The study also included an integrative review of the regulatory framework. The criteria for selecting legal documents were as follows: documents relevant to the research topic and available in the public domain on the official websites of government bodies and intergovernmental organizations. In addition to cases, an integrative review of technical documents, guides, and other information on the technical capabilities of AI in the field of government administration was utilized. This selection of sources was based on documents and content from the official websites of technology companies providing AI solutions for the public sector.

A significant part of the study involved an integrative case review, which allowed for the deconstruction of cases to identify the main components of AI-driven government services designs during secondary analysis. Case selection was based on reports on business media websites, news media websites, and media specializing in technology. Furthermore, the results of the preceding Integrative Literature Review of scientific sources were used for case selection.

In the integration of the review results, structural-functional and systemic approaches were primarily used. The systemic approach views the components of AI-driven government services implementation practices as a system consisting of interconnected components with their own characteristics and features, allowing for the examination of the emergence of designs. The structural-functional approach, in turn, views each component of AI-driven government services implementation designs as a contributor to the overall understanding of the design system's integrity. Combined, these approaches allow for an examination of the diversity of areas and methods of applying AI in government services. Working with these approaches enabled, for example, the identification of a taxonomy of various classes of AI-driven government services and the categorization of the main areas of AI-driven government services implementation.

The study also employed general scientific methods: comparative approach; analysis; synthesis; induction and deduction; formal-logical approach; secondary analysis of scientific data; the method of apperception, which represents the accumulation of knowledge through the interpretation of new information obtained from other sources; and the method of secondary analysis of empirical (including statistical) data.

3 Results

Strategic Vision and Institutionalization. When discussing aspects of designing AI-driven government services such as institutionalization and strategic vision, it is essential to refer primarily to official documents of national strategies for artificial intelligence development.

The first in time and most detailed is the Chinese strategy, "Plan for the Development of a New Generation of Artificial Intelligence", dated July 8, 2017. Among other things, the Chinese strategy includes a separate section describing the vision for AI implementation in government processes and public services. AI is intended to promote the "intellectualization of social governance". The Chinese strategy highlights the following main areas: Firstly, the "smart court", which involves the application of artificial intelligence in evidence collection, case analysis, reading and analysis of legal documents, and the implementation of intelligent judicial dispute resolution systems. The strategy also covers other areas of government services, such as intelligent transportation, smart cities, public security, environmental protection, military-civilian integration in AI, intelligent infrastructure, and AI-based predictive planning [12].

In the Russian national strategy for the development of artificial intelligence until 2030, adopted in 2019 (with amendments from 2024), there is a discussion of the need to stimulate the implementation of artificial intelligence technologies in the economy and social sphere without a clear strategy and conceptual framework regarding the areas of AI implementation in government management and services. One of the main tasks is highlighted: ensuring centralized development and dissemination of standardized solutions in government bodies, other state agencies, and organizations based on trusted artificial intelligence technologies. There is also a separate emphasis on the need to create a comprehensive system of regulatory framework for public sector related to the development and use of artificial intelligence technologies, ensuring the security of such technologies' application [13]. However, a separate strategic "challenge" for the Russian Federation is noted: the low level of implementation of artificial intelligence technologies in public administration. It should be summarized that the strategy of the Russian Federation, unlike the Chinese one, is more of a list of regulatory issues, as well as issues related to national security, without providing a strategic vision, specification of areas and methods of implementing AI technologies in government services, and specific sectors of government management.

In the document "Maintaining American Leadership in Artificial Intelligence" [14] it is stated that the United States needs to maintain its leadership in the development of AI technologies and stimulate the development of these technologies. However, there is no separate emphasis on the strategic vision for the implementation of AI-driven government services, or on the areas and sectors of government management where AI implementation is necessary.

The European Commission also has a roadmap and a strategic approach to the implementation of AI in European Union countries. Primarily, work is being done in the area of developing and synchronizing regulatory frameworks by all members of the European Union [15]. There is no unified roadmap or strategic vision for the implementation of AI-driven government services. However, the European Commission is implementing a structured risk-oriented approach to AI, which will be further applied by this research [16].

Thus, at the outset of deploying AI-driven government services, China possesses the most clearly empirically oriented strategic vision for utilizing AI in public services, while other centers of influence are focused on the general formation of the regulatory framework, regardless of the integration of AI into government services. However, when discussing the formal regulatory and legal institutionalization of AI-driven government services, all states have significant gaps (although all strategies emphasize the need to intensify the process of forming the regulatory framework in the field of AI), which will further find reflection in other components of designs. Primarily, this includes the absence of regulatory and legal clarifications regarding the accountability of AI and its legal subjectivity. The AI Index Report 2024, conducted by Stanford University, undertook an analysis of legislative documents encompassing the term "artificial intelligence" across 128 nations spanning the period from 2016 to 2023. Among these nations, 32 have enacted a minimum of one bill directly pertinent to artificial intelligence. Cumulatively, these countries have endorsed a total of 148 bills addressing various facets of artificial intelligence [17]. The dynamics of the number of adoptions of laws related to ai is upward, which signals that we are only in the process of resolving these issues.

Taxonomy of Classes and Levels of AI Responsibility in the Decision-Making Chain of AI-Driven Government Services. AI-driven government service designs can be classified based on the level of AI accountability in the decision-making chain. This classification can be represented pyramidically, where at the top of the pyramid there will be full autonomy of AI in decision-making, while at the bottom, AI's access to decision-making will not be delegated at all.

At the highest level, the decision-making process is entirely delegated to AI. The class of such autonomous AI in the pyramid of AI-driven government services can metaphorically be called "AI-captain". With AI of high autonomy class, the aforementioned problem of institutionalizing AI accountability arises, as AI does not possess legal subjectivity in any legislation worldwide. Therefore, if decision-making authority is fully delegated to AI in the manner of an AI captain, in case of an error, there will be no responsible legal subject and accountability. Decisions of the AI-captain class can be attributed to a project carried out by the Chinese government in collaboration with the tech giant Alibaba. In the city of Hangzhou, China, AI-based traffic management systems are used to monitor and control traffic flow. These systems analyze real-time traffic data from cameras and sensors to autonomously optimize traffic signal timing, detect accidents, and forecast congestion. While traffic control operators are present in the traffic management center in case of emergencies, the AI primarily makes decisions on traffic regulation autonomously. As a result, traffic flow is improved, reducing travel time and mitigating congestion-related issues [18].

The second class of decision-making autonomy is the "AI navigator", which offers a ready-made solution, but its approval is carried out by a citizen (recipient of government services), an official, a collective decision, or another institutionalized method. Thus, a subject of accountability emerges, who either accepts or rejects the AI-proposed solution. An example of such a solution can be Gotham by Palantir [19], an AI-based operating system that offers various response scenarios to military tactical and strategic questions, leaving the final decision on adopting a particular scenario to command and official personnel. Speaking of the demand for such solutions, in 2023, the US Defense Department entered into a $250 million deal with Palantir, involving a partnership in the field of defense and military AI services [20].

The next class, "AI advisor", assumes that the AI offers a set of configurations of possible solutions and their variables, but the selection of the most optimal solution, adjustment of parameters of proposed solutions, and its approval are carried out by a citizen (recipient of government services), an official, a collective decision, or another institution. This category includes chatbots. For example, the Singapore government has implemented virtual assistants powered by AI to provide citizen services and answer queries. For instance, "Ask Jamie" is an AI chatbot available on government websites that assists citizens in finding information and completing transactions with various government agencies [21].

The fourth class is the «AI observer». This type autonomously analyzes the environment and data, signaling the occurrence of various triggers. Control and response to the signal remain with an official, a collective decision, or another institution. For example, The Barcelona City Council employs AI for predictive maintenance of public infrastructure such as streetlights and sewage systems. By analyzing data from sensors embedded in infrastructure, AI algorithms can predict when maintenance is required, allowing for proactive repairs and cost savings [22].

The fifth class of AI is termed "working hands". This class of AI performs complex tasks such as analyzing large datasets, which would require significant human resources but do not entail significant responsibility for making final decisions or producing a finished product. The results of AI activities undergo review by an official, a collective decision, or another institution. For example, The UK Visas and Immigration (UKVI) department uses AI to analyze supporting documents submitted with visa applications. The system, known as the "streamlined assurance process", automatically checks documents for authenticity and validity, streamlining the visa application process and reducing the workload on human assessors [23]. Even at this level of autonomy within the AI class, the public raises concerns about AI decisions. For example, the AI algorithm utilized by UKVI is accused of bias. In response to these allegations, the UK Home Office "has insisted that the algorithm is used solely to allocate applications and does not ultimately make decisions on them. The final decision remains with human caseworkers and not machines" [24].

And finally, the very last, lowest level class of AI in terms of its involvement in decision-making is the «routine assistant». It performs routine tasks that do not involve decision-making. For example, the government of Albania will use ChatGPT to translate thousands of pages of European Union legal acts and regulations into Albanian, and then integrate them into existing national legal acts [25]. In this case, AI performs routine work far from the level of decision-making, and the process itself involves reviewing and controlling the results of AI activity at all stages of the procedure, with the final integration of the results being left to institutional mechanisms.

The Level of Publicity of Ai-Driven Government Services. Is one of the components of the integration design of Ai-driven government services. Firstly, there are exclusively closed services (for official use only) (for example: defense, security, intelligence). Secondly, hybrid Ai-driven government services can be identified, assuming that citizens receive the final decision or government service, in the process of which AI and a human are jointly involved (for example: obtaining documents, where the document is prepared by AI, but signed by a real official). Thirdly, there are absolutely public Ai-driven government services, where citizens receive government services by directly interacting with AI (for example: AI-based chatbots facilitating navigation on government service websites).

The Level of Criticality Of AI Errors and Risks. Is one of the most important criteria in designing Ai-driven government services. For example, if an AI-advisor level chatbot suggests an incorrect solution to a citizen regarding navigation on government service websites, the consequences would be much less critical compared to a decision made in the realm of defense or law enforcement agencies. Thus, all areas of implementing Ai-driven government services can be ranked according to the level of error criticality.

Undoubtedly, resolving this task requires multiple rounds of consultations with experts in each of the areas of AI implementation in government services. However, at the pre-project level, one can utilize the classification proposed by the European Commission in the «AI Act» [16]. Technologies AI used in critical infrastructure or decision-making fall into the "high-risk" category, where citizens' lives, health, rights, freedoms, and opportunities may be endangered. The "limited risk" category includes issues related to the lack of transparency in AI activities. For instance, when using artificial intelligence systems such as chatbots, people should be aware that they are interacting with a machine to independently verify the final decision. Finally, "minimal risk or absence thereof" refers to AI with minimal risk, such as video games with integrated AI or spam filters.

Sovereign AI and Public-Private Partnerships. Are important components in the design of Ai-driven government services [26]. For instance, the Los Angeles Police Department (LAPD) utilizes PredPOL, AI-based predictive policing software. It analyzes data such as reports of past crimes, locations, and times to predict where crimes are likely to occur. This helps law enforcement agencies allocate resources more effectively to prevent crime and enhance public safety. It's important to note that PredPOL is developed by the commercial public company SoundThinking, Inc., which commercially provides access to its high-tech solutions in public safety technologies to both private and public entities [27]. This case, along with examples like Palantir's partnership with the US Defense Department in military AI, exemplifies effective public-private partnerships in the implementation of Ai-driven government services.

In turn, there exists another approach that involves the emergence of sovereign AI. Sovereign artificial intelligence refers to AI that is owned and controlled by a single state, and it has significant implications for national security, governance, and international relations. The concept of sovereign artificial intelligence has gained attention in the context of national strategies for the development and use of AI technologies [28–30]. As countries seek to harness the potential of AI for economic, military, and societal advancement, the development of sovereign AI capabilities has become a focal point of strategic planning and policy formulation [31, 32]. The intersection of artificial intelligence and national sovereignty has prompted discussions on ethical principles, governance, and the regulation of AI in the context of national defense and security [32, 33]. The deployment of AI technologies in military applications and the modernization of firepower weapon equipment have underscored the significance of sovereign AI in shaping the future landscape of warfare and security [34].

The component of AI sovereignization and public-private partnership in this area is difficult to differentiate, as it entails a dilemma.

On one hand, effective partnerships with private companies grant the state access to a plethora of competitive technological solutions. Today, major technology companies are driving forces in the industry, making a strategy of cooperation between governments and corporate technology giants appear most productive in the short term, providing access to cutting-edge hardware and software complexes for deploying Ai-driven government services. For example, according to media reports, Microsoft, in collaboration with OpenAI, plans to launch a data center project by 2028, which could cost as much as 100 billion dollars and include an artificial intelligence supercomputer called "Stargate"

[35]. If such investments were made by states using taxpayers' funds, these expenses might appear unreasonable to the wider public.

Indeed, we can observe many governments successfully collaborating with technology companies to establish Ai-driven government services. For example, the Japanese government partnered with NEC Corporation to develop AI-powered disaster response systems of the «AI-advisor» class [36]. These systems utilize satellite imagery, social media data analysis, and machine learning algorithms to assess damage, coordinate rescue efforts, and provide real-time situational awareness during natural disasters [37].

The market offers a wide range of solutions from technology companies for building Ai-driven government services. For instance, IBM alone provides ready-made products based on AI to establish a comprehensive ecosystem of Ai-driven government services. These include IBM MaS360 for protecting devices, applications, and government sector data [38], IBM Maximo for optimizing operations in managing government assets [39], an AI-powered chatbot assistant IBM Watsonx for citizen interaction 24/7 [40], IBM Flashsystem for exploring options for infrastructure modernization and managing large government datasets [41], and finally, IBM watsonx.governance as an integrated platform for managing and monitoring the activities of all Ai-driven government services, including managing AI models from third-party providers [42].

Almost all technological giants also offer their sets of applications, infrastructure solutions, and technologies for building government AI services, which speaks to the competitiveness and potential of this sector of development.

On the other hand, the arguments presented above regarding the sovereignty of AI in critical areas do raise significant questions about strategic security and state development. Moreover, risks such as the bankruptcy of AI solution provider companies, data leaks, infrastructure dependence, and the risk of commercial espionage also lean towards states designing sovereign AI development. For instance, the founder of the technology company Oracle, Larry Ellison, stated in a recent interview: "Every government, pretty much every government, is going to want a sovereign AI cloud" [43].

The Technical and Technological Domains of Ai-Driven Government Services. Constitute another component of their designs based on the technical characteristics of the solutions. Bernd W. Wirtz, Jan C. Weyerer, and Carolin Geyer highlight ten technical areas in which AI serves the government: AI-Based Knowledge Management, AI Process Automation Systems, Virtual Agents, Predictive Analytics & Data Visualization, Identity Analytics, Cognitive Robotics & Autonomous Systems, Recommendation Systems, Intelligent Digital Assistants (IDA), Speech Analytics, and Cognitive Security Analytics & Threat Intelligence [44]. Today, six years after the original publication, it is necessary to supplement the list with multimodal AI, which simultaneously interacts with several of the aforementioned areas, offering more complex and comprehensive solutions (a real-world example being the previously mentioned IBM watsonx.governance).

Sectoral Areas of Government Services. Finally, one of the most important components of implementation designs is the sector of government services that is planned to be modified using AI. The following areas can be highlighted.

AI for Public Health can analyze health data to track and control disease outbreaks, monitor the effectiveness of public health interventions, and personalize health recommendations for individuals [45–47]. AI for Public Safety and Law Enforcement can analyze crime data to predict and prevent crime, optimize resource allocation for emergency services, enhance surveillance systems, and identify suspects through facial recognition [48, 49]. AI for Public Education: AI-powered adaptive learning platforms can provide personalized learning experiences for students. AI can also automate administrative tasks, assist in grading, and provide educational content recommendations [50, 51]. AI for Public Transportation can optimize traffic flow, improve public transportation systems, enable autonomous vehicles, and enhance logistics and supply chain management [44, 52, 53]. AI for Urban Planning can analyze data to optimize city infrastructure, improve waste management, monitor environmental factors, and enhance disaster response planning [54–57]. AI for Social Services can streamline the delivery of social welfare programs, identify individuals in need of assistance, personalize support services, and detect cases of fraud or abuse [58, 59]. AI for Government Operations can automate routine administrative tasks, improve data management and analysis, enhance cybersecurity measures, and provide virtual assistance for citizen inquiries and support [60, 61]. AI for Environmental Protection can analyze environmental data to monitor pollution levels, predict natural disasters, manage wildlife conservation efforts, and optimize energy consumption [62–64]. AI for Emergency Response: AI-powered systems can analyze emergency calls to prioritize response times, coordinate resources during disasters, and provide real-time updates to emergency responders [65–67]. AI for Legal Services can assist in legal research, document analysis, contract review, and case prediction, improving the efficiency and accuracy of legal processes [68, 69]. AI for E-Government Services can improve the accessibility and efficiency of government services through automated forms, virtual assistants, and personalized recommendations [2, 70]. AI for Public Finance Management can assist in fraud detection, risk assessment, and financial forecasting for government budgets [71, 72]. AI for Strategic Planning and Decision Making can assist military commanders and policymakers in strategic planning, scenario analysis, and decision-making processes by analyzing vast amounts of data and providing insights and recommendations [73–76]. AI for Autonomous Systems can enable the development of autonomous military and civil systems, such as unmanned aerial vehicles (UAVs), unmanned ground vehicles (UGVs), and autonomous ships, for tasks like surveillance, reconnaissance, and logistics support [77]. AI for Intelligence Analysis can analyze large volumes of intelligence data, including imagery, signals, and human intelligence, to support intelligence analysis, threat assessment, and situational awareness [78, 79]. AI for Cybersecurity can enhance cybersecurity measures by detecting and mitigating cyber threats in real-time, identifying vulnerabilities, and optimizing incident response [80, 81]. AI for Logistics and Supply Chain Management can optimize military and civilian logistics and supply chain management by predicting demand, optimizing inventory levels, and identifying efficient transportation routes [71, 82, 83]. AI for Counterterrorism and Counterinsurgency can support counterterrorism and counterinsurgency efforts by analyzing patterns of activity, detecting anomalies, and identifying potential threats in urban environments [84, 85]. AI for Border Security can enhance border security through the use of surveillance systems, biometric identification technologies, and predictive analytics to detect and prevent illegal border crossings and smuggling activities [86, 87]. AI for Humanitarian Assistance and Disaster Response can assist in humanitarian assistance and disaster response efforts by analyzing satellite imagery, social media data, and other sources to assess damage, prioritize response efforts, and coordinate resources effectively [88, 89].

Indeed, these are just some of the widely discussed areas of designs for utilizing Ai-driven government services, which will surely be significantly expanded in the future. Even this number of areas already greatly increases the variability of design possibilities.

4 Discussion and Conclusions

The structural-functional deconstruction of implementation practices, cases, and discourses in the main part of the work allows for the identification of the main components of designs, the aggregate of variations of which constitutes the diversity of approaches to the implementation of Ai-driven government services.

By examining current cases and practices of implementing Ai-driven government services, it can be concluded that the development of a single unified and most universal design for the implementation of Ai-driven government services appears utopian for several reasons. Firstly, the entire field under consideration is dynamically evolving, and we are likely at the beginning of the AI development journey, making standardization challenging. Secondly, the entire area of implementing Ai-driven government services serves as a kind of sandbox, where governments and the private sector experiment with various technical capabilities, institutional frameworks, and regulatory approaches. Thirdly, there is no unified consensus regarding the regulatory framework, ethical aspects, and other components. Fourthly, the diversity of variations in design components is indeed extensive, which, on one hand, prevents standardization of approaches in a single design but allows for a more precise tuning of the components of this design to align with the service's goals and objectives, technological and infrastructural capabilities, as well as the regulatory environment.

However, the identified components of the designs, as highlighted in the research results, will enable the development of a more structured approach to designing such services, allowing for their more precise adaptation to the goals and objectives of the service, technological and infrastructural capabilities, as well as the regulatory environment within which the service is designed.

For instance, the component of strategic vision varies significantly in terms of goal-setting and understanding Ai-driven government services in different centers of power (such as the United States, the Russian Federation, the European Union, and China). It is evident that work on fine-tuning this component will continue. Similarly, the situation is true for regulatory frameworks, where efforts to develop and adjust them are ongoing among all interested parties.

The component of AI responsibility in decision-making chains is also variable. Six main classes of AI have been identified, ranging from the most autonomous to those lacking autonomy in decision-making: "AI captain", "AI navigator", "AI advisor", "AI observer", "AI working hands", and "AI routine assistant". This component is interrelated with components such as risk level, institutionalization and regulation, technical and infrastructural capabilities, as well as the overall goal-setting of the service implementation. It is worth noting separately that the application of AI class "AI captain" for providing government services seems the most utopian and risky given the current level of development of the regulatory framework, gaps in ethical aspects, and the rapid pace of AI technology development.

However, as we can see in the cases mentioned earlier, they are sometimes used in real-world practices of Ai-driven government services, although humans are still present to intervene in case of critical errors. Nevertheless, it will be difficult to determine who is responsible for incorrect decisions made using AI, even if we are talking about AI class "working hands". Thus, until we reach a consensus on the regulatory framework for AI in general and Ai-driven government services in particular, AI at all stages of operation should be supervised by humans to avoid critical risks and errors. However, here arises a paradox, as human control and supervision of AI may require more resources (primarily human and time resources) than the initial execution of the AI-assigned task.

The component of publicness in Ai-driven government services also increases the variability of design approaches, as it encompasses both fully public AI services for citizens, hybrid services, and "internal" (or "for official use") AI services. The risk component and the level of AI error criticality also allow for better structuring of the system for developing designs for the implementation of government AI services. Risk is ranked from "high" to "minimal risk or absence thereof", making the application of certain classes of AI in designs with high and limited risk levels unacceptable.

The component of the relationship between AI sovereignty and public-private partnerships also contains a dilemma regarding the relationship between the technical, technological, and infrastructural capabilities of deploying government AI services and governments' dependence on third parties and associated risks.

The identified components of technical and technological capabilities in the field of AI are likely to be supplemented with the development of AI technologies, which will also introduce variability into the designs for the implementation of Ai-driven government services. Similarly, the sectoral areas for potential implementation of Ai-driven government services will multiply with the development of technologies, the development of regulatory frameworks, and a common understanding of the field.

All of this together opens up extensive possibilities in designing the implementation of Ai-driven government services. Variations of the identified components in the study will allow for a more structured description of existing designs in the future, as well as a more systematic and structured design of new ones. It should be noted that each of the components is likely to become a separate area for research in the foreseeable future, multiplying the variability and possibilities of designing the implementation of Ai-driven government services. Additionally, there are still many questions and white areas for researchers, officials, governments, practitioners, and most importantly, consumers of Ai-driven government services (i.e., citizens). Achieving consensus on these matters requires cooperative efforts and further research.

Acknowledgments. The author acknowledges Saint-Petersburg State University for a research project 116471555.

References

1. Berryhill, J., Heang, K., Clogher, R., McBride, K.: Hello, world: artificial intelligence and its use in the public sector. OECD Working Papers on Public Governance (2019)
2. Yigitcanlar, T., Li, R., Inkinen, T., Paz, A.: Pubic perceptions on application areas and adoption challenges of AI in urban services. Emerg. Sci. J. **6**(6), 1199–1236 (2022)
3. Robles, P., Mallinson, D.: Catching up with AI: pushing toward a cohesive governance framework. Polit. Policy **51**(3), 355–372 (2023)
4. Gualdi, F., Cordella, A.: Artificial intelligence and decision-making: the question of accountability. In: Proceedings of the 54th Hawaii International Conference on System Sciences, pp. 2297–2306 (2021)
5. Katekar, V.: Public value-creation through application of artificial intelligence (AI) in covid-19 management: policy lessons from India. Indian J. Public Adm. **70**(1), 63–81 (2023)
6. McBride, K., Noordt, C., Misuraca, G., Hammerschmid, G.: Towards a systematic understanding on the challenges of procuring artificial intelligence in the public sector (2021)
7. Bullock, J.: Artificial intelligence, discretion, and bureaucracy. Am. Rev. Public Adm. **49**(7), 751–761 (2019)
8. Sigfrids, A., Nieminen, M., Leikas, J., Pikkuaho, P.: How should public administrations foster the ethical development and use of artificial intelligence? A review of proposals for developing governance of AI. Front. Hum. Dyn. **4** (2022)
9. Zuiderwijk, A., Chen, Y.C., Salem, F.: Implications of the use of artificial intelligence in public governance: a systematic literature review and a research agenda. Gov. Inf. Q. **38**(3), 101577 (2021)
10. Snyder, H.: Literature review as a research methodology: An overview and guidelines. J. Bus. Res. **104**, 333–339 (2019)
11. Torraco, R.J.: Writing integrative literature reviews: Guidelines and examples. Hum. Resour. Dev. Rev. **4**(3), 356–367 (2005)
12. Notice on the development plan of the new generation of artificial intelligence.https://www.gov.cn/zhengce/content/2017-07/20/content_5211996.htm. Accessed 25 Mar 2024
13. National stratagy for the development of artificial intelligence for the period until 2030. http://www.kremlin.ru/acts/bank/44731. Accessed 25 Mar 2024
14. Maintaining American Leadership in Artificial Intelligence. https://www.federalregister.gov/documents/2019/02/14/2019-02544/maintaining-american-leadership-in-artificial-intelligence. Accessed 25 Mar 2024
15. European approach to artificial intelligence. https://digital-strategy.ec.europa.eu/en/policies/european-approach-artificial-intelligence. Accessed 26 Mar 2024
16. AI Act. https://digital-strategy.ec.europa.eu/en/policies/regulatory-framework-ai. Accessed 26–27 Mar 2024
17. AI Index Report 2024. https://aiindex.stanford.edu/report/. Accessed 27 Mar 2024
18. Alibaba's 'City Brain' is slashing congestion in its hometown. https://edition.cnn.com/2019/01/15/tech/alibaba-city-brain-hangzhou/index.html. Accessed 22 Mar 2024
19. Gotham. The Operating System for Global Decision Making. https://www.palantir.com/platforms/gotham/. Accessed 22 Mar 2024
20. Palantir Wins $250 Million AI Deal With US Defense Department. https://www.bnnbloomberg.ca/palantir-wins-250-million-ai-deal-with-us-defense-department-1.1977297. Accessed 22 Mar 2024
21. 'Ask Jamie' Virtual Assistant. https://www.tech.gov.sg/products-and-services/ask-jamie/#:~:text=The%20Government%20Technology%20Agency%20of,services%20and%20improve%20service%20delivery. Accessed 22 Mar 2024

22. Ortega-Fernández, A., Martín-Rojas, R., García-Morales, V.J.: Artificial intelligence in the urban environment: smart cities as models for developing innovation and sustainability. Sustainability **12**, 7860 (2020)
23. Visa Processing Algorithms. https://hansard.parliament.uk/commons/2019-06-19/debates/7B667153-E403-430C-8784-489D90717085/VisaProcessingAlgorithms. Accessed 22 Mar 2024
24. AI system for granting UK visas is biased, rights groups claim. https://www.theguardian.com/uk-news/2019/oct/29/ai-system-for-granting-uk-visas-is-biased-rights-groups-claim#:~:text=The%20Home%20Office%20has%20insisted,and%20not%20machines%2C%20it%20said. Accessed 22 Mar 2024
25. Albania to speed up EU accession using ChatGPT. https://www.euractiv.com/section/politics/news/albania-to-speed-up-eu-accession-using-chatgpt/. Accessed 22 Mar 2024
26. Maximize limited patrol and analyst resources for highest impact. https://www.soundthinking.com/law-enforcement/resource-deployment-resourcerouter/. Accessed 21 Mar 2024
27. About sound thinking. https://www.soundthinking.com/company/. Accessed 21 Mar 2024
28. Dillon, S., Dillon, M.: Artificial intelligence and the sovereign-governance game. In: Cave S., Dihal K., Dillon D. (eds) AI Narratives: A History of Imaginative Thinking about Intelligent Machines, pp. 333–356 (2020)
29. Tapalova, O., Zhiyenbayeva, N.: Artificial intelligence in education: AIED for personalised learning pathways. Electron. J. E-Learn. **20**(5), 639–653 (2022)
30. Filgueiras, F.: Designing artificial intelligence policy: comparing design spaces in Latin America. Latin Am. Policy **14**(1), 5–21 (2023)
31. Al-Suqri, M., Niaz, H.: A comparative analysis of information and artificial intelligence toward national security. IEEE Access **10**, 64420–64434 (2022)
32. Taddeo, M., McNeish, D., Blanchard, A., Edgar, E.: Ethical principles for artificial intelligence in national defence. Philos. Technol. **34**(4), 1707–1729 (2021)
33. Kurki, V.: The legal personhood of artificial intelligences. Theor. Leg. Personhood 175–190 (2019)
34. Hou, Y., Wang, Z., Yang, Z., Zhai, E.: Artificial intelligence technology pushes forward the modernization of firepower weapon equipment. In: Workshop on Electronics Communication Engineering. pp. 107–113 (2023)
35. Microsoft, OpenAI plan $100 billion data-center project, media report says. https://www.reuters.com/technology/microsoft-openai-planning-100-billion-data-center-project-information-reports-2024-03-29/. Accessed 21 Mar 2024
36. NEC develops technology for disaster damage assessment using a Large Language Model (LLM) and image analysis. https://www.nec.com/en/press/202308/global_20230825_02.html. Accessed 21 Mar 2024
37. Using large language models and image analysis for disaster damage assessment. https://techwireasia.com/08/2023/how-to-use-large-language-models-and-image-analysis-for-disaster-damage-assessment/. Accessed 21 Mar 2024
38. Manage and protect government employees' devices, apps and data. https://www.ibm.com/products/maas360/government. Accessed 21 Mar 2024
39. Government asset management with IBM Maximo Application Suite. https://www.ibm.com/products/maximo/public-sector. Accessed 21 Mar 2024
40. AI-powered government chatbots for 24/7 citizen support. https://www.ibm.com/products/watsonx-assistant/government. Accessed 21 Mar 2024
41. Government storage solutions with IBM Storage FlashSystem. https://www.ibm.com/flashsystem/government
42. watsonx.governance. https://www.ibm.com/products/watsonx-governance. Accessed 21 Mar 2024, 23 Mar 2024

43. Oracle's Larry Ellison thinks every government will want to build a 'sovereign' AI cloud in the future. https://www.cnbc.com/2024/04/07/oracle-chatgpt-and-the-sovereign-cloud-nations-will-seek-in-future.html. Accessed 21 Mar 2024
44. Wirtz, B., Weyerer, J., Geyer, C.: Artificial intelligence and the public sector—applications and challenges. Int. J. Public Adm. **42**(7), 596–615 (2018)
45. Tran, B., et al.: Global evolution of research in artificial intelligence in health and medicine: a bibliometric study. J. Clin. Med. **8**(3), 360 (2019)
46. Mucci, A.: Incorporation of artificial intelligence in healthcare professions and patient education for fostering effective patient care. New Dir. Adult Continuing Educ. **2024**(181), 51–62 (2024)
47. Fisher, S., Rosella, L.: Artificial intelligence for public health: priorities for successful use by public health organizations. Res. Square (2022)
48. Cath, C: Governing artificial intelligence: ethical, legal and technical opportunities and challenges. Philos. Trans. Roy. Soc. Math. Phys. Eng. Sci. **376**(2133), 20180080 (2018)
49. Dennehy, B, et al.: Artificial intelligence (AI) and information systems: perspectives to responsible AI. Inf. Syst. Front. **25**(1), 1–7 (2022)
50. Hamal, O., et al.: Artificial intelligent in education. Sustainability **14**(5), 2862 (2022)
51. Zouhaier, S. et al.: The impact of ai implementation in higher education on educational process future: a systematic review. Res. Sqare (2021)
52. Shahraz, M.: Intelligent transportation systems: an overview of current trends and limitations. Int. J. Sci. Res. Eng. Manage. **06**(12), 128–146 (2022)
53. Abduljabbar, R., Dia, H., Liyanage, S., Bagloee, S.: Applications of artificial intelligence in transport: an overview. Sustainability **11**(1), 189 (2019)
54. Yiğitcanlar, T., Desouza, K., Butler, L., Roozkhosh, F.: Contributions and risks of artificial intelligence (AI) in building smarter cities: insights from a systematic review of the literature. Energies **13**(6), 1473 (2020)
55. Yiğitcanlar, T., Kankanamge, N., Regona, M., Maldonado, A., Rowan, B., Ryu, A., et al.: Artificial intelligence technologies and related urban planning and development concepts: how are they perceived and utilized in australia? J. Open Innov. Technol. Mark. Complexity **6**(4), 187 (2020)
56. Cugurullo, F.: The rise of AI urbanism in post-smart cities: a critical commentary on urban artificial intelligence. Urban Stud. **61**(6), 1168–1182 (2023)
57. Kamrowska-Załuska, D.: Impact of AI-based tools and urban big data analytics on the design and planning of cities. Land **10**(11), 1209 (2021)
58. Tomašev, N., Cornebise, J., et al.: Ai for social good: unlocking the opportunity for positive impact. Nat. Commun. **11**(1), 2468 (2020)
59. Schmager, S.: Exploring citizens' stances on AI in public services: a social contract perspective. Data Policy **6**, 19 (2024)
60. Arslan, A., et al.: An empirical model for exploring AI in government: putting socio-technological systems perspectives into use. Int. J. Comput. Technol. **21**, 14–25 (2021)
61. Mikhaylov, S., et al.: Artificial intelligence for the public sector: opportunities and challenges of cross-sector collaboration. Philos. Trans. Roy. Soc. Math. Phys. Eng. Sci. **376**(2128), 20170357 (2018)
62. Vinuesa, R., Azizpour, H., Leite, I., Balaam, M., Dignum, V., Domisch, S., et al.: The role of artificial intelligence in achieving the sustainable development goals. Nat. Commun. **11**(1), 1–10 (2020)
63. Perucica, N., Andjelkovic, K.: Is the future of AI sustainable? A case study of the European union. Transf. Govern. People Process Policy **16**(3), 347–358 (2021)
64. Vagin, S., Klimenko, V., Telegina, Z., Aleksashina, T.: Improving environmental decision-making in environmental business-management using big data and AI. Front. Environ. Sci. **10**, 112–127 (2022)

65. Velev, D., Zlateva, P.: Challenges of artificial intelligence application for disaster risk management. Int. Arch. Photogram. Remote. Sens. Spat. Inf. Sci. **48**, 387–394 (2023)
66. Abid, S., et al.: Toward an integrated disaster management approach: how artificial intelligence can boost disaster management. Sustainability **13**(22), 12560 (2021)
67. Mesicek, L., Bae, K., Ko, H.: Ai advisor platform for disaster response based on big data. Concurr. Comput. Pract. Exp. **35**(16), 34–47 (2021)
68. Janeček, V., Williams, R., Keep, E.: Education for the provision of technologically enhanced legal services. SSRN Electron. J. (2020). https://doi.org/10.2139/ssrn.3736101
69. Floridi, L.: Artificial intelligence as a public service: learning from Amsterdam and Helsinki. Philos. Technol. **33**(4), 541–546 (2020)
70. Koc, A.: The national technology initiative for digitalization in the public sector. Proj. Manag. J. **53**(5), 428–441 (2022)
71. Dwivedi, Y., Hughes, L., Ismagilova, E., Aarts, G., Coombs, C., Crick, T., et al.: Artificial intelligence (AI): multidisciplinary perspectives on emerging challenges, opportunities, and agenda for research, practice and policy. Int. J. Inf. Manage. **57**, 101994 (2019)
72. Kumari, B., Kaur, J., Swami, S.: Adoption of artificial intelligence in financial services: a policy framework. J.Sci. Technol. Policy Manage. **15**(2), 396–417 (2022)
73. Johnson, J.: Delegating strategic decision-making to machines: dr. Strangelove Redux? J. Strategic Stud. **45**(3), 439–477 (2020)
74. Stone, M., Aravopoulou, E., Ekinci, Y., Evans, G., Hobbs, M., Labib, A., et al.: Artificial intelligence (AI) in strategic marketing decision-making: a research agenda. Bottom Line Manag. Libr. Financ. **33**(2), 183–200 (2022)
75. Payne, K.: Artificial intelligence: a revolution in strategic affairs? Survival **60**(5), 7–32 (2018)
76. Huang, M., Rust, R.: Artificial intelligence in service. J. Serv. Res. **21**(2), 155–172 (2018)
77. Jerbi, D.: Exploring the latest frontiers of artificial intelligence: a review of trends and developments. TechRxiv (2023). https://doi.org/10.36227/techrxiv.22717327
78. Blanchard, A., Taddeo, M.: The ethics of artificial intelligence for intelligence analysis: a review of the key challenges with recommendations. Digit. Soc. **2**(1), 12 (2023)
79. Vogel, K., Reid, G., Kampe, C., Jones, P.: The impact of AI on intelligence analysis: tackling issues of collaboration, algorithmic transparency, accountability, and management. Intell. Natl. Secur. **36**(6), 827–848 (2021)
80. Zeadally, S., Adi, E., Baig, Z., Khan, I.: Harnessing artificial intelligence capabilities to improve cybersecurity. IEEE Access **8**, 23817–23837 (2020)
81. Sarker, I., Furhad, H., Nowrozy, R.: AI-driven cybersecurity: an overview, security intelligence modeling and research directions. Sn Computer Science **2**(3), 173 (2021)
82. Modgil, S., Singh, R., Hannibal, C.: Artificial intelligence for supply chain resilience: learning from covid-19. Int. J. Logist. Managem. **33**(4), 1246–1268 (2021)
83. Richey, R.: Artificial intelligence in logistics and supply chain management: a primer and roadmap for research. J. Bus. Logist. **44**(4), 532–549 (2023)
84. Uddin, I., Zada, N., Aziz, F., Saeed, Y., Zeb, A., Shah, S., et al.: Prediction of future terrorist activities using deep neural networks. Complexity **1**, 1–16 (2020)
85. Schulte P.: Future war: AI, drones, terrorism and counterterror. Handbook of Terrorism and Counter Terrorism, pp. 416–433. Edward Elgar Publishing (2019)
86. Kerimovs, A.: Artificial intelligence (AI) model development framework for the protection of state borders, with a focus on analyzing behavioral patterns. Global J. Comp. Sci. Technol. **1**, 1–8 (2024)
87. Nazmul, A.M.: Artificial intelligence (AI) and future immigration and border control. Int. J. Multidisc. Res. **5**(5), 1–7 (2023)

88. Bari, L.: Potential use of artificial intelligence (AI) in disaster risk and emergency health management: a critical appraisal on environmental health. Environ. Health Insights **17**, 135–148 (2023)
89. Thekdi, S., Tatar, U., Santos, J., Chatterjee, S.: Disaster risk and artificial intelligence: a framework to characterize conceptual synergies and future opportunities. Risk Anal. **43**(8), 1641–1656 (2023)

Modelling the Media Content Propagation in Complex Social Networks Based on Quantitative Characteristics of Web Search Queries

Alexey Faizliev[1], Sergei Sidorov[1(✉)], and Sophia Tikhonova[2]

[1] Faculty of Mathematics and Mechanics, Saratov State University, Saratov 410012, Russia
{faizlievar,sidorovsp}@sgu.ru
[2] Faculty of Philosophy, Saratov State University, Saratov 410012, Russia

Abstract. A novel susceptible–infected model on graphs was examined for modeling information diffusion in social networks. We assumed that the dynamics of web search queries on a specific topic can be an adequate reflection and proxy approximation for the quantitative representation of the information propagation process in complex social networks. Therefore, we reject the hypothesis of homogeneous mixing and consider the network structure, focusing on information propagation in scale-free networks. We apply the proposed model to analyze the phenomenon of media content propagation in social networks, which is projected onto quantitative characteristics of web search queries.

Keywords: Social networks · Information diffusion · SI model · Complex networks · Search queries

1 Introduction

Modeling the processes of information dissemination in social networks and communities is a valuable task. However, it is often difficult, if not impossible, to quantify the amount of network users that receive an information at a given point in time, became interested in it and continued to spread it. In our study, we propose a new model of information dissemination in social networks that considers the structural characteristics of the networks, among the elements and nodes of which the process of diffusion will occur.

In our study, we treated a social network in a broad sense. This is not restricted by, online service or website, but also a social structure that implies relationships (friendships, work, etc.) between offline agents. At the same time, television, radio and other media are also components of such an information dissemination network.

Moreover, we propose to use temporal data on the number of web-queries on a given topic as an approximate characteristic of the number of network users who got interested a given information. Note that quantitative data on web-queries is easily available and can be obtained from a variety of web-search services. We also believe that an user of a social

A. Chugunov et al. (Eds.): DTGS 2024, CCIS 2445, pp. 93–104, 2025.
https://doi.org/10.1007/978-3-031-90720-3_7

network who had received a message on a certain topic or media object (film, book, pop artist, media phenomenon, etc.), if interested, may conduct an additional search through a web search engine service with a certain probability. Therefore, we assume that the number of web-search queries should be proportional to the number of social network users who have became interested information on a certain topic. Therefore, to assess the quality of the proposed model, we can use time series of the number of queries on a given topic.

Our assumption about the relationship between the relative search volume obtained using Google Trends and the relative volume of social media posts is supported by a number of papers [1, 2]. Previous work by [3] demonstrated that television advertising or sponsorships can drive consumer searches online. In our opinion, television can be considered as a hub (the vertex with a large number of connections) in the information dissemination network.

The curve describing the information diffusion in social networks can be represented as an S-shaped line that shows the dependence between the total number of the social network users who have received a message on a specific topic over time [4]. This curve can be roughly divided into three segments, corresponding to three stages of the diffusion process:

- In the initial stage, only a small portion of social network users possess specific information, often referred to as "innovators". These innovators then spread this information by publishing it on their social media pages, making it accessible to their followers, primarily their close contacts. Subsequently, users who have been exposed to this information (topic) continue to propagate it further through the social network, using their contact list and followers. During this timeframe, the curve begins to slowly grow from the start of the segment to its end.
- In the second stage, the growth curve accelerates significantly and enters an exponential mode. This is when the largest increase in the number of users receiving the information occurs. The increase in the speed of information propagation is driven by a large number of users who have not yet received this information.
- Then the curve enters a saturation mode, leading to a slowdown in the rate of information propagation. This occurs because the majority of network users have already received this information and/or lost interest in it.

The process of information diffusion in a social network has the same features as the epidemic spread of diseases. Different diffusion models, including the Bass model, the Gompertz model, and others [5, 6] have been developed over the years. Scientists have widely applied these models and their variations to analyze various phenomena [7–10]. A crucial step is to compare multiple models to study a specific dataset and identify the advantages and disadvantages of each method. In recent years, the study of information propagation in social networks has become one of the main topics due to their ability to provide scholars with vast amounts of data [11–15].

Unfortunately, existing models focus mainly on the early stages of information propagation. In our research, our goal is to model the behavior on the later stages of an information diffusion process. Recent studies have shown that network structure has a strong influence on the characteristics of information dissemination in networks. Therefore, in this work we exploit a model that takes into account the network structure. We reject the hypothesis of homogeneous mixing and focus on information diffusion in scale-free networks.

The paper contains four sections. The classical SI (Susceptible–Infected) information diffusion model is described in Sect. 2. The SI information diffusion models on graphs are presented in Sect. 3 [30]. Section 4 includes a description of the data and empirical results obtained using the considered models. This paper is a continuation of our previous research [30]. In the current study, we demonstrate that our new SI-type graph model can be used to analyze the phenomenon of content distribution in social networks, the projection of which are Internet search queries.

2 SI Model

To describe the information diffusion, three main logistic models are commonly employed: the SI, SIS, and SIR models [16]. These models help us to understand the fundamental principles of information propagation. All of these models describe an S-shaped curve that reflects the information spreading among groups of users in social networks.

The SI model is a simple intuitive model that helps to describe the information diffusion in social networks [17–19]. According to the model, users of social networks who actively participate in the discussion of a specific topic can be classified into two main categories: the first group consists of information disseminators who publish messages related to a given topic, while the second group consists of users who have not yet received the information on the topic and have not yet participated in its dissemination. The growth of the first group in the SI logistic model can be described via the differential equation:

$$\frac{dI(t)}{dt} = \beta\langle k\rangle\frac{S(t)I(t)}{N}, \tag{1}$$

where

- N is the total number of the network users,
- $S(t)$ is the number of users who have not received any news message and do not possess information related to the given topic at time t (such users are referred to as susceptible),
- $I(t)$ is the number of users who have received a news message on the topic and continue to spread it at time t (such users are referred to as informed),
- β is the probability of information transmission, i.e. the likelihood that a user who receives a message will be interested in the topic and will transmit it or its derivatives to other users in the network per unit time,
- $\langle k\rangle$ is the average number of contacts among users in the social network.

If we denote $s = s(t) = S(t)/N$ and $i = i(t) = I(t)/N$ the fractions of susceptible and informed users at time t, respectively, then Eq. (1) can be rewritten as follows:

$$\frac{di}{dt} = \beta\langle k\rangle si = \beta\langle k\rangle i(1-i), \tag{2}$$

where the product $\beta\langle k\rangle$ represents the rate of information propagation. This first-order differential equation with the initial condition $i_0 = i(0)$ can be solved analytically.

3 Information Diffusion on Networks

3.1 SI Model on Graphs

It should be noted that the most of existing models do not consider the structure of the contact network, while it plays an important role in the spread of information and its dynamics. The main assumption of such models is that any network user can transmit certain information to any other user with equal probabilities (the hypothesis of homogeneous mixing) and that all users have approximately the same number of contacts (friends, followers). However, these assumptions do not hold in real social networks: a message posted by a user in a social network is only accessible to their friends (followers), i.e. information spreads through a complex network of contacts. Moreover, such contact networks typically exhibit scale-free properties, so the average number of connections for a user is not sufficient to describe their topology.

The inadequacy of the fundamental assumptions led to a thorough reconsideration how to model the information propagation in real social networks. This reevaluation began with the works of R. Pastor-Satorras and A. Vespignani [20], who expanded the basic epidemic models to account for the network's topological characteristics. The information propagation, as well as the optimal conditions for its spread and the emergence of super-spreaders, have been extensively explored in the field of network science concerning the spread of dangerous viruses, pathogens (as well as disinformation or rumors) [21]. The authors of [22] investigated the influence of the network community structure on percolation using the classical SIR epidemic model. It was concluded that the spread within communities is highly dependent on network density [23, 24], and the boundaries between communities are the most significant factor in epidemic spread, regardless of community size and shape. In particular, the study [25] examines the spread of epidemics using the adjacency matrix of the graph.

In paper [26], a new SIR model was presented for studying the spread of rumors. This model explicitly takes into account the location of objects, as well as the connections and interactions between them. Experiments showed that the presence of a social network accelerates the spread of rumors. However, the authors did not consider the influence of connections in the social network, which have a significant impact on the process of rumor propagation.

Wu and Chen [27] improved the SIR model by applying their integrated methodology for analyzing the spread of opinions and ideas on web forums. This enhanced model was confirmed on real data taken from a web forum of a major retail company as well as a general political discussion forum. Their experimental results also demonstrated that this SIR model effectively handles the spread of topics on web forums.

Bao et al. [28] investigated the mechanism of information propagation using heat transfer methods in conjunction with the connections between network nodes to model information diffusion in social networks. Their model depends on the network structure, as the proposed mechanisms are determined by the states and degrees of the network nodes.

In the paper [29], a model of information propagation based on the principles of heat transfer is presented. It is assumed that the diffusion mechanism in the model depends on the number of interactions for a specific node with its neighbors. Experiments on real social network datasets demonstrated the effectiveness of this model. The authors also developed algorithms for identifying the top k nodes influenced by marketing information.

In this study, a SI type model and its variations are presented, which are applied to the analysis of information propagation dynamics on random graphs of different types, as well as on real social networks. Our goal is to develop new models that take into account the specific characteristics of graph topology.

To build a model of information propagation on a network, we will refer to Eq. (2) of the classical SI model (the model does not take into account the network structure). However, it is worth noting that during the spread of information on the network, users with a greater number of connections have a higher probability of coming into contact with an already informed user, and therefore, they also have a higher probability of possessing the information. In light of this, the mathematical formalization should consider a degree of each node as an implicit variable. For this purpose, a block approximation of the degree can be applied, which distinguishes nodes based on their degree and assumes that nodes with the same degree are statistically equivalent. To denote this approximation, let us denote

$$i_k = \frac{I_k}{N_k}, \tag{3}$$

the fraction of informed nodes of degree k among all N_k nodes of degree k in the network. The overall fraction of informed nodes is equal to the sum of all informed nodes of degree k: $i = \sum_k p_k i_k$, where p_k is the probability that a randomly chosen node has degree k. Taking into account the different degrees of nodes, the SI model for each degree k taken separately can be written as follows

$$\frac{di_k}{dt} = \beta(1 - i_k)k\theta_k. \tag{4}$$

This equation has a similar structure to the classical SI model (4) that was described earlier: the level of information propagation is proportional to the parameter β and the fraction of nodes of degree k that are not yet informed, which is equal to $1 - i_k$. However, there are several significant differences:

- The average degree $\langle k \rangle$ in (2) is replaced by the actual degree k of each node in (4).
- The density function θ_k represents the fraction of informed neighbors of a susceptible node with degree k. Thus, θ_k is simply the fraction of informed nodes i_k. However, in a network environment, the fraction of informed nodes in the immediate vicinity of a node may depend on its degree k and time t. Researching the density function θ_k can help in understanding the dynamics of information propagation in a network.
- While (2) describes the behavior of the entire system with a single time-dependent equation, (4) represents a system of $k_{\max}$ interconnected equations, where each degree present in the network requires its own equation.

In the paper [22], the behavior of i_k was studied during initial time periods. In our work, we extend the formalism studying the information propagation at all temporal stages of its penetration into the network.

As discussed earlier, to compute i_k, it is necessary to first determine θ_k. In the case of the absence of degree correlations in the network, the probability that a link leads from a node of degree k to a node of degree k' does not depend on k. Therefore, the probability that a randomly chosen edge points to a node of degree k' is an excess degree:

$$\frac{k' p_{k'}}{\sum_k k p_k} = \frac{k' p_{k'}}{\langle k \rangle}, \tag{5}$$

where p_k is the fraction of nodes with degree k.

It is quite obvious that at least one connection of each informed node is linked to another informed node that has transmitted information. Based on this, in the study [22], the authors assumed that the number of available channels for information transfer in the future is equal to k'. Thus, the density function θ_k can be defined as follows:

$$\theta_k = \frac{\sum_{k'} (k' - 1) p_{k'} i_{k'}}{\langle k \rangle}. \tag{6}$$

It should be noted that such an assumption is simplified and may be applicable only in the initial stage of information propagation.

Returning to Eq. (6), it should be noted that if there are no degree correlations, then $\theta = \theta_k$ will not depend on k. Therefore, when differentiating (6), we obtain:

$$\frac{d\theta}{dt} = \sum_k \frac{(k-1) p_k}{\langle k \rangle} \frac{di_k}{dt}. \tag{7}$$

Using (4) and (7), we get:

$$\frac{d\theta}{dt} = \sum_k \frac{(k-1) p_k}{\langle k \rangle} \beta (1 - i_k) k \theta. \tag{8}$$

It is quite obvious that at the initial stage of information dissemination (when t is small), the proportion of informed nodes is significantly less than one, and the multiplier $(1 - i_k)$ can be neglected. In the study [22], it is noted that in this case, the proportion of informed nodes can be explicitly expressed. In our specific case, we cannot neglect the multiplier $(1 - i_k)$.

Thus, we obtain a system of $k_{\max}$ interconnected equations:

$$\begin{aligned} \theta &= \tfrac{\sum_k (k-1) p_k i_k}{\langle k \rangle}, \\ \tfrac{di_k}{dt} &= \beta (1 - i_k) k \theta, \; k = 1, \ldots, k_{\max}. \end{aligned} \tag{9}$$

3.2 A Novel SI Model on Graphs

Now we assume that the number of available channels for information transmission increases along with the growth of users' awareness in the network over time. As more and more nodes become informed, the number of channels for information transmission in the future also increases. As a result, the density function θ_k can be defined as follows:

$$\theta_k = \frac{\sum_{k'} k'(t, \beta) p_{k'} i_{k'}}{\langle k \rangle}. \tag{10}$$

The number of channels $k'(t)$ available for information transmission in the future can be described by a function dependent on time t and the probability of information propagation β. This function can be approximated as follows:

$$k'(t,\beta) = k'(1 - \beta^{c(\beta)t}) \tag{11}$$

where $c(\beta) = a\beta + b$ is a linear function of β. The coefficients a and b, which were determined empirically are equal to $\overline{a} = 2.8$, $\overline{b} = 0.06$.

Thus, we obtain a system consisting of k_{max} interconnected equations:

$$\begin{aligned} \theta &= \frac{\sum_k k(1-\beta^{c(\beta)t})p_k i_k}{\langle k\rangle}, \\ \frac{di_k}{dt} &= \beta(1 - i_k)k\theta, \; k = 1, \ldots, k_{\max}. \end{aligned} \tag{12}$$

The results of solving Eqs. (9) and (12), as well as Eq. (2), will be presented later using the example of media content propagation in social networks.

4 Analysis of the Phenomenon of Media Content Propagation in Social Networks

In this section, we will test the adequacy of our proposed novel SI model for predicting the number of social media users who have became interested information on a particular topic. We assume that the number of such users is proportional to the number of web-search queries on the network. Therefore, to assess the quality of the proposed model, we used time series of the number of queries on a given topic, obtained using the Google Trends search web service. Quantitative data on web queries can also be obtained using the Yandex Wordstat search web service. We will also examine the classical SI model (which does not consider the contact network structure) and the graph-based model proposed in [22] from the point of view of the spread of media content in social networks. The results of the models considered in the current study for different types of random graphs (Barabási–Albert and Erdős–Rényi) are presented in paper [30].

For the comparative analysis of the approaches proposed in the study, we will consider the following approximating differential equations (models):

1. The classical SI model, which does not take into account the network structure, can be represented by the following equation:

$$\frac{di}{dt} = \beta\langle k\rangle i(1 - i).$$

   For convenience, let's call this model "SI".
2. The SI model on a network, proposed in [22], can be described by the following equations:

$$\begin{aligned} \theta &= \frac{\sum_k (k-1)p_k i_k}{\langle k\rangle}, \\ \frac{di_k}{dt} &= \beta(1 - i_k)k\theta, \; k = 1, \ldots, k_{\max}. \end{aligned}$$

   For brevity, let's call this model "SI on network".

3. The approximating version of the SI model on graphs, taking into account the change in the number of information transmission channels over time, can be represented by the following equations:

$$\theta = \frac{\sum_k (k-1) p_k i_k}{\langle k \rangle},$$
$$\frac{di_k}{dt} = \beta(1 - i_k)k\theta, k = 1, \ldots, k_{\max}.$$

For brevity, we will call such a model as "SI approximation".

To compare models, three metrics will be used: the mean absolute error (MAE), the mean square error (MSE) and the mean absolute percentage error (MAPE):

$$MAE = \frac{1}{n}\sum_{i=1}^{n} |y_i - x_i|, MSE = \frac{1}{n}\sum_{i=1}^{n} (y_i - x_i)^2, MAPE = \frac{100\%}{n}\sum_{i=1}^{n} \left|\frac{y_i - x_i}{x_i}\right|,$$

where y_i is the forecast at time-step i, x_i is the observed value at time-step i, while n is the length of the time series.

The chosen objects of study is the dynamics of interest among social network users in six media products of popular culture. Among them is a Soviet film that is considered as a classic of Soviet cinema and holds significant cultural importance – The Irony of Fate, or Enjoy Your Bath! (1975). Our analysis also includes the American miniseries Chernobyl (HBO, 2019), which reexamines the standard image of the Empire of Evil. The Russian film World Champion (2021) aims to preserve the ambivalent image of the USSR while eliminating traditional negative mythologies. The Russian series Vampires of the Middle Belt (2021) romanticizes Soviet everyday life, using the symbolism of childhood, but maintains an anti-Soviet stance towards the political regime of the USSR. Another Russian series, The Boy's Word: Blood on the Asphalt (2023) presents a retrospective of the 80s Soviet reality, defining the "Kazan phenomenon". The video game Atomic Heart by Mundfish Studio (2023) has a Soviet atmosphere and invokes a romantic techno-aesthetic.

To conduct testing of models on web-search queries on various topics such as Atomic Heart, Chernobyl, World Champion, The Boy's Word and Vampires of the Middle Zone, a graph was created that has properties similar to real networks. Additionally, a random graph was generated using the Barabási–Albert model for web-search queries related to the film The Irony of Fate (see Table 1).

Table 1. Characteristics of graphs for testing models on web-search queries.

Graph	Number of Nodes	Number Edges	Density	Average degree	Power law exponent γ
Scale-free	1912	31299	0.017	32.74	1.7
Barabási–Albert	210	1025	0.047	9.76	3

For each of the web-search queries, we experimentally determined the probability of information propagation, β. Figures 1 show graphs depicting the trajectories of the accumulated share of web-search queries on different topics, as well as model trajectories that assume information propagation on a network with a scale-free structure. From the graphs, it can be seen that the trajectories proposed by our model are closest to the benchmark trajectories. Furthermore, it can be confidently said that the dissemination of information about the series *Vampires of the Middle Belt* does not utilize a network structure.

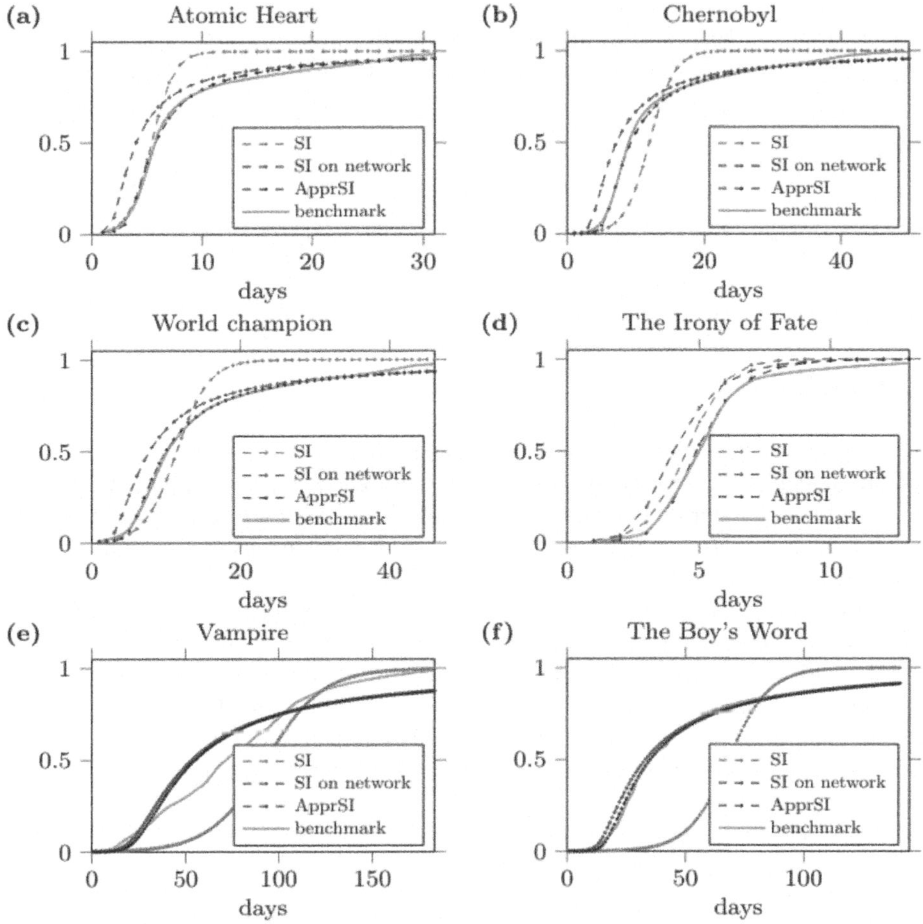

Fig. 1. Trajectories of information diffusion for different models for (a) Atomic Heart (game), $\beta = 0.03$, (b) Chernobyl (series), $\beta = 0.017$, (c) World champion (movie), $\beta = 0.014$, (d) The Irony of Fate (movie), $\beta = 0.14$, (e) Vampires of the middle zone (series), $\beta = 0.002$, (f) The Boy's Word (series), $\beta = 0.0075$.

Table 2 gives estimates of model accuracy for various web-search queries. It can be noted that our proposed novel model gives the best accuracy for all metrics, with the exception of *The Boy's Word* series for the MAPE metric. Moreover, on average, the

MSE of the novel model is by an order of magnitude less than that of the model "SI on network".

Table 2. Comparison of model accuracy.

Models	SI			SI on network			ApprSI		
Metrics	MAE	MSE	MAPE	MAE	MSE	MAPE	MAE	MSE	MAPE
Atomic Heart	0.09	0.01	29.4	0.06	0.01	13.1	0.02	0.00	4.5
Chernobyl	0.09	0.02	26.9	0.04	0.01	19	0.02	0.00	6.2
World champion	0.09	0.01	23.3	0.05	0.01	16.8	0.01	0.00	5.17
Tre Irony of Fate	0.08	0.01	38.1	0.06	0.01	19.0	0.02	0.00	7.34
Vampire	0.11	0.02	37.4	0.09	0.01	22.3	0.08	0.01	22.4
The Boy's Word	0.21	0.08	44.2	0.02	0.00	6.27	0.02	0.00	9.6

5 Conclusion

In this paper, we have proposed a new model that differs from existing models, allowing for the modeling of information diffusion at both early and late stages of propagation. Additionally, our model takes into account the network structure when modeling differential equations. We reject the hypothesis of homogeneous mixing and focus on information diffusion on networks with a scale-free structure.

We test and compare the dynamics of information propagation using our proposed model with other existing models. Based on the assumption that the dynamics of web-search queries are a reflection of the diffusion of information through complex social networks with a scale-free structure, we test various diffusion models in their ability to predict the trajectories of web-search queries on various topics. The web-search query trajectories proposed by our model are closest to the benchmark trajectories.

Acknowledgments. The work was supported by the Russian Science Foundation, project 22-18-00153.

References

1. Mukherjee, P., Jansen, B.J.: Correlation of brand mentions in social media and web searching before and after real life events: phase analysis of social media and search data for super bowl 2015 commercials. In: 2015 IEEE International Conference on Data Mining Workshop (ICDMW), pp. 21–26 (2015). https://doi.org/10.1109/ICDMW.2015.60
2. Mukherjee, P., Jansen, J.: Conversing and searching: the causal relationship between social media and web search. Internet Res. **27** (2017). https://doi.org/10.1108/IntR-07-2016-0228

3. Zigmond, D., Stipp, H.: Assessing a new advertising effect: measurement of the impact of television commercials on internet search queries. J. Adv. Res. - JAR **50** (2010). https://doi.org/10.2501/S0021849910091324
4. Rogers, E.: Diffusion of Innovations, 5th edn. Free Press, New York (2003)
5. Berestycki, H., Desjardins, B., Weitz, J., Oury, J.M.: Epidemic modeling with heterogeneity and social diffusion. J. Math. Biol. **86** (2023). https://doi.org/10.1007/s00285-022-01861-w
6. Gompertz, B.: On the nature of the function expressive of the law of human mortality, and on a new mode of determining the value of life contingencies. In a letter to Francis Baily, Esq. F. R. S. &c. by Benjamin Gompertz, Esq. F. R. S. Philos. Trans. Roy. Soc. London **2**, 252–253 (1833). https://doi.org/10.1098/rspl.1815.0271
7. Bertotti, M.L., Modanese, G.: On the evaluation of the takeoff time and of the peak time for innovation diffusion on assortative networks. Math. Comput. Model. Dyn. Syst. **25**(5), 482–498 (2019). https://doi.org/10.1080/13873954.2019.1660997
8. Bahrami, S., Atkin, B., Landin, A.: Innovation diffusion through standardization: a study of building ventilation products. J. Eng. Technol. Manage. **54**, 56–66 (2019). https://doi.org/10.1016/j.jengtecman.2019.11.001
9. Rakesh, K., Anuj Kumar, S., Kulbhushan, A.: Dynamical analysis of an innovation diffusion model with evaluation period. Bol. Soc. Paranaense Mat. **38**(5), 87–104 (2020). https://doi.org/10.1016/j.jengtecman.2019.11.001
10. Modanese, G.: The network bass model with behavioral compartments. Stats **6**(2), 482–494 (2023). https://doi.org/10.3390/stats6020030
11. Zheng, J., Xu, M., Cai, M., Wang, Z., Yang, M.: Modeling group behavior to study innovation diffusion based on cognition and network: an analysis for garbage classification system in shanghai, china. Int. J. Environ. Res. Public Health **16**(18) (2019). https://doi.org/10.3390/ijerph16183349
12. Cramer, M., Almeida, F., Wendl, M., Anderson, M., Rautianinen, R.: Innovation diffusion in an agricultural health center: moving information to practice. J. Agromed. **24** (2019). https://doi.org/10.1080/1059924X.2019.1592046
13. Yang, W., Yu, X., Zhang, B., Huang, Z.: Mapping the landscape of international technology diffusion (1994–2017): network analysis of transnational patents. J. Technol. Transf. **46**(1), 138–171 (2021). https://doi.org/10.1007/s10961-019-09762-
14. Akinyemi, O., Harris, B., Kawonga, M.: Innovation diffusion: how homogenous networks influence the uptake of community-based injectable contraceptives. BMC Public Health **19** (2019). https://doi.org/10.1186/s12889-019-7819-5
15. Boumaiza, A., Abbar, S., Mohandes, N., Sanfilippo, A.: Innovation diffusion for renewable energy technologies, pp. 1–6 (2018). https://doi.org/10.1109/CPE.2018.8372592
16. Bewley, R., Fiebig, D.G.: A flexible logistic growth model with applications in telecommunications. Int. J. Forecast. **4**(2), 177–192 (1988). https://doi.org/10.1016/0169-2070(88)90076-3
17. Griliches, Z.: Hybrid corn: an exploration in the economics of technological change. Econometrica **25**(4), 501–522 (1957). https://doi.org/10.2307/1905380
18. Gruber, H., Verboven, F.: The diffusion of mobile telecommunications services in the European union. Eur. Econ. Rev. **45**(3), 577–588 (2001). https://doi.org/10.1016/S0014-2921(00)00068-4
19. Bass, F.M.: A new product growth for model consumer durables. Manage. Sci. **15**(5), 215–227 (1969). https://doi.org/10.1287/mnsc.15.5.215
20. Lee, M.K., Cho, Y.: The diffusion of mobile telecommunications services in Korea. Appl. Econ. Lett. **14**, 477–481 (2007). https://doi.org/10.1080/13504850500461431
21. Zhang, X., et al.: Multiplex network reconstruction for the coupled spatial diffusion of infodemic and pandemic of COVID-19. Int. J. Digit. Earth **14**(4), 401–423 (2021). https://doi.org/10.1080/17538947.2021.1888326

22. Pastor-Satorras, R., Vespignani, A.: Epidemic spreading in scale-free networks. Phys. Rev. Lett. **86**, 3200–3203 (2001). https://doi.org/10.1103/PhysRevLett.86.3200
23. Eryarsoy, E., Delen, D., Davazdahemami, B., Topuz, K.: A novel diffusion-based model for estimating cases, and fatalities in epidemics: the case of covid-19. J. Bus. Res. **124**, 163–178 (2021). https://doi.org/10.1016/j.jbusres.2020.11.054
24. Dimarco, G., Perthame, B., Toscani, G., Zanella, M.: Kinetic models for epidemic dynamics with social heterogeneity. J. Math. Biol. **83**(1), 1–32 (2021). https://doi.org/10.1007/s00285-021-01630-1
25. Gómez, A., Oliveira, G.: New approaches to epidemic modeling on networks. Sci. Rep. **13** (2023). https://doi.org/10.1038/s41598-022-19827-9
26. Wang, J., Wang, Y.Q.: Sir rumor spreading model with network medium in complex social networks. Chin. J. Phys. **53**(1), 1–21 (2015). https://doi.org/10.6122/CJP.20140906
27. Woo, J., Chen, H.: Epidemic model for information diffusion in web forums: experiments in marketing exchange and political dialog. SpringerPlus (5), 66 (2016). https://doi.org/10.1186/s40064-016-1675-x
28. Bao, H., Chang, E.Y.: AdHeat: an influence-based diffusion model for propagating hints to match ads. In: Proceedings of the 19th International Conference on World Wide Web, WWW 2010, pp. 71–80. Association for Computing Machinery, New York (2010). https://doi.org/10.1145/1772690.1772699
29. Doo, M., Liu, L.: Extracting top-k most influential nodes by activity analysis. In: Proceedings of the 2014 IEEE 15th International Conference on Information Reuse and Integration (IEEE IRI 2014), pp. 227–236 (2014). https://doi.org/10.1109/IRI.2014.7051894
30. Sidorov, S., Faizliev, A., Tikhonova, S.: An extension of the susceptible-infected model and its application to the analysis of information dissemination in social networks. Modelling **4**(4), 585–599 (2023). https://doi.org/10.3390/modelling4040033

Argumentative Networks: Individuation and Solidarity in Persuasive Communication

Leonid Smorgunov(✉)

St. Petersburg State University, St. Petersburg, Russia
l.smorgunov@spbu.ru

Abstract. The article analyzes the argumentative structure of network communicative persuasion using the example of the social network "Mash on the Moika". The main idea of the article is that reasoning, as an argumentative process of seeking justifications, is not based solely on logocentrism and can involve the intuitive acceptance of arguments for values, justifications, preferences and opinions. In this case, the argumentative mechanism for substantiating judgments correlates well with the network concept of communication due to the fact that networks are not only a simple transmitter of information, but also contain a structure that ensures the choice of arguments by the very fact of the design features of the communication process - the relative position of nodes/vertices and connections. Argumentation in the network is provided by two main processes of individuation and network solidarity: the higher the intensity indicators of the processes, the more grounds for structural argumentation. A structural approach to network argumentation is represented by the analysis of network metrics, which includes indicators of individuation (eigenvector centrality, average path length, closeness centrality) and network solidarity (density, closeness centrality, assortativity, modularity). Network analysis was carried out using the Gephi and Python programming languages.

Keywords: Networks · Argumentation · Argumentative Network · Individuation · Solidarity · Network Structural Characteristics · Mash on the Moika

1 Introduction

The expansion of the composition of participants in political choice increased the role of diversity of knowledge and opinions in the justification, which led to the concept of the "smart set", which ensures the correct choice by reducing its overall error through random mass participation. Communication is not only the exchange of information to achieve consensus about the true result of a discussion, but to a large extent reasoning as an argumentative process of searching for justifications, which may be based on logocentrism, and may include the intuitive acceptance of arguments in favor of values, requests, preferences, opinions. This argumentative reasoning develops the concept of communication in the direction of searching for principles other than the reflexive rationality of the first developers of the rational model of reasoning [1]. It is important to

A. Chugunov et al. (Eds.): DTGS 2024, CCIS 2445, pp. 105–115, 2025.
https://doi.org/10.1007/978-3-031-90720-3_8

note that the argumentative mechanism for asserting judgments correlates well with the network concept of communication due to the fact that networks are not only a simple transmitter of information, but also contain a structure that ensures the choice of arguments by the very fact of the design features of the communication process - the relative position of nodes and connections. A feature of the new mechanism of network communication is its ability to provide an argumentative component of reasoning, which is due to its structural adequacy of the human ability to generate arguments based on intuitive choice. Network dynamics of communication introduces its own characteristics into this process.

In this sense it is necessary to distinguish two dominant directions of network research, which differ in the way they consider network connections and their functions: connectionist and structuralist views [2]. The connectionist (or relational) perspective suggests the networks are channels that facilitate the flow of relational resources such as information, experience, or support [3]. These resources are transferred through interactions among network members, and thus differences in (behavioral) outcomes can be explained by members' differential exposure to or access to these resources. Lidsay Levitan writes that the people around us have a profound influence on our political views and the strength of them, such that people whose social networks include diverse viewpoints have weaker and less deeply held views than those who are surrounded by like-minded people. In particular, those embedded in networks that are heterogeneous in views are more open to changing their views. The nature and mechanisms of influence of this network on openness to attitude change remain unclear. In a survey experiment, he examined two mechanisms proposed in previous literature: (1) social hesitation caused by disagreement among network members and (2) social constraints to maintain similar views. The results strongly support social constraints and are ambiguous regarding the formation of social doubts [4: 957–975].

At the same time, the structuralist approach pays attention to the role of various components of network in influencing support or refutation of arguments and views. Particular importance is attached, for example, to self-organization: "We prove," write Dario Madeo and Chiara Mocenni, "that players may partially or fully cooperate whether self-regulating mechanisms are sufficiently stronger than social pressure. The proposed model can explain unconditional cooperation (strong self-regulation) and unconditional defection (weak self-regulation). For intermediate selfregulation values, more complex behaviors are observed, such as mutual defection, recruiting (cooperate if others cooperate), exploitation of cooperators (defect if others cooperate) and altruism (cooperate if others defect)" [5: 1]. Such phenomena lead to transitions between different game structures in accordance with changes in system parameters and cooperation between players. The topology of connections between players is crucial when self-regulation and its associated costs are sufficiently low. This is particularly true for a population organized in a random network with a scale-free distribution of connections: "the regular networks are in general the least cooperative since the distinction between lowly and highly connected players vanishes. Hence, it can be concluded that cooperation is more likely in heterogeneous network structures" [6 Ibidem: 9]. It should be noted that there are other morphological characteristics of the network that have a decisive influence on the flow of information and the formation of individuation and network solidarity. The epistemological bias here is associated with the role of network channels of information dissemination, epistemic persuasion and the formation of knowledge based on the logic of reasoning and inference. As a rule, various models of persuasive communication, strategic communication, etc. are formed in this vein. In the structural tendencies of considering network political communication, which are very few in number, the design of networks as a space of political communication is studied. In this regard, persuasive communication is built rather on argumentative strategies generated by such characteristics of networks as cohesion, assortativity, modularity, centrality (in its various meanings and metrics).

2 Based Idea of Network Persuasion: Individuation and Solidarity

Network communities arises on the basis of transversal interactions and persuasion due to a flexible system of roles and functional differentiation. The transformation of the mechanisms of persuasive communication is associated not only with the mobility of the content of communication messages (factors of morality, psyche, logic and political situation), but also with the active use of complex network communication design (virulence, diffusion, centrality, openness, controllability, assortativity, modularity). The main idea of the article speaks of the commensurability of the network design of persuasive communication, focused on individuation and the formation of a stable value system of general civic solidarity.

It is significant that in the process of network participation the importance of individuation becomes increasingly revealed when networks accumulate in their space the potential energy of the collective, ready for action under the influence of an individual attack. Here the idea of Gilbert Simondon begins to appear, which connects the processes of individuation and the formation of a collective through transduction into the space of individualizing collectives. What the developing individual is destined for constitutes his existence in the collective. The collective is not a collectivist generalization of individuals through induction, but the result of the opening (transduction) of individuation in "correspondence with the collective." "The collective is not a substance or a form anterior to the individuated beings that would compel them, penetrate them, or condition them: the collective is the communication that envelops and resolves individual disparations as a presence that is the synergy of actions, the coincidence of futures and pasts as an internal resonance of the collective" [7: 242]. In this regard, the modern stage of communication becomes trans-stabilization, suggesting a state filled with the potential of new formations in the process of movement of individuation towards solidary groups.

Mutual trust also implies a more effective way to spread solidarity. An important advantage of the network structure is the reduction of the costs of mutual persuasion. In networks, there is intense interaction between its participants, allowing each of them to observe a different high-quality communication practice due to the openness of communication boundaries. In this regard, networks facilitate the direct transmission of this experience and serve an important function of demonstrating the spread of network communication. Networks usually arise around innovative communication centers – posts, commentators, the positions of which can be structurally measured by indicators of centrality, authority, hubs, etc. Such a center ensures the life cycle of a network organization, and therefore the possibility of disseminating communication innovations.

3 Description of the Research Object

To study the processes of individuation and solidarity, this study takes VKontakte the information community "Mash on the Moika" with a predominant participation of young people under 35 years of age. It was created on March 4, 2019 as a news channel about the life of St. Petersburg and the region. As of May 2024, this community had more than two hundred twenty-nine thousand subscribers. Unlike other news communities, Mash on the Moika is characterized by high traffic and extends beyond the designated region.

The data was downloaded from the corresponding community of the VKontakte social network using parsers written in the Python programming language. Network consist of posts and commentators who leave comments on them, as well as comments on other comments, contributing to the process of deliberation, also the likes. Communication channels are weighted: posts have a weight of 3, comments on posts and other comments have a weight of 2, likes on posts and commentators have the weight - 1. The research design of this paper involves (1) the conceptualization of network communication, (2) the construction of graphs to clarify the features of network communication designs, (3) quantitative analysis of the network to clarify the role of the most influential participants and their impact on individuation and solidarity arising during network communication, (4) calculation of the most important structural indicators (degree centrality, betweenness centrality, PageRank, clustering and modularity coefficients, assortativity and so on), influencing the possibility of argumentation in the network. Argumentation in the online communities manifests itself where is great thematic diversity and active commentators with high rates of betweenness centrality, who are connecting links within the network [8, 9]. Individuation can be measured by eigenvector centrality, average path length, and closeness centrality. Network solidarity is measured by the tendency to form groups, the presence of nodes with non-zero betweenness centrality scores, a network with high density scores, proximity centralization, and negative assortativity (disassortativity). Network analysis was performed using Gephi and Python programming languages.

Data downloaded from the news community "Mash on the Moika" (news of St. Petersburg) for the period 01.02.2023–01.03.2023, made it possible to form a directed graph with 14498 nodes, 57358 edges and 29 subgroups identified based on the calculation of the coefficient modularity. This network covers a variety of topics: from local urban problems of the functioning of schools and kindergartens to the national problem. However, what is qualitatively new in this network is the behavior of active commentators, who not only leave comments under posts, but also conduct extensive deliberations, supporting or denying what other participants say in the comments. In fact, the role of moderator was transferred to active commentators of the network "Mash on the Moika". Table 1 shows the network metric of "Mesh on the Moika", which will be used to characterize various network argumentative properties. It shows not only the metric average data, but also the ranks of data that have a non-zero value.

Table 1. Network Metrics of the "Mash on the Moika"

Measures	Data	Ranks (non-zero value)
Nodes/edges	14498/57358	
Likes/com-com/post-com	0,87/0,05/0,07	
Indegree	3,91	1–691
Outdegree	3,91	1–308
Degree	3,91	
Density	0,0001	
Betweenness Centrality	1434,47	0,038–883874,3
Closeness Centrality	0,606	0,109–1
PageRank	0,0017	0,000027–0,0086
Eigenvector centrality	0,0037	0,00073–1
Assortativity	-0,3	
Modularity	0,37	
Clustering coefficient	0,03	0,00016–1
Authority	0,0015	0,000001–0,188
Hub	0,0026	0,000001–0,239
Average path length	4,421	
Diameter	13	

4 Structural Characteristics of Argumentation in the Social Networks

4.1 The Network Density and Argumentation by the Speed of Information Dissemination

Self-motivated communication in the network corresponds to the logic of connective action, based on the processes of self-organization in networks [10]. In this respect, the network represents a new topology of social connections, allowing individuation to manifest itself in a collective form. The density of the network space plays a significant role in both individuation and community consensus. It is measured not only by the presence of connections between all network vertices, but also by the nature of the distance between them, the speed of signal propagation and confirmation of their acceptance. A number of researchers study the spatial distribution of social activity, paying particular attention to the distances between specific people as network users with whom they communicate. The shortness of distances between network vertices (geodesic distance) is of particular importance in communication networks, creating the effect of rapid "infection" of the network space. But the diameter of the network, as the longest shortest distance between pairs of network vertices, is a factor in the movement of messages, indicating the degree of manifestation of the "small world" phenomenon.

Indicators of the maximum or average distance between network actors indicate the ability of participants to interact and affect their trust in each other. For "Mash on the Moika", the average shortest path between vertices is 4.421 (i.e., a little over four links), while the network diameter (longest shortest path) is 13 links. For such a large network, this metric indicates the presence of a "small world" phenomenon. As Carrasco, Miller, and Wellmann note, "the results strongly suggest that, although the spatial distribution of social interaction has idiosyncratic characteristics, there are several systematic effects associated with the characteristics of egos, alters, and their personal networks that affect the spatial distribution of relationships, and which can aid understanding of where people perform social activities with others" [11: 114].

4.2 The Centrality of the Vertices and Individuation

The positions of actors in the network, the speed of information dissemination, and the intensity of communication depend on a number of indicators of the centrality of the location of network vertices - by proximity, by the importance of neighbors, by density, etc. Centrality, as Mark Newman notes, is an important measure of the position of a vertex in the network and has many dimensions, which allow us to understand the processes of interaction on the network, the ability to receive information, be prestigious, etc. [12: 159]. Of course, in political discussions, better-connected people do not benefit equally from the potential influence that comes from their more central location in the network.

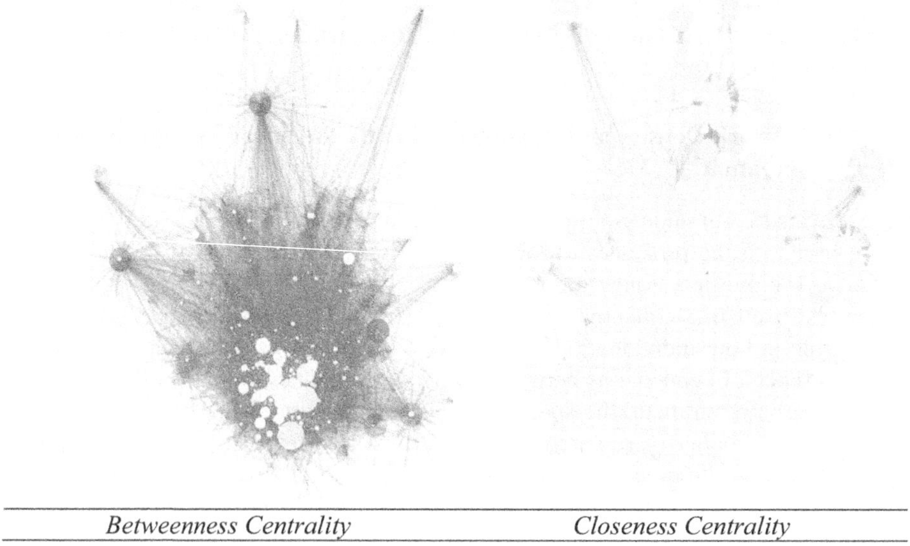

Fig. 1. Centrality in "Mash on the Moika" Network

As highlighted in some studies, network position influences the differential distribution and acceptance of information and arguments. For example, "individuals with high indegree centrality or high betweenness centrality may not approach political discussions in the same manner and thus capitalize equally on their influential network locations. Though both types of individuals may engage in political discussion more often than less well-connected persons, those high in indegree centrality may be less likely to embrace the social risk inherent in those discussions whereas those high in betweenness centrality may be more tolerant of that risk" [13: 378]. Figure 1 provides visual information about the two types of centralities for the "Mash on the Moika" network.

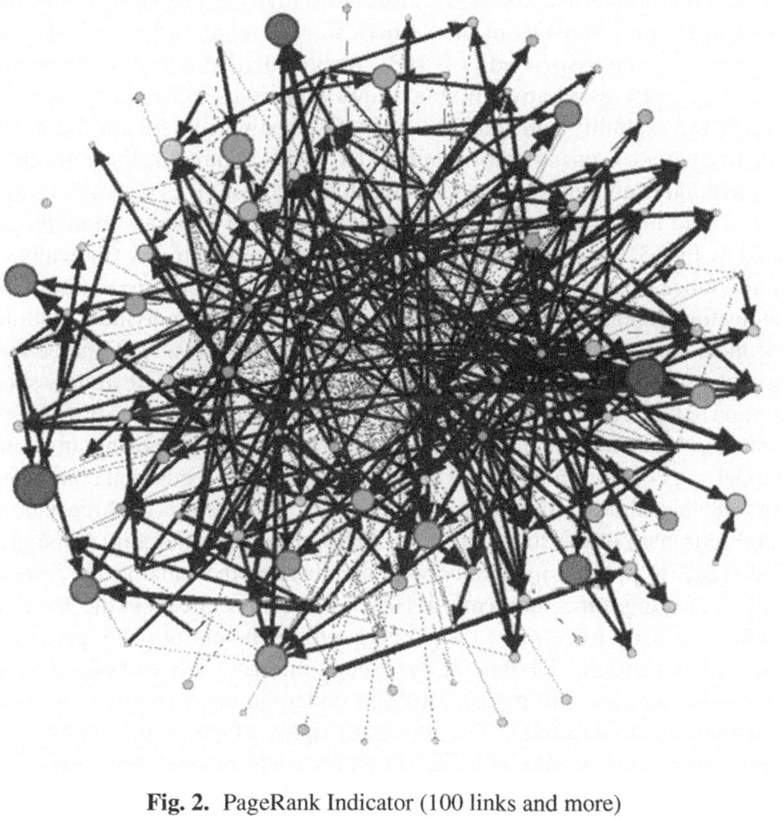

Fig. 2. PageRank Indicator (100 links and more)

Betweenness centrality refers to the degree to which a vertex lies on a path between other vertices. It averages 1434.47, with a rank from 0.038 to 883874.3. As a rule, commentators take this position, connecting various groups within the network. Closeness centrality measures the average distance from one vertex to other vertices. The higher the indicator, the less capable this vertex is of quickly disseminating information. For the network under study, the average closeness centrality is 0.606, and the rank is from 0.109 to 1. According to this indicator, posts are the active disseminators of information.

This is also evidenced by post authority data, which is much higher than the network average of 0.0015. And finally, the PageRank indicator (Fig. 2), which ranks vertices in accordance with how often a network user, following links, will get to a given vertex. For "Mash on the Moika", the average is 0.0017, the advantage in this sense lies with posts, rather than commentators and likes.

4.3 Network Assortativity and Modularity for Argumentation

Assortativity/disassortativity is an important indicator of argumentative networks, which serves to assess the level of network solidarity. Assortativity indicates the homogeneity of the vertices included in the network. Disassortativeness indicates diversity in the network. In structural terms, assortativity/disassortativity is measured by the similarity of the structural characteristics of the vertices (for example, the degree of vertices) to which the vertices are associated [14: 203]. Argumentative networks show high rates of assortativity, since assortative mixing allows arguments to be accepted with a high level of self-referentiality and individuation of reasoning. "Mash on the Moika" is a disassortative network, its indicator is minus 0.3. In this regard, the three groups of users (posts, commenters and likes) of course have diversity that gives rise to disassortativity. However, within the various classes represented in the network, assortativity grows, as evidenced by Fig. 3, which visually presents Eigenvector Centrality (indicators centrality by importance of neighbors) and betweenness centrality for three classes (modules). Thus, indicators of homophily and endogenous cooperation in individual modules of the network under study indicate the formation of a cooperative culture of interaction, which influences the acceptance of argumentation in a dispute. Some researchers specifically pay attention to this feature of networks when studying communication processes in complex contexts: "The aim… is to present a contribution… by proposing an evolutionary game model of cooperation that takes into account the self-regulation characteristics of the actors and the cultural pluralism of societies". So, they focuses on three major sources of cultural pluralism of the social group…: "**Homophily.** Homophily is the propensity of an individual to prefer connections with members of the same group instead of the out-groups… **Endogamic cooperation.** Here we use this concept in the broad sense, to denote the propensity to be more cooperative with members of one's group than with members of other groups. **Civicness.** Any social interaction is embedded in a web of institutions—formal and informal norms and underpinning meanings that make individual actions interconnected….The model is highly effective in describing the real behavior of interacting people living in a complex environment" [15: 2–3].

Associated with assortativity is a measure of modularity. Modularity is a measure of the structure of networks or graphs, designed to measure the strength of a network's partitioning into modules. Networks with high modularity have dense connections between nodes within modules, but weak connections between nodes in different modules. Mark Newman writes: "Modularity is a measure of the extent to which like is connected to like in a network. It is strictly less than 1 and takes positive values if there are more edges between nodes of the same type than would expect by random chance. It can also take negative values if there are fewer such edges than we would expect by chance" [16: 205]. Modularity is a significant indicator of the acceptance of arguments in a group. Positive modularity promotes the dissemination and acceptance of valid arguments. This is not

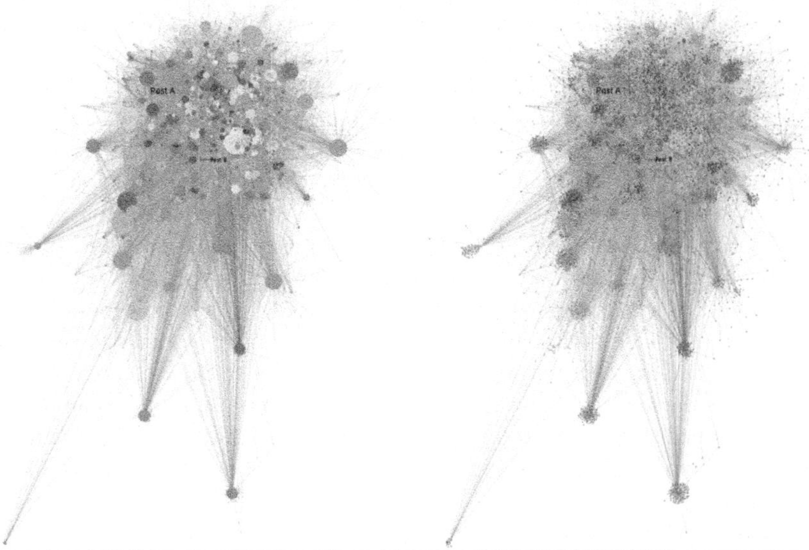

Eigenvector Centrality *Betweenness Centrality*

Fig. 3. "Mash on the Moika" Modularity (classes 2,3,4)

contradicted by the provisions of Sperber and Mercier's theory of argumentative reasoning, according to which in group discussions one participant with the correct answer can convince a group unanimously insisting on the wrong answer, even if he was initially less confident than other members of the group [1]. The modularity indicator for "Mash on the Moika" is 0.37. This network has 29 classes, distributed differently due to connections internal to the classes and external to them. However, internal connections still dominate. This is confirmed by Fig. 3 for both posts and commenters.

5 Discussion and Conclusions

The general model of persuasive communication in a network context could be built on two inference mechanisms in reasoning processes - epistemic, based on the logic of evidence, and argumentative, based on the intuitive acceptance of the structures of deliberative interaction in networks. The article uses an argumentative strategy of persuasion through the use of structural characteristics of networks. Just as the public press, radio and television created their structural mechanisms of persuasion, so too do networks influence the communication strategy of users. A network message becomes a belief in the process of such development of network mechanisms of socialization (networking persuasion), which contribute to the individuation of values and the formation of network solidarity as a resonant potential for individuation. Argumentative mechanisms associated with producing, understanding, and accepting arguments relied on processes of individuation and network solidarity. Individuation was measured by network metrics such as eigenvector centrality, average path length, and closeness centrality. Network solidarity was expressed by a tendency to form groups, the presence of vertices with non-zero betweenness centrality indicators, a network with high density indicators, closeness centralization and negative assortativity (disassortativity). The study of network designs of persuasive communication based on network analysis allowed us to conclude that there are two direct mechanisms of influence on the value attitudes and network socialization of users. The first mechanism is influence through the active role of a moderator who leads deliberation, pushing group members to active communication. In this case, the network should be characterized by a high degree of self-organization, and the moderator should have a position of direct contact with users (high indicators of proximity centrality). In fact, the act of communication on the part of the moderator simply signals to the rest of the discussion participants (the readers) that their message has been "processed" and taken into account. The second mechanism assumes the active role of the users themselves, which is accompanied not only by slacktivism, which has a positive effect on the acceptance of arguments within and outside the group, but also by a more developed system of groupings in the network, which confirms the hypothesis about the greater role of cohesion rather than the heterogeneity of network contacts for communication.

Computer technology or computing "may be the fourth great field of science, along with the physical, biological and social sciences" [18: 369]. Social computing involves connections between social behavior and computing systems, or communication and computing. The combination of various computer services aimed at conscious communication, capable of changing content on the basis of cooperation, today has a direct impact on democratic procedures and the formation of publicity. Social computing expands the concept of democracy by incorporating the criterion of publicly accessible network communication into the process of grounding political truth. The virtualization of communication between government authorities and citizens has only partially moved into the online network space. On the one hand, the range of communication platforms is expanding, into which transport, recreational facilities, museums, shopping centers, etc. are turning. On the other hand, there is a tendency towards the formation of new zones of public control and correction of communication, the closing of space within individual digital communities, the privatization of public spaces, etc. These political risks of digitalization must be taken into account. However, in general, digitalization has a transformative effect on the organization of public power, transforming it into an open space for argumentative communication between citizens.

References

1. Mercier, H., Sperber, D.: Why do humans reason? Arguments for an argumentative theory. Behav. Brain Sci. **34**(2), 57–74 (2011)
2. van der Heijden, M., Schalk, J.: Network relationships and standard adoption: diffusion effects in transnational regulatory networks. Public Adm. **98**(3), 768–784 (2020)
3. Lin, N.: Social Capital: A Theory of Social Structure and Action. Cambridge University Press, Cambridge (2001)
4. Levitan, L.C.: Social constraint and self-doubt: mechanisms of social network influence on resistance to persuasion. Polit. Psychol. **39**(4), 957–975 (2018)

5. Madeo, D., Mocenni, C.: Self-regulation versus social influence for promoting cooperation on networks. Sci. Rep. **10**(4830), 1–18 (2020)
6. Ibidem
7. Simondon, G.: Individuation in Light of Nations of Form and Information. Transl. by T. Adkins. University of Minnesota Press, Minneapolis (2020)
8. Granovetter, M.S.: The strength of weak ties. Am. J. Psychol. **78**(6), 1360–1380 (1973)
9. Grandjean, M.A.: Social network analysis of Twitter: mapping the digital humanities community. Cogent Arts Human. **3**(1), 1–14 (2016)
10. Bennett, L.W.: Segerberg, A: The logic of connective action. Inf. Commun. Soc. **15**(5), 739–768 (2012)
11. Carrasco, J.A., Miller, E.J., Wellman, B.: How far and with whom do people socialize? Empirical evidence about distance between social network members. Transp. Res. Rec. **2076**(1), 114–122 (2008)
12. Newman, M.: Networks, 2nd edn. Oxford University Press, Oxford (2018)
13. Miller, P.R., Bobkowski, P.S., Maliniak, D., Rapoport, R.B.: Talking politics on Facebook: network centrality and political discussion practices in social media. Polit. Res. Q. **68**(2), 377–391 (2015)
14. Madeo, D., Salvatore, S., Mannarini, T., Mocenni, Ch.: Modeling pluralism and self-regulation explains the emergence of cooperation in networked societies. Sci. Rep. **11**, 19226 (2021)
15. Denning, P.: Computing science: the great principles of computing. Am. Sci. **98**(5), 369–372 (2010)

Citizens' Social Rating in the Era of Digitalization: The First Experience and Its Perception

Alexander V. Sokolov(✉) and Egor Grebenko

Demidov Yaroslavl State University, 10, Sovetskay Street, 150003 Yaroslavl, Russia
alex8119@mail.ru

Abstract. The transformation of communication and the development of new forms of interaction between people and organizations in the digital space have increased the importance of modern digital services and platforms. A feature of their operation is the collection and accumulation of big data about users. At the same time, the observed trend towards the development and creation of digital ecosystems has highlighted the importance of working with large amounts of data that remain from any user actions in the digital space and characterize them by a variety of parameters. Such data allows their holders to process and group information about users and their actions in the online environment. Therefore, based on working with this data, organizations can carry out social rating and determine the formats of communication with each individual, provide him with certain preferences or, conversely, limit him in any actions.

Based on this, this article presents the results of a study conducted to identify the relationship between the current processes of digitalization and the potential implementation of social rating systems. The empirical basis of the study is interviews with 34 experts, another study with a sample of 10 experts, and a series of 3 focus groups among citizens. The results obtained made it possible to identify the features of the formation and functioning of modern digital services in Russia, as well as to determine the attitude of citizens to digital technologies and social rating processes based on their interactions with these digital resources. At the same time, despite the active use of digital services and ecosystems, citizens are wary of the introduction of large-scale social rating systems, seeing them as a threat to their personal freedoms and privacy.

Keywords: Digitalization · Social Rating · Internet · Digital Service · Communication · Interaction

1 Introduction

In the modern world, where information is becoming more accessible and technology is developing rapidly, the idea of evaluating and monitoring people's behavior using a social rating system is becoming increasingly relevant. Therefore, digitalization has created conditions for the development and implementation of rating systems for people and organizations.

A. Chugunov et al. (Eds.): DTGS 2024, CCIS 2445, pp. 116–128, 2025.
https://doi.org/10.1007/978-3-031-90720-3_9

In Russia, the issue of the introduction of social rating continues to be actively discussed. At the same time, in 2019, the legal basis for the functioning of large-scale assessment systems was laid, which is disclosed in the National Project "Digital Economy". The discourse on the potential introduction of social rating systems in Russia is mainly represented by two opposing points of view. Proponents of this system see it as an opportunity to increase the efficiency of the state, improve the quality of life of citizens and encourage law-abiding behavior. Opponents fear a violation of confidentiality, discrimination against certain groups of the population and the use of the system as a tool of social control.

It is important to understand that social rating is a tool that can be used both to address a wide range of social issues and to optimize public policy. Its effectiveness and fairness will directly depend on how the issues of ensuring the transparency of the system, minimizing the risks of data leakage and discrimination, creating a system for appealing evaluation results and ensuring the participation of citizens in decision-making regarding social rating will be resolved. Despite the fact that the future of social rating systems remains unclear, today it is safe to say that they are capable of having a significant impact on the political life of both individual countries and the entire world community as a whole. Therefore, today it seems relevant to study potential rating and evaluation systems for citizens, as well as to understand the prospects for their use in the framework of interaction between government and society.

2 Theoretical Framework

In the modern world, digitalization plays an increasingly important role in various spheres of society. With the development of technology and the increasing availability of the Internet in countries around the world, more and more information about people is becoming available online. Easily generated and collected Big Data in the digital space is becoming a valuable resource for their owners, turning into a new raw material of the XXI century [1]. As a result, a "new social order is being formed, based on constant monitoring and offering unprecedented opportunities for social discrimination and influencing behavior" [2]. Commercial structures have realized that they can profit not only from the services directly provided, the goods produced, but also the data they receive from their customers [3]. A striking example of the use of Big Data for social transformation is the integrated Smart City technology, which allows to eliminate many problems of the functioning of agglomerations and improve the quality of life of people [4].

This situation makes it possible to obtain big data and use it, among other things, to create different ratings based on big data. Digitalization helps automate the rating process, which makes it faster and more efficient. Automatic data processing allows you to detect connections and trends that might have gone unnoticed during manual analysis. As a result, the discussion of a new problem is being updated – the possibility of ensuring the security of using digital services and data confidentiality [5].

Big Data-based ratings are evaluation systems that use large amounts of data to analyze and rank objects or subjects according to certain criteria. Such ratings can be applied in various fields, from social networks [6] and online stores [7], finance [8] and business [9], to healthcare [10], education [11], urban [12] and public administration [13]. The process of creating ratings based on big data usually involves collecting, storing, processing and analyzing large amounts of information that can be obtained from various sources such as Internet traffic, transactions, new media, mobile devices, etc. After processing, the data is used to identify patterns, trends, correlations and predict the behavior of objects.

The field of activity for collecting and processing data for compiling various ratings is highly professional. It is dominated by international rating agencies [14].

To date, it can be stated that these processes are beginning to be projected directly onto specific individuals, thereby forming the process of social rating of citizens. These ratings are an assessment and ranking of individuals based on their behavior, actions and relationships. Digital technologies make it possible to analyze numerous volumes of personalized data, including information about content consumption, social media activity [15], purchases, behavior in various situations [16], etc.

Thus, a social rating is a system for evaluating human behavior and activity in society, providing for the opportunity to influence the format of interaction with other people, digital services of an organization, the ability to access certain resources or impose restrictions in various spheres of life.

The most developed is the Chinese experience of social rating. The social credit system is considered here as an instrument of social management strategy [17]. At the same time, despite many contradictions and ethical conflicts, this system receives a fairly high level of public support [18]. This system is gradually developing and the phenomenon of "Qianke" has been formed in the criminal legal system of China, which involves rating not only the individual (criminal) himself, but his relatives and friends [19]. Thus, the rating of one individual affects the rating of others.

It can be said that ratings based on big data are a powerful tool for decision-making and process optimization [20], but their use should be carried out with special attention to legal and ethical aspects, especially when ratings are social and aimed at a person. It is necessary to take into account issues of privacy and data security in order to avoid possible abuses and violations of citizens' rights, it is important to take into account possible biases and errors that may arise due to the quality of the data or the algorithms used.

3 Research Methods

The purpose of the article is to identify the features of the phenomenon of social rating of citizens. For an adequate and detailed analysis of it, several tasks were set during the study:

- to identify the impact of digitalization on the formation and development of social rating systems for citizens;
- to identify the features of existing citizen rating systems;
- to assess citizens' perception of existing social rating systems.

In order to achieve the goal and complete the tasks, a set of sociological studies was conducted.

The study is based on empirical data obtained as a result of a series of two interviews with experts on formalized questionnaires. The first interview was conducted among 34 experts, where the features of the processes of digitalization and digital transformation of modern society were revealed, as well as the role of modern online services and platforms in the formation of digital ecosystems was determined (spring 2023). The 34 experts included both researchers dealing with the use and implementation of modern digital technologies in the political process, as well as specialists working with digital services and platforms in their professional activities. For a more objective assessment of the development of digital ecosystems in politics, experts representing state and municipal institutions, specialists working in commercial enterprises (mainly engaged in digital technologies), as well as representatives of non-profit organizations were interviewed.

The second interview was conducted among 10 experts who identified trends and features of the formation of social rating systems (February-March 2024). The sample included specialists who work with digital services and platforms in their professional activities.

Also, a significant part of the data was obtained during a series of 3 focus groups (February 2024), the respondents of which were citizens (residents of the city of Yaroslavl). Focus groups made it possible to identify citizens' perceptions of modern digitalization achievements and determine their attitude to social rating systems. The representativeness of the sample of participants is determined by the formation of each focus group according to age and social characteristics that advise the general characteristics of the demographic population. The first focus group consisted of participants between the ages of 18 and 30. The second group was recruited from participants aged 31 to 55 years. The third group included participants over the age of 56. Each focus group consisted of 9–10 people. There were almost equal numbers of male and female representatives in each group. The focus groups were held according to a pre-formed list of questions.

Thus, the logic of collecting empirical data assumed the following construction:

- collection of data and assessments from the expert community on the problems of digitalization and its impact on the process of formation and development of social rating of citizens;
- collecting data from citizens as an object of social rating to assess the effects of digitalization and the first examples of social rating systems.

Thus, data were obtained from both carriers of specialized knowledge and ordinary people themselves.

4 The Results of the Study

4.1 Digitalization and Development of Digital Systems

The development of modern society is inextricably linked with the use and implementation of digital technologies in the life of a modern person. Thus, experts note positive changes as a result of the digitalization of modern society, especially in the social and economic spheres ("Today it is simply impossible to imagine the activities of a modern person and his life without the use of digital technologies," the expert believes).

Positive changes in the life of society are also noticeable with the advent of new digital technologies and the parallel improvement of communication mechanisms between subjects of various relationships. The sphere of online interaction between individuals and organizations through digital platforms and services stands out especially today. It is also important to increase the accessibility and intensity of interactions related to the adaptation of digital platforms to mobile devices, which simplifies access to the digital space and the service sector (including those provided by commercial organizations).

At the same time, it is important to note that experts tend to separate the concepts of "digitalization" and "digital transformation", and digitalization, in their understanding, is a common process affecting the modern digital life of the whole society, and digital transformation is a key "mechanism" for achieving objective results in changing the ways of functioning and interaction of government and society. Moreover, digital transformation must be systematic, which ultimately contributes to the formation of a completely new form of organization that carries out its activities at the digital level. Therefore, these processes are not only inextricably linked, but are crucial in the development of a digital society. The emergence of new ways of communication in society, including through digitalization and digital transformation, modernizes and changes the system of relationships between individuals, expanding the potential for the realization of public and personal interests. Therefore, modern society is constantly adapting to the processes of digitalization and digital transformation, which is natural within the current reality based on the increasing role of digital technologies in people's lives ("People are forced to adapt to changes related to digitalization. Otherwise, they risk being out of access to the system of distribution of benefits and resources," - the expert's opinion).

Digitalization processes in politics can be considered separately. Thus, the introduction of digital services simplifies the mechanisms of interaction between government and society, leveling many barriers to offline interaction ("Digitalization cannot but affect politics. Politics, like society, is forced to respond to trends set by the introduction of new technologies," - expert opinion). On the other hand, some experts gave examples of digitalization of the internal activities of authorities related to the implementation of their current tasks (for example, the introduction of electronic document management). Based on this, the introduction of digital services and platforms in politics is an integral part of the development of Russian society, which will eventually improve the mechanisms of digital interaction based on the need for digital communication in the current realities of digital technology development. It is important to note that the development of modern services and platforms determines the formation of modern digital ecosystems that allow you to include digital systems that are different in their functionality and structure. The most successful experience in implementing such digital ecosystems is demonstrated by domestic companies such as Yandex, Beber, VK, and Tinkoff.

According to experts, the main obstacle to the creation and use of digital ecosystems is the technological complexity of implementing large-scale projects and products. Thus, most of the developments are already used in the digital ecosystems of large companies that not only own patent rights, but also "holders" of a huge number of highly qualified personnel capable of creating and maintaining complex digital systems. This also creates a request (and in the situation of public administration, due to its peculiarities, a problem) to attract specialists to develop such technologies in the political sphere. In particular, the state is not able to offer IT specialists the same favorable and competitive conditions and remuneration. Nevertheless, we can observe the successful implementation of large-scale digital public service delivery systems created by the state. Such a system is the portal "Public Services", which allows authorities and citizens to interact within a complex digital system based on the provision of services to citizens in various spheres of social, economic and political life of modern society. It is not only advanced for Russian society, but is also recognized as a successful platform (with the makings of a digital ecosystem) implemented by the state ("Public services is probably the only platform that can be called an ecosystem in politics or at least a service that has the functionality inherent in full-fledged digital ecosystems," the expert believes).

The use of an ecosystem approach to the assessment of digitalization reveals a number of disadvantages of the development of digital technologies in the business environment and in the field of public administration. The public sector has significant differences with business, which has not only succeeded in creating real digital platforms and services, but is also moving towards the formation of complex digital systems ("Business, due to its peculiarity, is constantly looking for ways to increase profits, is actively developing digital technologies by adapting them in its activities. The state is clearly lagging behind commercial organizations in speed and reaction when introducing new technologies," - expert opinion).

This is mainly due to the difference in the goals of implementing digital ecosystems. The state does not seek to make a material profit from the introduction of digital technologies, but only tries to simplify and improve communication and interaction with citizens. Businesses, based on the laws of competition, strive to make a profit or a competitive advantage with any introduction of modern digital technologies, which in itself encourages them to introduce increasingly complex and technologically advanced forms of interaction with consumers (users). In fact, we can say that the creation of digital ecosystems in politics depends on the very subjectivity of political actors and their desire not only to verbalize political goal-setting, but also their real intention to implement it in order to ensure their own dominance and design a society corresponding to their interests. At the same time, experts are unequivocally confident that large-scale digital ecosystems in politics and business will become the next stage of digitalization of society. In particular, the prevailing view is that sooner or later any digital services and platforms will transform into full-fledged digital ecosystems that allow users and organizations to carry out any interaction within the digital space. At the same time, the forms of offline interaction will be minimized or completely absent. The development of digital technologies in politics is already becoming an objective process in which society and the state are forced to meet the demands and challenges of the time. The need to introduce and develop digital ecosystems is already evident in many countries of the world, and in the future the use of digital technologies will be perceived as a natural mechanism of interaction between government and society.

4.2 Social Rating and Assessment Systems

The development of technologies and digital services makes it possible to involve and accumulate a significant number of citizens in the digital space, which creates new opportunities for the implementation of control and evaluation systems. Such systems are already being actively implemented in commercial enterprises and, according to experts, they are successfully used in the processes of interaction with citizens. Rating systems are structures that determine the format of interaction between the rated person and the rating person based on his position in the system. Vivid examples of rating are: ratings of passengers and drivers in taxis (Yandex. Taxi; Maxim, etc.); marketplaces (Wildberries; Ozon, etc.); platforms for placing ads and providing specialized services (Avito; Go.Russian Federation; Профи.ги). At the same time, the areas that affect modern social rating systems are so large-scale that it allows us to talk about the widespread use of assessment systems for citizens based on their interactions with each other and commercial organizations ("A lot of things are evaluated, sometimes a person simply does not realize that he is subject to assessment and that this assessment somehow affects him" - opinion an expert).

According to experts, such a sharp increase in the use and implementation of rating systems in the commercial environment is caused by the desire of businesses to optimize the allocation of resources in the process of constantly increasing demand for services ("Large companies understand the need to optimize their interaction with customers and maximize profits. In this regard, they will use a wide range of tools, including those based on digital technologies" - expert opinion). Rating systems allow not only to determine whether an individual or an organization should enter into direct interaction (provision or receipt of a service) based on the position of the person being evaluated in the rating system (in this case, the rating can determine the reliability of a person), but also to determine the format of interaction that will be established between the parties. For example, if a person has a desire to purchase a specific product on a digital marketplace and offers from several sellers are available to him, then he will be able to determine which of them he will interact with (that is, purchase the product) based on the rating of sellers. The reverse interaction is built in a similar way. For example, knowing the rating of an individual, the organization determines the speed of providing services to him, or even restricts the provision of services. Based on this, rating systems are actively used today in various areas of interaction between citizens and organizations, but they are especially actively implemented where there is a need to establish the "reliability" of the provider or recipient of the service. If the reliability of a service representative can be easily determined based on the feedback and ratings of other users, then the reliability of a consumer is determined by criteria based on his past interactions in the provision of the same or similar services. A striking example here is the citizens' credit rating system (credit history). Having gained access to the history and rating of the borrower, the lender can determine not only whether to provide credit services in general, but also calculate the minimum/ maximum loan amount. Taxi drivers act in a similar way, who, after reviewing the passenger's rating, can determine whether it is worth providing transportation services to him or not. What is in the first case that in the second case, rating systems allow service representatives to determine the degree of "reliability" of the consumer and indicate the degree of risk of loss of resources when entering into direct interaction ("An organization or another person needs an assessment to understand the degree of their risk when contacting him. Therefore, rating is an opportunity to choose the best and most reliable," - expert opinion).

At the same time, there are not as many social rating systems initiated by the state today as in the commercial environment. This is due to a number of factors, the main one of which, according to experts, is again the complexity of the technical support of large-scale social rating systems. If the rating systems used in the business environment determine only part or individual interactions of citizens, then the systems implemented by the state by their nature imply coverage of wide spheres of citizens' life activities, allowing them to determine their social status already within the framework of the whole society. A striking example, according to experts, is the social credit system in China, where an attempt is being made to introduce large-scale assessment systems based on social interactions of citizens (When talking about social rating, the first thing that comes to mind is China. At the same time, their assessment system seems to an ordinary person from other countries to be something scary and utopian," the expert's opinion). The system not only allows you to determine the degree of "reliability" of a person as a citizen, but also determines the range of incentives and restrictions available to him based on his position in the rating. Despite the obvious objections of experts on the ethical side of using such a social rating system (Of course, social rating in China raises many legal and simply human issues, which remain secondary within the Chinese political system. It is difficult to imagine such systems in our country or in another country," - the expert's opinion), they nevertheless agree that the system has the potential to be effective in conditions of limited resources and increasing demand for public services (this is especially true for states with a broad social security system).

Therefore, the processes of digitalization and digital transformation have not only created the basis for the modernization of digital communication of citizens, but also resulted in the formation of an environment for the development of social rating systems based on the increasing interactions of individuals in the digital space. Moreover, the development of digital technologies has made it possible to collect, store, analyze and process big data necessary for the functioning of social rating systems. The accumulation of a significant number of users around services, platforms and digital ecosystems allows you to create databases based on all user interactions with systems, and therefore rank them based on these interactions.

4.3 Perception of Digitalization and Social Rating Processes by Citizens

For modern citizens, the achievements of digitalization have already become an integral part of life. It is safe to say that the vast majority of citizens use modern digital technologies and their large-scale participation in online communication processes. Moreover, the Internet is becoming a means of achieving not only personal goals, but also professional and career goals ("I use my smartphone daily, if not constantly. As it is impossible to be at work without access to the network, so at home when you need to talk to someone or solve some problem," - the opinion of a focus group participant).

Middle-aged and younger people can hardly imagine a day without using a digital device and accessing the global network. It can be noted that the communications of the modern generation are actively carried out on social networks and messengers, which, in their opinion, corresponds to the modern rhythm of life, where it is necessary to quickly and timely receive a response to a request or take the necessary action. This manifests itself not only in personal life, but also in work and study. Working citizens actively use digital services to perform professional tasks, moreover, the level of proficiency in surfing the Internet determines the success of the task. For representatives of educational institutions, the use of digital services and platforms determines not only communication with teachers, but also becomes the main tool for achieving educational goals.

Representatives of the older generation still see the Internet and modern digital technologies as a mechanism to simplify communication with the environment, rather than a universal tool of everyday life. Despite the presence of obvious barriers to the use of digital technologies, the main of which are the difficulty in mastering complex navigation algorithms on the Web and in modern Internet access devices, the older generation still uses the so-called "necessary minimum" of technologies to meet the requirements of modern digital society. It is also interesting that older people are already aware of the increased role of the Internet and digital technologies in the life of a modern person, which is a certain incentive for them to become more involved in the digital environment (although it is difficult for me to understand all the features of the Internet and social networks, even I have to master these technologies in order to to talk to relatives or make an appointment at a polyclinic," - the opinion of a participant in the retirement age focus group).

Despite citizens' perception of digitalization as a positive process that allows them to solve everyday tasks through digital technologies, they still feel some fears associated with the increasing role of digital technologies in modern human life. Thus, the younger generation is characterized by fear associated with the possibility of replacing humans with artificial intelligence technologies, which in the future will deprive them of opportunities to achieve career goals and full-fledged self-realization in society. A common fear for young and middle-aged people is the potential threat of being completely left without Internet technologies. They can no longer imagine life without communication on social networks and the consumption of content from digital services. For all ages, the main fears are the threat of personal data leakage and increasing cases of online fraud. Despite these fears, we can say that people are still quite loyal to the Internet and the achievements of digitalization. The information they receive on the global network is actively used by them to make decisions that determine their life priorities. Therefore, the Internet is becoming an opportunity for modern citizens to fill the information vacuum that may arise in cases of a lack of necessary data ("It's convenient when you don't know something or doubt something. You can always contact the search engine and get the necessary information. Actually, everything can already be solved through a smartphone," - the opinion of a focus group participant).

If we talk about the rating processes, it can be noted that citizens are aware that their actions in the digital environment can be evaluated. But despite their awareness, they have little interest in the value of their own rating. This applies to almost all ages, but most of all it is typical for the older generation, who devote less time to the digital environment and are accustomed to face-to-face interaction formats. Also, citizens do not attach importance to ratings for their lives, except for those who had to deal with the consequences of their position in the rating system when providing specific services (for example, a person wanted to take out a loan from a bank, and he was interested in the credit rating to understand how high his rating was and whether he would be approved for a loan). In general, the potential negative consequences that can cause difficulties for people in the process of interacting with evaluators are an incentive for them to change their rating (for example, the desire to increase the accident-free rating in order to get more favorable terms for CTP).

Despite the fact that people do not define ratings as an important part of their lives, they realize that rating systems can influence specific situations that determine advantages in the processes of interaction with the evaluator ("I basically never thought about the fact that part of my actions is being evaluated. Nevertheless, it is important to me if this assessment somehow affects my future," - the opinion of a focus group participant). Therefore, awareness of the assessment may cause them to feel anxious if the position in the rating does not have obvious advantages in a particular situation (for example, a low grade at school or university may worry the student if it affects the machine or other types of rewards). But, even with knowledge of their assessment and position in the rating, citizens rarely communicate with the evaluator. People are not very interested in evaluation systems, criteria, and what the evaluator is guided by when ranking. Citizens resort to interaction only in cases when, in their opinion, the assessment turns out to be unfair or incorrect ("I once passed a test in my organization and did not agree with the final assessment. Therefore, I turned to those who organized the test.", - the opinion of a participant in the focus group). Most often, citizens are in contact with specific individuals, and not with companies (representatives of companies). A striking example is the discussion of the final assessment with a teacher as part of an educational activity or with an evaluator as part of testing employees in organizations. The most common channel of communication with organizations is electronic appeals to support services. People's experience shows that companies, in general, demonstrate openness and transparency in the criteria of social rating, although some criteria raise questions about the fairness and appropriateness of their use. Often, such a perception is subjective and is determined by the worldview of each individual or is based on the prevailing circumstances of each individual situation. It is interesting that some people perceive interaction with the evaluator as a disregard for the dignity of the individual, manifested in the subjectivity of perception of one person by another ("In general, I believe that it is wrong to evaluate a person's entire life, it is beneath human dignity," - the opinion of a focus group participant). This view is more typical for older people, when, as representatives of the middle and younger ages, they are not inclined to be interested in the reasons for the assessment.

Based on the above, we can say that citizens somehow have some ideas about the processes of social rating. Moreover, they realize that they encounter them in everyday life, although not everyone understands to what extent they are involved in assessment systems. It is also interesting that some simply do not notice the rating systems or do not perceive them at all as something that affects their lives, but when the position in the rating determines the negative or positive consequences of interaction, they try to take the necessary actions to correct it.

5 Discussion

The conducted research made it possible to achieve the set goals. It is important that the results of the conducted interviews of experts and focus groups are correlated. This, in turn, confirms the evaluative judgments of experts and citizens' perceptions regarding digitalization and its impact on the formation of social rating systems for citizens. The use of sociological research methods made it possible not only to describe the current picture of the development of social rating systems, but also to identify the real ideas of citizens about them. Therefore, the significance of this study lies not only in the fact that the analysis and conclusions contained therein give a general idea of social rating systems, but also allow us to assess the potential and risks of their implementation at the present stage of society's development.

Despite the results obtained, the study has several limitations and potential opportunities for further research on the relevant topic. First of all, it is possible to note the complexity of the study of the phenomenon of social rating due to the lack of a variety of real examples of the implementation of assessment systems at the state level. At the moment, the only real experience and case of a large-scale social rating system remains the social credit system in China. Secondly, due to the lack of public access to the description of criteria and justification of rating in some commercial organizations, it seems difficult to consider the operating rating systems in Russia. At the same time, it is obvious that business structures are innovators in the introduction of digital technologies and methods for evaluating personnel and consumers of their services. Thirdly, there is currently no clear regulation of how social rating systems should function, who will administer them, what methods of data collection and processing will be used, what boundaries and restrictions for rating will be, how transparent the procedure and its results will be.

In further research, it is interesting to consider the ethical, legal and technical aspects of social rating of citizens. Although this study partially addresses the issues of the fairness of assessment and the legality of the use of rating of a person and organizations, nevertheless, further analysis based on a disciplinary approach will allow us to form a more objective picture regarding the moral and ethical side of social rating systems.

Based on the above, we can identify a number of questions for further research, the answers to which will allow us to reveal in more detail the social rating systems of citizens:

- Who and how will implement and administer social rating systems for citizens?
- What are the limits/boundaries when collecting and processing personal data of citizens for rating?
- How public and open can the process of social rating of citizens and its results be (the assessments themselves and the position of individual citizens in the rating)?
- To what extent and how social rating systems can be integrated into public administration?

6 Conclusions

Digitalization and digital transformation of society, on the one hand, simplify the life of a modern person, making various services more accessible and expanding the opportunities for people to interact in an online environment. On the other hand, they create conditions for the introduction of social rating systems that determine the formats of communication between individuals and organizations within the framework of their interactions. The development of digital services and platforms, as well as the potential growth of the role of digital ecosystems, predetermine the introduction of assessment systems that make it possible to rationalize user interactions in the provision and consumption of services. The need for effective use and allocation of resources within the framework of the functioning of social support mechanisms for the population pushes modern states to think about the introduction of large-scale social rating systems. The example of China and its social credit system demonstrates not only some experience in using these systems, but also allows it to be broadcast and used in those countries where the demand for social rating systems is high.

Despite the fact that rating systems are already actively used in the commercial environment (for example, ratings of taxi drivers, marketplaces) and are gradually being implemented by the state, they still remain difficult to scale due to technical limitations and ambiguous perception by the population. Although people's attitudes towards the achievements of digitalization are positive, they have a number of concerns due to the increasing role of digital technologies in people's lives. Such concerns are associated not only with distrust of the assessment system and the evaluator, but also with the ethical side of using large-scale social rating systems that broadcast their effect to all citizens and cover various aspects of human life (without taking into account their characteristics). Therefore, digitalization and social rating systems should be developed taking into account ethical standards and maintaining a balance between the interests of the state and the rights of citizens.

Social rating of citizens, like any other assessment system, may contain errors and distortions. For example, it may not take into account differences in socio-economic status and cultural characteristics between different population groups, especially in multinational States. In addition, rating systems can be manipulated and influenced by political parties, the state and other interest groups, which can negatively affect the democracy of the political system and the processes of coordinating the interests of various groups. Therefore, the implementation of rating systems should take into account a number of factors, such as the objectivity of evaluation criteria, transparency and accessibility of information, the use of modern technologies, etc. Only in this case, rating systems will be able to become an effective tool for evaluating public opinion and the work of government agencies. Thus, today we are witnessing the emergence of a new way of interaction between the state and society, citizens, commercial and nonprofit organizations. The qualitative implementation of this process can determine the adequacy of building a new socio-political structure of society in the era of digitalization.

Acknowledgements. The research was funded by Russian Science Foundation, research project No. 24–28-00728, https://rscf.ru/en/project/24-28-00728.

References

1. Bannister, J., O'Sullivan, A.: Big Data in the city. Urban Stud, **58**(15), 3061–3070 (2021). https://doi.org/10.1177/00420980211014124
2. Couldry, N., Mejias, U.A.: Data colonialism: rethinking big data's relation to the contemporary subject. Television New Media **20**(4), 336–349 (2019). https://doi.org/10.1177/1527476418796632

3. West, S.M.: Data capitalism: redefining the logics of surveillance and privacy. Bus. Soc. **58**, 20–41 (2019)
4. Kong, L., Woods, O.: The ideological alignment of smart urbanism in Singapore: critical reflections on a political paradox. Urban Stud. **55**(4), 679–701 (2018)
5. Flyverbom, M., Deibert, R., Matten, D.: The governance of digital technology, big data, and the internet: new roles and responsibilities for business. Bus. Soc. **58**(1), 3–19 (2019). https://doi.org/10.1177/0007650317727540
6. Graham, T., Rodriguez, A. The sociomateriality of rating and ranking devices on social media: a case study of reddit's voting practices. Social Media + Soc. **7**(3) (2021). https://doi.org/10.1177/20563051211047667
7. Yerzhanova, S., Jazykbaeva, B., Smailova, L.K.: Development of e-commerce and rating of online retail stores. Issues Sustain. Dev. Soc. **2**, 110–118 (2021)
8. Natsypaeva, E.A. Banks in social networks: specifics, problems, current ratings. Ind. Econ. Manag. Technol. **2**(2), 129–136 (2022)
9. Gazizullin, R.I.: Rating of social responsibility of business: concept, structure, prospects. Prob. Econ. Legal Pract. **4**, 55–60 (2023)
10. Lazarevič, P., Quesnel-Vallée, A.: Rating Health and rating change: how Canadians rate their health and its changes. J. Aging Health **35**(7–8), 535–542 (2023). https://doi.org/10.1177/08982643221119654
11. Zenkov, A.R.: Ratings as a tool for adapting vocational education to the challenges of post-industrial employment. Soc. Labor Res. **1**(46), 117–127 (2022)
12. Lyaskovskaya, E.A., Khudyakova, T.A., Schmidt, A.V.: Improving the rating of Russian smart cities. Econ. Reg. **4**, 1046–1061 (2022)
13. Kabanov, Y., Chugunov, A.V.: Specifics of electronic management in the subjects of the Russian Federation: pilot analysis of regional ratings and statistics. Int. J. Open Inf. Technol. **11**(12), 138–142 (2023)
14. Köcher, S., Köcher, S.: The mode heuristic in service consumers' interpretations of online rating distributions. J. Serv. Res. **24**(4), 582–600 (2021). https://doi.org/10.1177/10946705211012475
15. Nieborg, D.B., Helmond, A.: The political economy of Facebook's platformization in the mobile ecosystem: Facebook Messenger as a platform instance. Media Cult. Soc. **41**(2), 196–218 (2019)
16. de Reuver, M., Verschuur, E., Nikayin, F., Cerpa, N., Bouwman, H.: Collective action for mobile payment platforms: a case study on collaboration issues between banks and telecom operators. Electron. Commer. Res. Appl. **14**(5), 331–344 (2015)
17. Hoffman, S.: Programming China: the Communist Party's autonomic approach to managing state security. Merics China Monitor **44**, 1–12 (2017)
18. Kostka, G.: China's social credit systems and public opinion: explaining high levels of approval. New Media Soc. **21**(7), 1565–1593 (2019). https://doi.org/10.1177/1461444819826402
19. Li, E.: The Qianke system in China: disorganisation, discrimination and dispersion. Criminol. Crim. Just. **23**(4), 568–587 (2023). https://doi.org/10.1177/17488958231161436
20. Hendrickx, F.: Social rating European. Labour Law J. **2**(2), 98–100 (2011)

Transport Environment of a Smart City: The Research of Alternative Approaches to Ensuring Punctuality of Terrestrial Urban Public Transport

Julia L. Sviridova[1], Elena V. Budrina[2], Larisa I. Rogavichene[2](✉), Anna S. Lebedeva[2], and Irina S. Rykova[3]

[1] RDN LLC, Saint-Petersburg, Russia
[2] State Marine Technical University, Saint-Petersburg, Russia
boudrina@mail.ru, rogavichene@list.ru, hebo@rambler.ru
[3] ITMO University, Saint-Petersburg, Russia
i.am.nosova@gmail.com

Abstract. The article presents the results of the study of alternative approaches to organizing priority pass of public land urban passenger transport (PLUPT), that can ensure punctuality (traffic strictly in accordance with the schedule). It is one of the most important parameters of the quality of the public passenger transport. The purpose of the study is to identify the most expedient approach to ensure the priority travel of public transport (PT) among the alternatives: priority due to the organization of allocated lanes; PT priority travel technology based on inductive loop transport detector; technology of priority transportation of PT based on Vehicle-to-Infrastructure (V2I) telematic technology. The used research methods include the analysis of regulatory and legal framework documentation, the results of surveys of passengers of public transport in Russia, the comparative analysis and expert assessment of the approaches based on formulated criteria (implementation conditions, service requirements, adaptability to the situation on the street road network (SRN), restrictions and barriers, disadvantages and negative consequences, implementation cost, impact on the improvement of PT punctuality), analysis of the used hardware and software systems. Based on the analysis of the advantages and disadvantages of the three approaches under consideration, it was found that the organization of the allocated lanes does not provide sufficiently optimal PT traffic conditions at the regulated intersection. The inductive loop transport detector approach is attractive in terms of cost and timing but is not scalable and has no additional potential for smart city development. The V2I-based approach is the most functional and provides high PT punctuality, but now it is the most expensive one and it is difficult to implement it. Based on all the considered conditions for the application of the approaches, it was identified that the most promising is the approach based on the V2I technology, which is the basis for the active development of intelligent transport systems (ITS) within the framework of the "smart" city concept.

Keywords: Transport System · Public Transport · Priority Pass · Vehicle-to-Infrastructure · V2I · Smart City

A. Chugunov et al. (Eds.): DTGS 2024, CCIS 2445, pp. 129–144, 2025.
https://doi.org/10.1007/978-3-031-90720-3_10

1 Introduction

The transport system (TS) is one of the key components that ensures the competitiveness, social and economic development of any region. Meanwhile, the active process of urbanization requires city officials to answer the questions regarding the choice of methods and means of managing transport systems [24]. The rapid growth of the traffic logjams, the increased number of the road accidents consequences and their severity, the increased noise and atmospheric pollution of the cities and other repercussions of urbanization that occur against the background of dense urban development and the difficulties of the street and road network modernization (SRN) force stakeholders and particularly executive authorities that form the transport policy of the city to choose innovative and high-tech approaches to optimize the operation of the transport system [6, 17]. Moreover, these approaches must comply with the concept of a "smart city" as a priority direction for the development of modern large agglomerations. According to this concept, the transport environment of a "smart city" should ensure a high degree of population mobility, safe and comfortable movement, accessibility of all types of transport, high-quality infrastructure provision, effective traffic management, sustainable development of urban transport with a high level of environmental safety. Fulfillment of these tasks requires a revision of existing approaches and the introduction of complex integrated management systems.

Such realities gave rise to several concepts and trends [26]. One of these concepts was embodied in term Intelligent Transport System (ITS), which means a system that "integrates modern information, communication, telematics and management technologies. It is designed for the automated search and adoption of the most effective scenarios for managing the transport system of the region, a specific vehicle, or a group of vehicles to ensure the necessary mobility of the population, maximizing the use of the road network, improving the safety and efficiency of the transport process, comfort for drivers and users of transport" [9, 12]. Another and even more wide concept of the "smart city" considers all urban systems as derivatives of a uniformed complex, which is a highly integrated and interactive information environment [20, 21].

Within the framework of the "smart city" concept an important role is given to public transport (PT), which can become a full-fledged binding mechanism in the urban mobility system while ensuring the optimal use of the SRN space, a high level of traffic safety, saving financial resources of the population, reducing the negative impact on the ecological environment [1, 4]. In this case, we are talking about such a type of public transport as public land urban passenger transport (PLUPT) - buses, trolleybuses, trams.

According to the data obtained by the Russian state research organization WCIOM (All-Russian Center for the Study of Public Opinion), which is located in Moscow, despite the significant potential of PT to unload urban SRN, the preference of Russians when choosing a type of transport for movement inside the settlements at the moment is as follows: 1) personal road transport (45% of respondents); 2) land-based urban public transport (23%); 3) minibuses (10%). The remaining share of respondents prefers such types of transport as taxi, metro, bicycle, carsharing and alternative (means of individual mobility - MIM) [31, 35]. There is an objective need to reorient the choice of the passengers from the individual (private) transport in favor of PT [1, 7, 8], otherwise, following the concept of a "smart city" will be difficult.

The above-mentioned questions are the subject of particular interest of the researchers. In Russia the issues of formation of the transport environment within the framework of the "smart city" concept, ITS and the PT system functioning are analyzed in the works of V.M. Vlasov [30], A.E. Goreva [13], I.A. Evstigneev [12], S.V. Zhankazieva [37], V.V. Zyryanova [38], V.A. Kremenets [18], Pugachiov I.N. [28] and others.

In S.A. Bolgov's works [3], the need for digitalization of transport is noted in order to develop the transport component of a smart city. A.V. Pirotskaya's works [23] are devoted to studying trends in the development of the "smart city" concept from the perspective of various specialists and representatives of society.

Among foreign authors, Berg J. & Ihlström J. [1], Kociánová A. [17], De Keyser O. & Hillewaere M. [10], Bhattacharjee S. [2], Przhibil P. & Svitek M. [27], Casey R. & Collura J. [7], Diakaki C. [11], Wang H.-C. [19], Wang R. [32] and others. However, no comparative analysis of the priority pass of PT technologies was carried out.

2 Materials and Methods

The purpose of this study is to determine the most appropriate approach for ensuring the priority pass of PT to improve its punctuality within the framework of the "smart city" concept.

The objectives of the study are:

- to identify key performance indicators of the PT system of the highest priority, which affect the degree of its attractiveness for passengers, consistent with the objectives of forming a "smart city";
- to offer alternative approaches to improve one of the most important indicators of the PT system quality performance;
- to conduct a comparative analysis of the alternative approaches to ensure the PT punctuality based on the developed criteria using the expert survey method.

The research methods used are the analysis of the regulatory legal acts [14, 23, 26] and the results of surveys of public transport passengers; the comparison of the existing alternative approaches to ensure punctuality of PT; analysis of the software and hardware market providing priority pass of PT; conducting an expert survey to assess the approaches that are under study in April 2022.

Based on an analysis of the list of conditions for transport services to the population presented in the official documents[1], key tactical requirements and target guidelines for ensuring the functioning and development of a modern urban transport system were identified, which formed the basis of this study.

The presented comparative analysis of approaches to ensure the priority pass of PT can become a theoretical basis for the implementation of specific projects in the field of

---

[1] GOST R 510096-96. Transport services. Terms and definitions; Order of the Ministry of Transport of the Russian Federation dated December 30, 2021, No. 482 "On approval of methodological recommendations for optimizing transport service systems in urban agglomerations, as well as the introduction of digital fare payment technologies and monitoring transport services for the population".

a "smart city" traffic management. However, the final decision will depend on the set of actual conditions of the SRN and the transport policy that is carried out.

3 Results

According to the GOST standard, the following groups of indicators are defined in the Russian Federation, according to which the quality of public passenger transport is assessed [14]:

- Information service: frequency of information transmission about departure and arrival of the vehicles; frequency of information transmission about the services provided to the passengers and their cost; frequency of information transmission about the location of buildings, communication means, etc.
- Comfort: space (volume) of area per passenger; frequency of vehicle cleaning; air temperature in the vehicle; illumination in the vehicle; acceptable values of noise, vibration, humidity; average (acceptable) filling of the vehicle interior.
- Speed: duration of the trip; average vehicle speed; frequency of the vehicle stops.
- Timeliness: the share of the vehicles sent on schedule; the share of the vehicles arriving on schedule; average intensity of traffic; maximum intensity of traffic.
- Safety: reliable operation of the vehicles; professional suitability of the transport service providers; readiness of the vehicle to perform a specific transportation.

It is important to note that the groups of criteria "speed" and "timeliness" are interrelated and essentially combined into a general criterion that can be designated as punctuality of the PT [10].

According to the international studies conducted after the active phase of COVID-19, the priority of PT performance indicators from the point of view of the passengers stands as follows (from the most to the least significant): 1) comfort; 2) intensity of the traffic intervals/PT punctuality; 3) travel time; 4) mobility of movement; 5) safety, etc. At the same time, before the start of the pandemic, the key parameter of the PT system was the intensity of the traffic intervals/punctuality (65% of the respondents) [31]. In general, domestic and international indicators of public transport performance do not contradict, but rather complement each other, and together can be used to assess the transport environment of a "smart city".

As for the transport situation in Russia, at the current moment there has been an increase in the number and duration of the traffic logjams in large cities (Moscow, St. Petersburg, Novosibirsk, Samara, Yekaterinburg, Rostov-on-Don, Nizhny Novgorod, Chelyabinsk, Kazan, etc.) [19]. It leads to a transport conflict resulting in the impossibility of providing the PT traffic strictly in accordance with the schedule along the route, and therefore a decrease in its attractiveness for the passengers, which does not meet the requirements of the "smart city" concept. In this regard, it seems reasonable to use measures to improve the quality of work of land urban public transport based on the organization of the priority pass.

Let us briefly describe the technologies by means of which the PT priority pass is ensured in comparison with other vehicles at the city SRN (Table 1).

Let us consider the approaches under the study more closely.

Table 1. Approaches to the organization of priority pass PLUPT

№	Column header	"Application point" on SRN	Method of impact on passing vehicles 2015	Methods used
1	Marked out lanes	Along the entire route	Static	Organizational
2.1	Based on transport detectors	At controlled junctions	Dynamic	Technical, technological
2.2	Based on V2I technology			

Source: Designed by the authors

First approach involves the organization of a separate special lane from the main section of the road network. The traffic on it is available only to a certain type of vehicles - city public transport. The prerequisites for the formation of such an approach were objective differences in the characteristics of the PT traffic compared to other vehicles on the SRN: relatively low speed, the need to constantly separate public transport from the main flow of transport (near stopping pavilions).

In fact, the allocation of a special lane for the public transport traffic ensures the division of the vehicle flows into relatively homogeneous ones due to the optimization of the traffic management scheme. It contributes to an increase in the punctuality of the operation of the PT and the transport system.

Another approach for ensuring the priority pass of PT is associated with the introduction of software and hardware complexes (SHC) while maintaining the specified conditions for organizing traffic (approach 2). Thus, approach 2.1 - a type of second approach - makes it possible to provide special conditions when overcoming the PLUPT of an adjustable intersection to ensure its traffic exactly in accordance with the specified schedule along the route. When analyzing this approach, the following are of interest: the selected type of transport detector; selectable method of traffic light regulation.

First of all, optimal in terms of the cost of the equipment, the reliability of the operation and solved transport problems is the use of an inductive loop transport detector (TD), which is a technical means of traffic management (TMTM). This type of TD is the inductive loop with a sensor element, which is put in the roadway in front of the stop lines at the adjustable intersections of the urban SRN. The inductive detector can identify such parameters as vehicle type, traffic flow intensity, congestion of traffic lane, average speed [8].

As for the traffic light control method, three scenarios are possible in this regard: the extension of the current green phase of the traffic light object (TLO) for the PT pass, the reduction of other TLO phases for accelerated transition to the next green phase and the most radical method is to skip the yellow phase. All these scenarios are aimed at priority of giving the way to PT at the intersection after its detection that means with minimal time losses [8, 38]. The possibility of changing the TLO operating mode directly depending on the current situation at the SRN is provided by the presence of the Automated Traffic Control System (ATCS) in the city.

Within the framework of the approach 2.2, the same traffic light control methods are available to ensure the priority pass, however the applied technical devices are fundamentally different [36]. To implement this approach, it is necessary to equip PLUPT vehicles and SRN sections along which they move with special telematics devices of the V2I complex, namely, OBU (On-Board Unit) on-board devices and RSU (Road-Side Unit) peripheral road devices. At the same time, interaction between vehicle objects occurs mainly not physically as in the case of the approach 2.1 but by transmitting data on the planned and actual location of the vehicle [25]. The operation of the priority travel system based on the V2I technology can be presented in the form of a diagram (Fig. 1).

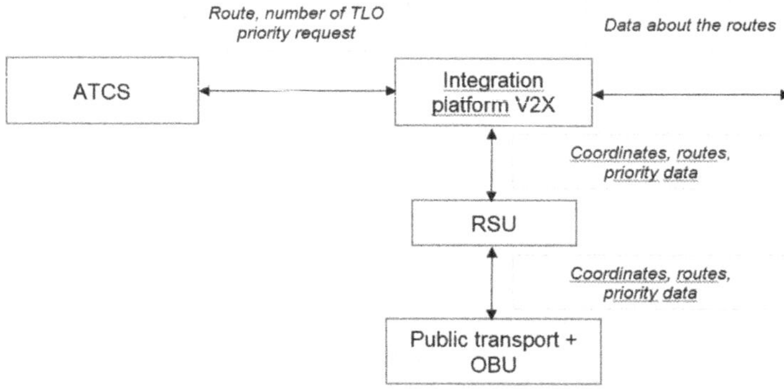

Fig. 1. The schematic representation of the system of the priority pass of public transport based on the V2I technology. Source: Designed by the authors.

These approaches to improving the quality of urban public transport (Table 1) can be considered as the alternative, since they are aimed at achieving one goal, but require various organizational, temporary, financial and other types of costs, as well as different levels of technological readiness of the transport system. In this regard it is proposed to conduct a comparative analysis, based on which it can be concluded about the main advantages, disadvantages and requirements (conditions) of the implementation of these approaches.

The comparison of the considered approaches for the organization of priority pass of public transport was carried out by interviewing some experts of the transport industry based on several criteria: the implementation conditions, the service requirements, the adaptability to the situation at the SRN, the limitations and barriers of the approach, the shortcomings and negative consequences of the approach, the cost of implementing SHC, the impact on the punctuality of the PT (Table 2).

On the next step questionnaire for a comparative analysis of 3 alternative approaches to ensuring the PLUPT punctuality was represented: based on dedicated lanes (1), based on the use detectors of transport of inductive loop type (2.1), based on V2I technology usage (2.2).

The experts were presented with the following requirements:

1. Experience in the transport field for at least 5 years, including today.

2. Complicity in a transport field project with the participation of government agencies (B2G project) in the development and implementation of intelligent transport systems, including the deployment of V2X technology.
3. Various job positions of experts in transport group (project manager; technical director; IT specialist; line engineer; representative of government agency).

Each expert assessed the three approaches according to criteria A-G, answering the presented questions. For criteria A, B, D-F evaluation scale was used from 1 to 5 (1 – lowest score, 5 – highest score), for C and G – an inverted scale was used from 1 to 5

Table 2. General description of the criteria for evaluation of approaches to ensuring PT priority pass

Designation	Criterion	Characteristic	Parameter
A	Conditions of the implementation	Requirements for the modernization of the road traffic management scheme, availability of the current ATCS and ITS as a whole	1. Existence of requirements for the traffic management scheme (TMS) 2. Existence of requirements for the TMTM 3. Level of city's ATCS development 4. Level of urban TS's digitalization 5. Providing an integrated approach to the organization of the TS
B	Maintenance requirements	The need to monitor and maintain the condition of equipment, SHC, etc	1. Existence of monitoring the technical condition of the PLUPT vehicles 2. Existence of an additional source of information about the SRN state 3. Possibility of improving passenger information services 4. Possibility of remote regulation and adjustment of the TMTM when violations are detected 5. Possibility of improving information services to the driver about the state of the situation on SRN

(*continued*)

Table 2. (*continued*)

Designation	Criterion	Characteristic	Parameter
C	Adaptability to the situation on the SRN	Consideration of the current transport situation on the SRN	1. Existence of additional equipment for tracking the location and follow the schedule of the PLUPT vehicles 2. Possibility of changing the operating mode of a TLO in advance depending on the location of the PLUPT vehicles 3. Possibility of changing the traffic conditions of the PLUPT depending on the traffic of SRN in online mode 4. Possibility of potentially changing the traffic conditions of other road users depending on the traffic of SRN in online mode 5. Possibility of feedback from the traffic management center (TMC)
D	Limitations and barriers	Availability of significant infrastructure and technical requirements	1. Existence of technical requirements for the roadway 2. Existence of requirements for traffic flow intensity parameters to implement the approach 3. Existence of requirements for the SRN traffic load 4. Existence of requirements for the SRN length to implement the approach 5. Existence of increased requirements for the data transmission system of the transport system to implement the approach

(*continued*)

Table 2. (*continued*)

Designation	Criterion	Characteristic	Parameter
E	Disadvantages and negative consequences	The presence of concomitant negative effects of the approach	1. Lack of benefit's leveling after merging traffic flows (at intersections and other sections of the SRN) 2. Aggravation of conditions for other types of transport movement on the SRN 3. Existence of a temporary negative impact on the current technical conditions of the SRN during implementing the approach 4. Changing routes / driving conditions for other road participants 5. The need to combine the approach with alternative ones to increase the effect of ensuring punctuality of the PLUPT
F	Implementation costs	Expected cost of approach implementation (equipment, SHC)	1. Existence of economies of scale (average costs reduction) as a result of implementation 2. Possibility of savings when implementing other road transport services 3. Possibility of savings by reducing the number of vehicles 4. Battery life of TMTM 5. New jobs creation in transport complex field

(*continued*)

Table 2. (*continued*)

Designation	Criterion	Characteristic	Parameter
G	Impact on the PT punctuality improvement	Expected speed increase / reduction of route time delays	1. Existence of a dependence of the PLUPT punctuality on other types of transport on the SRN 2. Possibility of targeted influence on the PLUPT movement to ensure punctuality 3. Dependence of PLUPT punctuality on traffic jams at signalized intersections 4. Possibility of collecting static data regarding the time of PLUPT vehicles movement along routes 5. Possibility of adapting PLUPT vehicle traffic conditions if the real traffic is ahead of schedule

Source: Designed by the authors

(1 – highest score, 5 – lowest score). In the process of analyzing the data obtained during the survey, the results for each criterion were summarized.

As part of the survey a comparative assessment of approaches to improve PT punctuality was obtained (Table 3), as well as an assessment of the significance of the identified criteria in terms of the transport system, implementation of the "smart city" concept and a general integral assessment of these approaches (Table 4).

Based on the obtained integrated estimates of three alternative approaches (Table 4), it is evident that in the context of average statistics of the state of the urban transport system, it is optimal to introduce an approach to ensuring priority PT access based on V2I technology.

The indicated approaches of ensuring priority passage of public transport 1, 2.1 and 2.2 can be considered as an "evolutionary development" of methods and tools for organizing a public transport system, since they, firstly, become more complicated from 1 to 2.2 in terms of their manufacturability, and, secondly, the more technologically advanced the approach to providing PT priority, the higher the actual (and potential) level of ITS development in the implementation area [9], which better satisfies the requirements of the "smart city" concept. However, when choosing one or another approach in organizing the urban safety system (including from the point of view of ensuring its punctuality), it is necessary to balance between "social efficiency" and economic efficiency.

Table 3. Expert evaluation of approaches according to criteria

Criterion/Approaches	Allocated traffic lanes					Based on transport detectors					Based on V2I technology				
	E1	E2	E3	E4	E5	E1	E2	E3	E4	E5	E1	E2	E3	E4	E5
A	4	3	3	2	4	4	4	3	4	5	5	4	4	5	4
B	3	2	3	2	2	2	2	3	2	3	3	4	4	3	5
C	5	4	4	5	5	2	1	2	1	1	1	1	2	1	1
D	1	2	2	1	2	3	2	4	4	4	4	5	5	5	4
E	4	4	3	4	3	1	1	2	3	1	5	4	4	5	4
F	1	2	1	1	2	3	2	2	1	2	4	5	4	5	5
G	2	2	3	2	1	2	2	3	2	2	1	1	2	1	2

Note: The rating scale: from 1 to 5, where 1 is the lowest rating for the criterion, 5 is the highest rating for the criterion. Criteria C, G are evaluated on an inverted scale, where 1 is the highest score of adaptability and effect on punctuality, respectively, 5 is the lowest

Source: Designed by the authors

Table 4. The integral evaluation of approaches according to criteria

Criterion/Approaches	Allocated traffic lanes		Based on transport detectors		Based on V2I technology	
	Avg. Value	Int. Value	Avg. Value	Int. Value	Avg. Value	Int. Value
A	3,2	9,6	4,0	12,0	4,4	13,2
B	2,4	3,84	2,4	3,84	3,8	6,08
C	4,6	7,36	1,4	1,82	1,2	1,92
D	1,6	3,2	3,4	6,8	4,6	9,2
E	3,6	8,64	1,6	3,84	4,4	10,56
F	1,4	3,08	2,0	4,4	4,6	10,12
G	2,0	4,8	2,2	4,84	1,4	3,08
Total:	18,8	40,52	17,0	37,54	24,4	54,16

Source: Designed by the authors

Thus, approach 1 provides a solution to a strictly defined problem – increasing the speed and timeliness of traffic movement due to its isolation from the general flow. At the same time, it seems to be the least expensive – since it does not require the city authorities to purchase additional road transport equipment, but it requires mainly organizational measures and minor changes to the SRN in the form of markings. Wherein this approach does not have additional potential for deploying ITS in the city.

Approach 2.1, the implementation of which requires the functioning of a city traffic control system, allows you to collect up-to-date data about road traffic state and transport flows, which can then be used to optimize traffic on large sections of the road network, and not only in relation to vehicles of the PLUPT (primarily this is about adaptive and coordinated traffic light regulation). This alternative approach is already more expensive than approach 1, since it requires the purchase of equipment – inductive detectors (the market price is 25,000 rubles, the need is determined by the number of controlled intersections and traffic lanes of the PLUPT); its implementation in the roadway and further maintenance, however, provides a wider range of opportunities for digitalization and optimization of the city's transport sector.

Approach 2.2 provides radically different opportunities for intellectualizing traffic. Thus, the solution to a specific task of improving traffic punctuality based on V2I technology can gradually develop into the mass introduction of V2V technology, which provides the possibility of "instant communication" between vehicles in traffic, as well as V2P technology, which ensures direct interaction between vehicles and pedestrians (cyclists, personal mobility aids users). These technologies in specialized literature and practice have received the complex name Vehicle-to-Everything (V2X). Their practical significance is determined by the possibility of developing new services and road transport scenarios: warning of the approach of another vehicle (including special vehicles)/pedestrian; warning about entering a speed limit/repair zone; assistance in choosing the speed of movement ("green wave"), etc. In fact, the introduction of V2I technology to ensure priority passage of public transportation can become the initial stage towards the development of a "smart city" based on ITS.

The cost of implementing this approach can be calculated based on the average market price of the V2I peripheral device: RSU - 160,000 rubles, the frequency of installation of the RSU along the route of the PLUPT – every 400–500 m, the average price of the on-board device (OBU) -100,000 rubles, which must be installed in each vehicle of the PLUPT. Despite the fact that ensuring punctuality based on V2I technology is indeed the most expensive technology presented at the implementation stage, it will create a "base" of connected vehicles and provide the main urban transport routes with appropriate peripheral equipment.

4 Discussion

According to the studies carried out by Berg J, Ihlström J, Kociánová A, Yakimov MR, the traffic of urban public transport exactly according to the schedule is one of the key indicators of the quality of the "smart city"'s transport system [1, 17, 34].

At the same time, De Keyser O, Hillewaere M, Audenaert P, Mayenhout B, Nelson E, Bullock D, Bhattacharjee S, Goetz A believe that the optimal results of the PT system functioning (in terms of punctuality and time spent by all road users) are provided if the PLUPT vehicle is detected before the regulated intersection in advance; and the specific conditions of traffic light control at this intersection in adaptive mode take into account the situation at the SRN [2, 10, 22].

According to the expert assessment of three alternative approaches carried out within the framework of the study, the optimal value for this indicator in the conditions of functioning of the urban ground passenger transport system is achieved when introducing the V2I technology (approach 2.2).

Yakimov M.P. also discovered that since the presence of an allocated PT lane (approach 1) as such does not guarantee the introduction of adaptive traffic lights and does not eliminate the problems of PT accumulation at intersections, this approach is not the most preferable [34]. This provision is confirmed by an expert assessment on criteria C (adaptability to the situation on the SRN) and G (impact on the increase in punctuality of the PT).

Approach to the priority travel 2.1 investigated by Casey R, Collura J, Diakaki C, Papageorgiou M, Dinopoulou V is based on the introduction of transport detectors (inductive loops) and allows to "adjust" the phases of the TLO operation through the ATCS subsystem. It is relatively inexpensive and quickly implemented (confirmed during the study by an expert assessment on criteria A - implementation conditions, B - service requirements, F - implementation cost), which is of interest for those regions and cities that are focused on achieving "rapid results" in the modernization of the transport system [7, 11].

To the disadvantages of this approach researchers De Keyser O, Hillewaere M, Audenaert P, Mayenhout B attribute the extremely limited distance of action of the used transport detectors (PT detection is possible only when approaching the regulated intersection directly) and the impossibility of extracting additional functionality in contrast to the solution based on V2I technology [10].

This approach makes it possible to provide the direct road users with the information about the current situation on the street's road network (in particular, passengers - about the exact time of arrival of public transport), the dispatch systems - about the PT traffic conditions both online and in the form of an array of archival data that can be used to optimize the traffic of the land urban public transport.

During the study there was demonstrated that the 2.2 approach considered in the works of Xie M, Ramanathan S, Rau A, Eckhoff D, Busch F, Wang R, Zhang X, Xu Z, Zhao X, Li X, Lee W-H, Wang H-C is a functionally improved version of the approach 2.1. It provides the ability to detect the approaching PT vehicle for several hundred meters and inform the driver about the priority provided and the recommended speed of movement [19, 32, 33].

Meanwhile, according to Gschwendtner C, Sinsel SR, Stephan A, Bohan M, Kousaridas A, Manolakis K, Eichinger J, Xu M this approach is the most expensive of the considered ones. It requires significant infrastructure, technical and technological transformations of the city's transport complex [4, 15]. This fact is also confirmed by the comparative expert evaluation (criteria B - service requirements, D - limitations and barriers, F - implementation cost).

However, from the point of view of implementing the concept of the "smart city" that is significantly based on an intelligent transport system, the 2.2 approach involves the massive deployment of the V2I technology. That is why it seems to be the most promising.

5 Conclusion

In the framework of the study, a comparative analysis of the approaches to organizing priority pass and ensuring punctuality of the PT operation was carried out. It has been demonstrated that these approaches meet the needs of the "smart city" transport systems of various levels of "technological readiness". The implementation of the approach of priority passage of public transport based on V2I technology will make it possible to increase the attractiveness of public transport for passengers by reducing travel time and increasing traffic safety, as well as increasing the efficiency of city traffic management, which, in turn, will have a positive impact on environmental safety and sustainable development of urban transport. In addition, the technical equipment of vehicles and the creation of a platform will ensure further digitalization of transport and integration of the transport system with other elements of the "smart city" through the transfer and analysis of data on the actual and forecast position of public transport.

The feasibility of introducing one of the approaches (from the point of view of traffic parameters) can be established by micro-modeling of traffic flows on a specific section of the SRN. Besides, possible limitations and problems that may appear during the implementation of the considered technology should be taken into account: the lack of continuous coverage of transport routes by communication networks of commercial operators, low level of urban TS readiness, common barriers to vehicle intellectualization, insufficient number and experience of national V2X equipment manufacturers, problems of information security. However, most of these problems are solving within the framework of the Transport and General strategy of RF, for example, within the framework of the Federal Information Infrastructure Project.

When justifying the socio-economical possibility and feasibility of implementing one of the approaches, it is necessary to consider:

- provision of the city and its transport complex with financial, personnel, technical and other resources;
- availability (level of development) of the ATCS and the ITS in the implementation city;
- the overall transportation strategy and policy of the city (traditional/innovative), following "smart city" concept.

Thus, the final decision on the implementation of one or another approach will be made by the executive branches of the transport sector of a certain territory based on a set of real conditions and the total cost. Expected benefits and effects of the implementation of one of the approaches considered will depend on the characteristics of the SRN section and the readiness of the city's transport system, the specifications of the equipment used, etc. [15].

The approaches considered and the results of the study may be of interest to transport sector executive branches; researchers of transport development issues; private organizations providing the development of projects in the field of transport development, production, supply, and commissioning of the TMTM, etc.

References

1. Berg, J., Ihlström, J.: The importance of public transport for mobility and everyday activities among rural residents. Swed. Natl. Road Transp. Res. Inst. **8**(2), 58–70 (2019)
2. Bhattacharjee, S., Goetz, A.: Impact of light rail on traffic congestion in Denver. J. Transp. Geogr. **22**, 262–270 (2012). http://dx.doi.org/10.1016/j.jtrangeo.2012.01.008

3. Bohan, M., Kousaridas, A., Manolakis, K., Eichinger, J., Xu, W.: Use cases, requirements and design considerations for 5G V2X. Comput. Sci. (1) (2017)
4. Bolgov, S.A.: The concept of "smart transport" in a "smart city". Sci. Educ. Transp. **1**, 196–197 (2022)
5. Brunner, H., Hirz, M., Hirschberg, W., Fallast, K.: Evaluation of various means of transport for urban areas. J. Energy Sustainabil. Soc. **8**, 9–20 (2018)
6. Cabrera-Arnau, C.: Urban population size and road traffic collisions in Europe. PLoS ONE **16**(8) (2021). https://doi.org/10.1371/journal.pone.0256485
7. Casey, R., Collura, J.: Advanced Public Transportation Systems: Evaluation Guidelines. USA, Washington D.C (1994)
8. Chao, S., Xiaohong, C., Michael, Z., Ze, H.: An evaluation method of urban public transport facilities resource supply based on accessibility. J. Adv. Transp. (2018). https://doi.org/10.1155/2018/3754205
9. Creß, C., Knoll, A.: Intelligent transportation systems using external infrastructure: a literature survey. Techn. Univ. Munich (3) (2022). https://doi.org/10.48550/arXiv.2112.05615
10. De Keyser, O., Hillewaere, M., Audenaert, P., Maenhout, B.: Optimizing the public transport priority at road intersections. IET Intel. Transp. Syst. **12**(8), 986–994 (2018). http://dx.doi.org/10.1049/iet-its.2018.5133
11. Diakaki, C., Papageorgiou, M., Dinopoulou, V., et al.: State-of-the-art and practice review of public transport priority strategies. IET Intell. Transport. Syst. **9**(4), 391–406 (2015)
12. Evstigneev, I.A.: Fundamentals of creating intelligent transport systems in Russian urban agglomerations. Moscow – Saint Petersburg, Russia (2021)
13. Gorev, A.E., Popova, O.V.: Development of urban passenger transport. City Transp. **2**(81), 45–47 (2019)
14. GOST R 51004-96. Transport services. Passenger Transportation. Nomenclature of quality indicators. Moscow, Russia (1997)
15. Gschwendtner, C., Sinsel, S.R., Stephan, A.: Vehicle-to-X (V2X) implementation: an overview of predominate trial configurations and technical, social and regulatory challenges. Renew. Sustain. Energy Rev. **145**, 110977(2021). https://doi.org/10.1016/j.rser.2021.110977
16. Kalašová, A.: Public transport as a part of shared economy. Arch. Autom. Eng. **85**(3), 49–56 (2019)
17. Kociánová, A.: Benefits of public transport priority at traffic signals: small town experience. In: 18th International Multidisciplinary Scientific GeoConference SGEM2018 (2018). https://doi.org/10.5593/sgem2018/6.3/S27.094
18. Kremenec, Y.A., Pecherskiy, M.P., Afanasjev, M.B.: Technical Means of Organizing Traffic. Russia, Moscow (2005)
19. Lee, W.-H., Wang, H.-C.: A person-based adaptive traffic signal control method with cooperative transit signal priority. J. Adv. Transp. (2022). https://doi.org/10.1155/2022/2205292
20. Mouratidis, K., Peters, S., Van Wee, B.: Transportation technologies, sharing economy, and teleactivities: implications for built environment and travel. Transoprt. Res. Part D: Transp. Environ. **92**, 102716 (2021). https://doi.org/10.1016/j.trd.2021.102716
21. Myeong, S., Park, J., Lee, M.: Research models and methodologies on the smart city: a systematic literature review. Sustainability **14**(3) (2022). https://doi.org/10.3390/su14031687
22. Nelson, E., Bullock, D.: Impact of emergency vehicle preemption on signalized corridor operation: an evaluation. Transp. Res. Rec. **1727**(1), 1–11 (2000). https://doi.org/10.3141/1727-01
23. Order of the Ministry of Transport of the Russian Federation of December 30, 2021 No. 482 On approval of guidelines for optimizing transport service systems for urban agglomerations, as well as introducing digital technologies for paying for travel and monitoring transport services for the population. Moscow, Russia (2021)

24. Pirotskaya A.V. Variety of approaches to studying the concept of "smart city". The fourth industrial revolution: realities and modern challenges. In: X anniversary St. Petersburg Sociological Readings: Collection of Materials of the International Scientific Conference, St. Petersburg, 13–14 April 2018, pp. 748–752. Federal State Autonomous Educational Institution of Higher Education "Peter the Great St. Petersburg Polytechnic University", St. Petersburg (2018). https://elibrary.ru/item.asp?id=35595492
25. Porciello, P., Henry, K.: A secure V2X connected vehicle transponder system for vehicle prioritization. In: Transportation Association of Canada and ITS Canada 2019 Joint Conference Exhibition (2019)
26. Policy Department for Structural and Cohesion Policies. The impact of emerging technologies on the transport system. European Union (2020)
27. Przybyl, P., Svitek, M. (eds.): Telematics in Transport. Russia, Moscow (2003)
28. Pugachev, I.N., Markelov, G.Y., Pavlenko, A.A.: Fundamentals of designing an intelligent control system for the city's road transport complexes. In: Improving the Organization of Traffic and Transportation of Passengers and Goods: A Collection of Scientific Papers Based on the Results of the International Scientific and Practical Conference. Belarus, Minsk (2014)
29. TomTom. Traffic Index. The Netherlands, Amsterdam (2021). https://www.tomtom.com/en_gb/traffic-index/ranking. Accessed 18 Apr 2022
30. Vlasov, V.M.: Application of Digital Infrastructure and Telematic Systems in Urban Passenger Transport. Russia, Moscow (2021)
31. VTsIOM. Data from a survey of Russians on public transport. Moscow, Russia (2021). Accessed 10 Apr 2022
32. Wang, R., Zhang, X., Xu, Z., Zhao, X., Li, X.: Research on performance and function testing of V2X in a closed test field. J. Adv. Transp. (2021). https://doi.org/10.1155/2021/9970978
33. Xie, M., Ramanathan, S., Rau, A., Eckhoff, D., Busch, F.: Design and evaluation of V2X-based dynamic bus lanes. IEEE Veh. Technol. Soc. Sect. (2021). https://doi.org/10.1109/ACCESS.2021.3117024
34. Yakimov, M.R.: Justification of the expediency of allocating lanes for the movement of route vehicles on the city's street and road network. Moscow, Russia (2016)
35. YOUMOBIL. Guidelines for the PT Decision Makers on Smart Rural Transport Tools. Italy, Genova (2022). https://www.interreg-central.eu. Accessed 02 May 2022
36. Zero-Sum ITS Solutions India Private Limited. Demonstration of a V2X System for the prioritization of Public Transportation Vehicles (Buses) on Bus Rapid Transport System corridor in Ahmedabad, India. Bengaluru, Karnataka (2022)
37. Zhankaziev, S.V., Vorobjev, A.I., Morozov, D.Y.: Trends in the development of autonomous intelligent transport systems in Russia. Transp. Russ. Federat. **5**(66), 26–28 (2016)
38. Zyryanov, V.V., Mironchuk, AA: Priority public transport: development of methods of organization. Transp. Russ. Federat. **3–4**(20–21), 22–25 (2012)

Author Index

A. Chugunov et al. (Eds.): DTGS 2024, CCIS 2445, p. 145, 2025.
https://doi.org/10.1007/978-3-031-90720-3

The manufacturer's authorised representative in the EU is Springer Nature Customer Service Centre GmbH, Europaplatz 3, 69115 Heidelberg, Germany. If you have any concerns regarding our products, please contact ProductSafety@springernature.com

Printed and bound by CPI Group (UK) Ltd, Croydon, CR0 4YY

30/09/2026

02225576-0010